V3?

D0864879

TWELV
NEW TESTAMENT

John A. T. Robinson

TWELVE MORE NEW TESTAMENT STUDIES

SCM PRESS LTD

334 01693 2

First published 1984
by SCM Press Ltd
26–30 Tottenham Road, London N1

Photoset at The Spartan Press Ltd
Lymington, Hants
and printed in Great Britain by
Billing & Sons Ltd
Worcester and London

CONTENTS

ACKNOWLEDGEMENTS

Thanks are due to the following publishers for permission to reprint some of the articles in thisa collection:

Messrs E. J. Brill, Leiden, for ch. 6.
Cambridge University Press, for chs. 2, 5, 9 and 10.
Mayhew McCrimmon Ltd and A. R. Mowbray and Co. Ltd, for ch. 7.
Mercer University Press, Macon, Georgia, for ch. 8.
Pilgrim Press, New York, for ch. 3.

PREFACE

In 1962 I garnered a collection of *Twelve New Testament Studies*, now long since out of print. Nearly a quarter of a century later I bring up the tally with twelve more. Where they have already been prepared for publication I print them with the kind permission of the journals of symposia concerned, to which reference is made at the beginning of each chapter, though at points I have modified them and brought them up to date. My reason for publishing them now is partly to be able to refer more briefly to some in my forthcoming Bampton Lectures on *The Priority of John*, due to appear in 1985.

I see that in 1962 I said I was deeply grateful to Miss Jean Cunningham of the SCM Press for her care in preparing the manuscript and making the index. I am happy after all this time to be able to say exactly the same thing today. She is a marvel actually to want to go on doing this tedious work in her retirement!

JOHN ROBINSON

ABBREVIATIONS

Ant.: Josephus, *Antiquitates Judaicae*
AV: Authorized Version of the Bible
Bibl: Biblica, Rome
BJ: Josephus, *De Bello Judaico*
BJRL: Bulletin of the John Rylands Library, Manchester
BZNW: Beihefte zur *Zeitschrift für die neutestamentliche Wissenschaft*, Berlin
CBQ: Catholic Biblical Quarterly, Washington, D.C.
EKK: Evangelisch-Katholischer Kommentar zum Neuen Testament, Zurich
ET: English translation
ExpT: Expository Times, Edinburgh
HE: Historia ecclesiastica
ICC: International Critical Commentary on Holy Scripture, Edinburgh and New York
JBL: Journal of Biblical Literature, Philadelphia et al.
JTS: Journal of Theological Studies, Oxford
NEB: New English Bible
NovTest: Novum Testamentum, Leiden
n.s.: new series
NTApoc: New Testament Apocrypha, ed. E. Hennecke and W. Schneemelcher, ET, 2 vols., London and Philadelphia 1963–65, repr. 1973–74
NTS: New Testament Studies, Cambridge
RHPR: Revue d'histoire et de philosophie religieuses, Strasbourg
RSV: Revised Standard Version of the Bible
SJT: Scottish Journal of Theology, Edinburgh
ZNW: Zeitschrift für die neutestamentliche Wissenschaft, Berlin

I

Hosea and the Virgin Birth

This piece, standing first not only because it is concerned with the first chapter of the New Testament but because it was written first, requires some explanation. It was first published as long ago as October 1948.[1] I did not include it in my original *Twelve New Testament Studies*, partly because it seemed to me too slight, but more because I had then become somewhat disillusioned with the approach it represented. This was the method of typological exegesis which views everything in the Old Testament in the light of the New and *vice versa*. There was nothing new in it. In fact it had a hoary history, along with allegorical exegesis, in the interpretation of Scripture from the earliest centuries of the church. But largely under the influence of W. Vischer's book, *The Witness of the Old Testament to Christ*[2] and the work of Austin Farrer, it caught on as a theological fashion in the 1940s and 1950s, particularly, as far as England was concerned, in Oxford. Taken to extremes, it saw an elaborate coding at work which supplied the clue to the mutual interpretation of the two Testaments. Thus every reference to Joseph of Arimathea, to give an instance from Farrer, was to be understood, because the evangelists would so have understood it, in the light of the patriarch Joseph. Now Austin Farrer was an original and a genius, though this did not to me make his exegesis of Mark along these lines any more credible. Of course, there was obviously truth underlying the method,[3] and no one could escape, say, the clearly intended pattern to be traced between the Temptation narrative of the gospels with its forty days of testing in the wilderness of Jesus called out of Egypt to be God's son (Matt. 2.15) with the Old Testament story of Israel so tested for forty years – especially since the replies of Jesus to the devil are all framed in quotations from Deuteronomy, reflecting the answers the old Israel was meant but

[1]*Theology* 52, 1948, pp. 373–5.
[2]ET (vol. 1 only), London 1949.
[3]For a balanced assessment, cf. that of the two (then) Oxford scholars, G. W. H. Lampe and K. J. Woollcombe, *Essays on Typology*, London and Naperville, 1957.

failed to give. So I had no hesitation in including my earlier such essay on 'The Temptations' in *Twelve New Testament Studies*.[4] But I subsequently became disenchanted with the method, not only because of the improbable extremes to which it could be pushed, but by discovering how easy it was to work. By sufficient selection of verses and manipulation of the order one could trace patterns and parallels almost everywhere, and, as Ronald Knox showed in parody, end up by proving Queen Victoria wrote 'In Memoriam'. So I decided to let 'Hosea and the Virgin Birth' rest in decent obscurity – not that, looking back, it does strike me that its connections are particularly far-fetched, especially in view of the church's explicit use of Hos. 1.10 and 2.23 to show that God's way of salvation in Jesus was nothing new or strange to the pattern of his dealings.

Subsequent reflection has however convinced me that there may have been deeper workings of truth here than I recognized. Perhaps the best way of drawing this out is first to reprint the original article, more or less as it stands, and then to refer to three passages in my later writings where explicitly or implicitly I have found myself driven back to reflect on it.

So here, first, is what I wrote more than thirty-five years ago.

It is becoming recognized that the function and purpose of scriptural quotation by the New Testament authors was not simply to provide snappily convincing proof-texts.[5] It was much more to expose the profound harmony of the events they had witnessed in these latter days with certain 'typical' dealings of Yahweh and his people in the past and to demonstrate their authenticity as saving acts of God by their congruity with what was already known of the peculiar characteristics of his working. There was a certain divine pattern which, like a water-mark, they believed could be detected repeating itself in any genuine piece of *Heilsgeschichte* or salvation history. The outlines of this pattern were given in the main in the events of Israel's national history, but they could equally well appear on the smaller scale of an individual's life.

There is one such individual life whose pattern is clearly regarded by the New Testament as a 'type' of divine action – the marriage-history of the prophet Hosea. Hos. 1.10 ('In the place where it was said to them, "You are not my people", it shall be said to them "Sons of the living God"') and 2.23 ('I will have pity on Not pitied, and I will say to Not my people, "You are my people"') are both cited by

[4]Pp. 53–60; reprinted from *Theology* 50, 1947, pp. 43–8.
[5]Especially, C. H. Dodd, *According to the Scriptures*, London 1952, New York 1953.

separate New Testament authors (Rom. 9.25f.; I Peter 2.10) to show that the method of the divine salvation which involved the nomination of the Christian church in place of the Jews as the people of the covenant was nothing strange to the ways of God. In fact, it was 'typical' of the way he worked. It is interesting to extend this line of thought beyond the immediate polemical issue with which the writers were concerned – namely, the status of Gentiles in the New Israel – and to view the congruity of the Incarnation itself, and especially of the Virgin Birth, with this particular 'type' of the divine method.

The 'type' may be described thus. God made men for a relationship of love with himself, of which the marriage-bond is the least inadequate human analogy. Men have repudiated that relationship with him, committed adultery against him. But, despite this unfaithfulness, God deliberately goes out to contract a formal relationship of marriage with them. He makes a covenant with them, to establish on the basis of law what as a fact of love no longer existed. This Hosea sees typified in God's injunction to him to take as his wife a woman known to be of loose morals. The purpose of this divine marriage is to have children, who are to represent the offspring and embodiment of unfaithfulness. Hosea is told to call his daughter and son 'No Pity' and 'No People': they are vessels of wrath, fitted to destruction, created by God to be the reminder of Israel's apostasy and the sign of her hopelessness. Yet the ultimate purpose of their creation is to be the instruments of God's mercy, to reveal the glory of his forgiving power, which, contrary to all desert and hope, justifies men by the action of free and unmerited grace. It is this divine favour or 'good pleasure' which calls 'her beloved who was not beloved' (2.23 LXX) and causes that 'in the place where it was said to them, "You are not my people," it shall be said to them "Sons of the living God"'. And this same sheer grace and undeterable love goes on to justify and receive back the wife too (the body of Israel), even though she has gone from iniquity to iniquity and requires to be purged and purified 'many days' (3.3f.).

Here, as it were, within the total divine strategy, is the blue-print for 'operation salvation', ready for the day when it shall be put into effect. It is the 'typical' action-pattern of the genuine divine ἀγάπη – deliberately choosing to work through a reversal of all human judgment, so as to reveal the more unequivocally the quality and greatness of its power. It is this action-pattern which the New Testament authors, and Paul in particular, see expressed supremely in the life and death of Jesus Christ, and which can legitimately be extended to the understanding of his birth.

The first and most indisputable fact about the birth of Jesus is that it occurred out of wedlock. The one option for which there is no evidence is that Jesus was the lawful son of Joseph and Mary. The only choice open to us is between a virgin birth and an illegitimate birth. This is not the place in which to argue the issue.[6] Suffice it to say that, whatever happened at the biological level, Christianity has had an interest in insisting upon the virgin birth as a symbol of truth that the Word was made flesh 'not of the will of man, but of God', that in Christ was to be seen something wholly new in history which could not be produced simply from within the natural process of generation.

But the relevant point here is that God elected in becoming incarnate to be born of a woman not in lawful wedlock. At once we have the scandal of the divine ἀγάπη revealing itself as an affront to all human righteousness. Joseph 'being a man of principle . . . decided to have the marriage contract set aside' (Matt. 1.19). The Jews found it impossible to accept a Messiah who had not even a father to give him a name. 'Is not this . . . the son of Mary?' (Mark 6.3). 'We are not base-born', they exclaim with scarcely veiled innuendo (John 8.41). But such is the quality of the divine good pleasure that it authenticates itself as genuine precisely in the offence of human and legal righteousness. God renews his covenant, his marriage-contract, with his people. In association with sinful human flesh is begotten one who, not only in his death but in his birth, bore the curse of the law, symbolizing in himself all that it meant to be No Pity, No People, Unbeloved and No Son. And yet, by the shocking verdict of God's good grace, it is he of whom it is declared, 'This is my beloved Son, in whom I am well pleased.' And through him, and that love 'to the end' which the Incarnation reveals, there is the promise too of the redemption of the mother, of the world that bore him — the right given to those who believe on his name themselves to become children of the living God.

Thus the typical pattern of God's redemptive work is repeated. What Hosea saw as promise the church sees as fact. Thus viewed, the Virgin Birth fits into that harmony which the New Testament writers detect as unifying both the former and the later acts of God, the old and the new covenants, in the single action-pattern of the divine love. It may also help us to understand aright the significance within the whole plan of campaign which Christ's manner of birth is meant to hold. Its lesson is not that the human partner in God's redeeming act must be morally fitted to the love that selects her (the doctrine of the Immaculate Conception). That is humanly impossible. Rather it is

[6]Cf., subsequently, my book *The Human Face of God*, London and Philadelphia 1973, ch. 2.

that God deliberately chooses the weak and the sinful things of this world to confound the mighty and convict the righteous.

So much for what I wrote then. Subsequently, in *The Human Face of God* (pp. 58–63), I came to the recognition that not only were two independent Christian writers using this parallel as apologetic for the utterly 'uncovenanted' fact that the Christian church included a Gentile element excluded altogether from the old people of God, but Matthew in his genealogy was using the same argument for including Jesus himself, who as 'the descendent of an irregular union' (Deut. 23.2) was ineligible not only for membership of Israel but *a fortiori* for messiahship. It is interesting that in face of Jewish slanders of illegitimacy Matthew does not take the line that these are pure fabrications, like the later allegations that the disciples stole the body of Jesus (28.13–15). On the contrary, he goes out of his way to admit the irregularity, far more than Luke, whose presentation *could* be interpreted on the hypothesis of pre-marital relations with Joseph, which so far from being a legal cause for breaking off a betrothal was later at any rate (Mishnah, *Kid.* 1) one way of effecting it. Matthew makes it quite clear that Joseph did not see himself as the father of the child, and he deliberately draws attention in his genealogy to four women of dubious sexual liaisons, who are strictly irrelevant to the genealogy, since this for the Jew has to be traced through the male side. He makes the point that the acknowledged presence (even by Jews) in the messianic lineage of Tamar, Rahab, Ruth and Bathsheba cannot invalidate the heritage, since God's purpose has not been denied by such dubieties in the past. He then crowns it with Mary, introduced by exactly the same formula, whom Joseph, as a man faithful to the law, wishes to put away. But the Holy Spirit directs otherwise, telling him to bestow upon him his name 'son of David' (Matt. 1.20), and thus incorporate him and his mother in the messianic line. Thus the scandal of the divine love is revealed as an affront to all legal righteousness, being vindicated in one who is born, as well as dies (Gal. 3.13), under the law's condemnation. It is a daring piece of apologetic, carrying the argument into the enemy's camp. It does not prove anything historically about Jesus' parentage – though it is surely an approach that would not have been resorted to had Christians simply been able to dismiss out of hand the Jewish slurs, of which we find plentiful evidence in the Talmud. Matthew's argument is that the possibility of his illegitimacy cannot be ruled out on the ground of inappropriateness, let alone impropriety. We shall never know humanly speaking who Jesus' father was. But can we be as free to be as indifferent as we are ignorant – on the ground that, as

Matthew boldly asserts, his 'divine' significance would be entirely unaffected? One suspects that most Christians would have difficulty in answering, Yes.

Then, secondly, in *The Roots of a Radical*,[7] after describing my own roots, I was addressing myself to the place of roots in the Christian heritage, especially for those in New Zealand who, like the Gentiles of the early church, felt *deraciné*. I was saying that roots are a matter neither for boasting (that was the answer of Paul before his conversion and of the Judaizers) nor for despising (that was the answer of the Gentiles who thought they could dismiss what the fullness of Israel meant to the Jew) but of being grafted, entirely without merit, into the richness of Abraham's stock, so that all his inheritance becomes that of Christians too.

But, I went on to say, the final answer to those who feel rootless and therefore worthless is that this condition was true of Christ himself. However one takes the stories of his birth, Jesus was without a father to give him his name (except purely legally). In a patriarchal culture to be known as 'the son of Mary' was a shaming appellation. And in his Jewish-Christian milieu Matthew regards it as the first charge against Christianity that he has to answer, devoting to it the whole of his opening chapter.[8] On the contrary, he says, Jesus' irregular birth was strikingly in line with God's εὐδοκία or good pleasure, deliberately to raise up children of promise to be 'sons of the living God', from outside the marriage-bond. In his interpretation of the gospel, as for Paul, nothing depends upon the 'righteousness of the law' but everything upon the 'putting right' of God. That Jesus himself was in the messianic line is a matter of sheer grace, not of right: it is 'against nature' (Rom. 11.24). Thus even Jesus, one may say, is 'justified by faith', the faithfulness of Joseph, who was prepared to believe God against all that principle would direct.

The third point at which I found my original article to be relevant was when I was arguing in a later essay in *The Roots of a Radical*, 'Honest to Christ Today' (pp. 72–7) about following the story line wherever it may lead. I had been questioning the 'two-storey'

[7]London and New York 1980, pp. 24–6.
[8]K. Stendahl, 'Quis et Unde?' in W. Eltester, ed., *Judentum-Urchristentum-Kirche: Festschrift für Joachim Jeremias*, BZNW 26, 1960, pp. 94–105, makes the important point that Matt. 1 does not describe the birth of Jesus – γένεσις in 1.18 meaning, not as it is usually translated 'birth', but the same as in 1.1, 'descent'. The actual birth is not reached till 2.1, the chapter in which he answers the second charge that he could not have been the Messiah because he did not come from Bethlehem but from Nazareth. He did both; but Matthew's answer is different from Luke's, in that he came first from Bethlehem and only subsequently (2.22f.) from Nazareth rather than *vice versa*.

christology of classical Catholicism and Protestantism in which Jesus has been presented as a divine Person who, by taking upon himself a second, human, nature as well as his own, is made up, physically or metaphysically, of two levels of substance or being which have to be held together without division or confusion. I was arguing on the contrary for a 'two-story' christology in which Jesus is an utterly normal human person to whose true nature and origin justice can be done only be telling two stories, using man-language and God-language, neither of which is true at the expense of the other and each of which we must be free to follow wherever the evidence takes us.

In some New Testament stories about him one set of language is at its maximum and the other at its minimum. Thus in the Ascension story the heart of the matter is the theological assertion that Christ is not only alive but Lord, and this is expressed in well-understood Old Testament symbolism of theophany.[9] The purely historical elements of movement in space and moment in time are at their minimum: the truth could be expressed without reference to a particular event (as, for example, in the affirmation that Christ fills all things in Eph. 4.8–10), though Luke links it to the tradition of a parting appearance of the risen Jesus (Acts 1.6–11 and in many manuscripts Luke 24.50). The Resurrection story is more complex. There are recognizable indicators of God-language (affirming that 'God is in this event') represented by angelic figures in dazzling dress, as in the Christmas story; but there is other vocabulary (of stones and shroud and sweat-cloths) which does not seem to belong to the same genre – as if to insist that there is *also* something purely historical that happened within the parameters of space and time. At this point and in this person the two meet. The first-fruits of the new creation are not simply to be apprehended from within the categories of the old, nor yet do they render them redundant. One cannot speak simply, as some would, of a 'physical' resurrection; for the body of the 'appearances' is not merely physical, whether for St Paul or for the evangelists: yet something outward and visible seems to have occurred, and not just, as Bultmann would have it, a change in the disciples' attitude.

There is a paradox here. On the one hand we can afford to be agnostic about what happened to the old body; for the truth of the Resurrection is not contained within it: we are speaking of a new order of being. For all we can be sure, as Ronald Gregor Smith scandalized many by insisting,[10] the bones of Jesus may still be lying

[9]Cf. J. G. Davies *He Ascended into Heaven*, London and New York 1958.
[10]*Secular Christianity*, London and New York 1966, pp. 103–6.

about somewhere in Palestine. And we must be *free* to say so. The 'divine' story could be perfectly compatible with this, just as it is in the classic paradigm of 'resurrection' in Ezek. 37, where the bones are there to be revivified. Yet there is also evidence to suggest, with such quasi-parallels as I adduced from Buddhism[11] and *possibly* reinforced by the Turin Shroud,[12] that the old body may not just have been left to decay but been absorbed or 'used up', as C. F. D. Moule has put it,[13] in the creation of the new. In each instance the relation of the two story-lines has to be judged on its merits. And this is where I return to the two that Matthew puts together in the genealogy of Jesus and his virginal conception.

In these two stories are set side by side what Jesus was 'according to the flesh' and 'according to the spirit', to use Paul's distinction in Rom. 1.3f. As the New English Bible translates it, 'On the human level he was born of David's stock, but on the level of the spirit – the Holy Spirit – he was declared Son of God' – though unlike Paul Matthew is concerned to push back the 'mighty act' which inaugurated the new creation behind the Resurrection to his birth. At one level Jesus comes out of the womb of Israel by the ordinary processes of generation and his lineage can be traced back through Joseph, though with more blots on the escutcheon, insists Matthew, than Christians – or Jews – unless pressed would be prepared to allow. He was not of sinless stock, but as Luke puts it, 'the son of Adam', with all that that implies. Yet on the other hand he represents a new start in the dealings of God with men. And these two aspects are both/and rather than either/or. Just as John insists that *as children of God* Christians are 'not born of any human stock, or by the fleshly desire of a human father, but [are] the offspring of God himself' (1.12f.), without implying that *as human beings* they are not born like everyone else, so to say of Jesus that he comes, 'from the Father', 'from heaven', and not 'from below', is in no way to deny that he *also* comes from Nazareth (1.46) and that his father and mother are well known (6.42; cf. 7.28). And for John too, if the irony is intended, this is compatible with his being born 'of fornication' (8.41).

Similarly Matthew holds together the tracing of his descent through Joseph (1.16) with the interpretation that he has no human father, and certainly not Joseph (1.18). Clearly if these are to be

---

[11]*The Human Face of God*, p. 139.

[12]See chapter 7 below.

[13]'St Paul and "Dualism": The Pauline Conception of Resurrection', *NTS* 12, 1965–6, pp. 118–23; reprinted in his *Essays in New Testament Interpretation*, Cambridge 1982, pp. 216–21.

taken as truths on the same level they are incompatible, as Luke, or
his scribe, saw (3.23), just as Genesis and Darwin are incompatible,
if taken as explanations on the same level of the 'how' of the first
creation. But, as the result of much honest wrestling, it has become
clear to most Christians that at different levels the latter two
accounts can both be true. One can be free to follow the scientific,
historical story to the limit (even to saying that the mechanism
operates on the apparently totally purposeless principles of 'chance
and necessity'), but *also* to say that it embodies the conviction that 'in
the beginning God created . . . '. More tardily has followed the
recognition that *how* the world ends (or when), whether with a bang
or a whimper or a nuclear holocaust, is still compatible with the
conviction that 'in the end God . . . ', and that equally the myths of
the End are not to be seen as competing scientific explanations.[14]
Much more slowly among devout churchmen has come the acknowledgment that it is possible to hold together the truth for which the
Virgin Birth story stands, namely, that the initiative of God in Jesus
cannot be accounted for *simply* within the categories of heredity and
environment, with the acknowledgment that these also play at their
proper level an essential, ambiguous and murky part.

For the author of Genesis there was no pressure to discern between
what was true at the theological level and what was true at the
geological. Similarly for Matthew there was no one to ask him
whether he meant what he wrote about the Virgin Birth to be taken
at the gynaecological level or at the interpretative – any more than
there was anyone to press Luke whether he was using 'son of' in the
same sense in the successive clauses of 3.38, 'son of Seth, son of
Adam, son of God'. But now we are being forced to discriminate if
we are not to be misunderstood. It becomes important to clarify
which 'story-line' we are following.[15]

I believe that we should recognize that all the gospel prologues
from the profound Johannine one (John 1.1–18) to the summary
Markan (Mark 1.1), with the Matthaean and Lukan birth-stories in
between, are primarily to be understood along the divine story-line,
setting within God's whole purpose from the beginning the history
that follows (though the history is to some extent to be found also in
the prologues, just as the theology is to be found in the subsequent

---

[14]For this see my first book, *In the End, God*, London and Chicago 1950; ²London
and New York 1968.
[15]One suspects that this is not such a modern problem as it may seem. The horror in
Islam at Jesus being called 'son of God' has probably all along stemmed from the belief
that Christians were really asserting physical filiation.

narratives). That is to say, they are answers to the question 'Who is this man?' at the level of spirit rather than of flesh. Matthew's particular answer is that in this event is to be seen a wholly new initiative, however much it also 'fulfils' the old, a 'virgin' start. By the happy chance that he was writing in Greek (for it does not work in the original Hebrew) he was able to take Isaiah's prophecy (7.14) about a young woman conceiving and bearing a son to refer to a technical virgin and so to turn the edge of Jewish slurs of sexual immorality. He *could* be speaking *both* theology and gynaecology. In the same way, the church was subsequently able to combine a literal interpretation of the Virgin Birth with its conviction that Jesus was 'complete in regard to his humanity' by attributing the whole of his manhood to Mary, because Aristotelian and medieval science postulated that the entire material substance of a person's humanity was derived from the mother's blood, the father's seed merely providing the impulse or trigger required to set it all in motion (the θέλημα of John 1.13). Indeed Aquinas specifically denies[16] that the miracle of the Virgin Birth included the creation of any new matter. We now know that genetics works differently. We have to postulate that half his genes were special creations or, to put it crudely, fakes, to make it look as if 'took after' someone on the male side (presumably Joseph) – whereas in reality he did not. It is all rather like God creating the rocks with the fossils in them to make it look as though evolution were true. And this position, however hopeful a refuge it looked to some nineteenth-century churchmen, was one in which we can now see it was impossible to rest. It confounds the story-lines.

But the need for 'coming clean', for getting out from behind the ambiguities, scientific or linguistic, is not necessarily a stumbling-block to faith. It can be an opportunity, as was shewn in the nineteenth century. We can be freed to see how both stories may be true, at different levels. It is possible to assert an act of 'new creation' in Christ. What Jesus stands for is a new divine initiative. Yet we are not forced to affirm this by suspending the biological processes or blurring the relationship between them and the spiritual. The second story can *also* be true and we are free to follow *its* argument wherever it leads. This is what Matthew in his day was daringly seeking to do, though he was able to have recourse to an ambiguity not open to us. Like our grandfathers, we have to face the choice: for knowledge brings a loss of innocence. I suggest that the parallel of

---

[16]*Summa Theologica* III. 32.4.

the Virgin Birth story with the marriage history of Hosea may be a way, and a thoroughly scriptural one, which can still liberate us to affirm the divine initiative without denying or covering up the other human or scientific story, which is as important, at this time of the dominance of microbiology, as when the discoveries of geology and the origin of species filled the popular mind a hundred years ago. Nothing too much should be rested upon the parallel. For it is an opening which has been with the church for some time, yet which it has been, and is likely to be, reluctant to explore.[17] Again, like many explorations in typology, it may be too far-fetched to bear much weight. Yet I have thought it worth re-opening and expanding the questions that the original article raised.

[17]Recognition that the women in Matthew's genealogy are there for their sexual irregularities goes back a long way. Thus Aquinas comments (*ST* III. 31.3 ad 5): 'As Jerome says on Matt. 1.3: "None of the holy women are mentioned in the Saviour's genealogy but only those whom Scripture censures, so that he who came for the sake of sinners, being born of sinners, might blot out all sin."' And he goes on to substantiate this in the case of the four women concerned – not in fact that Scripture does censure them so much as commend them for their astuteness (See *The Human Face of God*, p. 59–61). Needless to say, Aquinas does not proceed to draw any implications with regard to the fifth woman, Mary.

2

The Parable of the Wicked Husbandmen: A Test of Synoptic Relationships[1]

The unfreezing of the synoptic problem in recent years, for which we must be particularly grateful to Professor W. R. Farmer's survey,[2] has been a healthy, if painful, experience. It is far too early yet to predict what new patterns, or modifications to previous patterns, will establish themselves. It is a time for rigorous testing out of suggestions that have disturbed, if not shaken, the critical consensus. What follows is but a small sample dip into the mass of material that needs to be looked at afresh.[3] The passage selected – what is commonly known as the parable of the Wicked Husbandmen[4] – merits attention for several reasons. It is as securely grounded in the tradition of Jesus' life and teaching as any other. It is among those listed by Farmer[5] where the verbal agreement between the three synoptists is so great as to make some theory of literary interrelationship inescapable. It has the advantage now of a 'fourth dimension' in a close but in all probability independent parallel in the Gospel of Thomas. Yet, rather surprisingly, it is not discussed by Farmer either in his new 'redaction of the synoptic tradition in Mark', though he analyses at length the incidents on either side of it,[6] or in his survey of the parables as

---

[1]First published in *NTS* 21, 1974–5, pp. 443–61.

[2]*The Synoptic Problem*, New York and London 1964. I am personally grateful to him too for unpublished material and for the trouble he has taken in correspondence.

[3]For a comparable study, cf. D. Wenham, 'The Synoptic Problem Revisited: Some New Suggestions about the Composition of Mark 4.1–34', *Tyndale Bulletin* 23, 1972, pp. 3–38.

[4]For a truer title, see below, p. 21.

[5]Op. cit., p. 208.

[6]Ibid., pp. 257–64.

important historical evidence for the manhood of Jesus.[7] So, despite the many previous treatments it has received, it may be justifiable to look at it once again for what light it may shed on the elusive solution to the oldest problem confronting gospel critics.

Our first task, without presupposing any particular pattern of dependence between the traditions, must be to try to establish what are the primary and what the secondary features in the story in its various versions (Matt. 21.33–46; Mark 12.1–12; Luke 20.9–19; Thomas 65).[8] This has already been done so thoroughly, notably by Dodd[9] and Jeremias,[10] that this section must largely consist of garnering and sifting the work of others. We may content ourselves with a fairly rapid survey of the different sections of the parable.

The context

The parable is unique in Mark in not being in a collection of parables (Mark 4) or a discourse (Mark 13), though it is introduced editorially with the formula, found also in 3.23 and 4.2, 'he began to speak to them ἐν παραβολαῖς', which may mean no more than 'parabolically'. In Luke too it stands by itself (where it is described as 'this parable') as the only parable in the Jerusalem ministry outside the apocalyptic discourse. Matthew, introducing it as 'another parable', places on each side of it the parables of the two sons and of the marriage feast (the latter itself conflated with that of the wedding garment). In Thomas it *follows* the parables of the rich fool and of the marriage feast, but has no context. In the synoptists it is part of Jesus' last challenge to the leaders of Israel, comparable with that of the shepherd in John 10.1–5.[11] Jeremias' assimilation of its point to that of so many other parables, 'it vindicates the offer of the gospel to the poor',[12] overlooks its distinctive setting. Hengel strongly supports Dodd[13] in supposing that there is every likelihood that this

---

[7]'An historical essay on the humanity of Jesus Christ' in W. R. Farmer, C. F. D. Moule and R. R. Niebuhr, eds., *Christian History and Interpretation: Studies Presented to John Knox*, Cambridge and Toronto 1967, pp. 101–26.

[8]I use the enumeration and the translation of this last in E. Hennecke, *NTApoc* I, p.518.

[9]C. H. Dodd, *The Parables of the Kingdom*, London 1935, New York 1936.

[10]J. Jeremias, *The Parables of Jesus* (ET London and New York ¹1954; ³1972). References are to the latter revised edition (German ⁸1970), unless indicated.

[11]Cf. my article 'The Parable of the Shepherd (John 10.1–5)' reprinted in *Twelve New Testament Studies* London and Naperville 1962, pp. 67–75. Contrast the responses ἔγνωσαν (Mark 12.12) and οὐκ ἔγνωσαν (John 10.6).

[12]Op. cit., p. 76.

[13]Op. cit., pp. 130–2.

particular parable has come down to us in its original context: 'Has not the uniqueness of Jesus' situation in his last conflict in Jerusalem determined the distinctiveness of this parable in comparison with the rest of the parables of Jesus?'[14] Indeed, T. W. Manson went so far as to say that 'criticism that rejects it will be capable of getting rid of anything in the Gospels'.[15]

In contrast with many of the parables, it remains explicitly addressed to the opponents of Jesus, a feature which Jeremias noted as a mark of authenticity. It is spoken to 'the chief priests, scribes and elders' (Mark 11.27),[16] who have no difficulty in recognizing it as told against themselves. Unlike all other parables of the same form – of responsibility delegated in absence (the servant entrusted with supervision, Matt. 24.45–51; Luke 12.42–46; the ten virgins, Matt. 25.1–13; the talents or pounds, Matt. 25.14–30; Luke 19.12–27; the doorkeeper, Mark 13.33–37; Luke 12.35–38) – it is unique in not being directed to the church and reapplied to the parousia. There is no suggestion of any reference but to God's dealing with the Jews in the history of his people Israel. Those like Kümmel[17] who view it as an allegory created by the Christian community for its own purposes must surely explain why it was not supplied with the setting to which the church found it relevant to adapt all the other similar stories of Jesus. If we really wish to see what the church did when it created an allegory on the same theme, we may compare the version (applied to fasting) in the Shepherd of Hermas (*Sim.* 5. 2.1–8), where the virtuous slave ends by being promoted fellow-heir with the son.

The introduction

The story starts in its most basic form: 'A man planted a vineyard and let it out to farmers and went away.' This is how it begins in Luke, who adds only χρόνους ἱκανούς, an easily recognizable editorial touch, both words being characteristically, and in combination uniquely,[18] Lukan. It is also how it begins in Mark, apart from an important insertion to be discussed shortly. Matthew qualifies the

[14]M. Hengel, 'Das Gleichnis von den Weingärtnern', *ZNW* 59 1968, pp. 1–39.

[15]*The Teaching of Jesus*, Cambridge 1935, p. 104.

[16]Matt. 21.45 'the chief priests and Pharisees; Luke 20.19 'the scribes and chief priests'.

[17]W. G. Kümmel, 'Das Gleichnis von den bösen Weingärtnern', *Aux Sources de la Tradition Chrétienne: Mélanges offerts à M. Goguel*, Neuchâtel and Paris 1950, pp. 120–31.

[18]Luke 8.27; 20.9; 23.8; Acts 8.11; 14.3; 27.9.

'man' as an οἰκοδεσπότης, as he does in the opening of his other parable
of the vineyard in 20.1. It is a favourite word of his,[19] and must be
presumed to be editorial. It is not taken up later in the parable,[20]
where, as in the other synoptic versions, the owner is styled ὁ κύριος τοῦ
ἀμπελῶνος. In Thomas the man is described as 'good'. This stress on
the contrast in character between owner and tenants is entirely natural
to the story, especially as most absentee landlords could be presumed
to be exploiters unless otherwise stated, and it may well be original.[21]
Thomas omits specific reference to the owner going away, but this is
implicit in the subsequent acts of sending and is hardly significant.

The major question in the introduction relates to the addition or
otherwise of the details clearly intended to call to mind the parable of
Isa. 5.1–7. Matthew and Mark, but not Luke and Thomas, insert after
the planting of the vineyard: 'and he put a wall round it, hewed out a
winepress, and built a watch-tower'. These details are immaterial to
the rest of the story. Their sole function seems to be to underline the
point (which is evident in any case) that 'the vineyard of the Lord of
hosts is Israel' (Isa. 5.7) and to stress the caring provision he has made
for his people. They look like allegorical additions, and, as Jeremias
points out,[22] the reference to the 'fence' depends on the use of the
Greek Bible[23] and Matthew's version shows even closer approxima-
tion to the phrasing of the LXX.[24] We may therefore be reasonably
confident in regarding the allusions as secondary to the story as Jesus
told it, though whether they formed an original part of the synoptic
version must be discussed later.

The number of servants sent

Mark has three singly, followed by 'many others'. Luke has three
single servants. Matthew has two waves of servants in the plural, the
second 'more than the first'.

It is generally agreed that Matthew is allegorizing (the former and
the latter prophets) and that Mark 12.5b ('and many more besides') is
a similar addition. Verse 5b destroys the construction of the sentence,

---

[19]Matt. 7 times; Mark 1; Luke 4.
[20]Contrast Matt. 20.11.
[21]So H. Montefiore in H. Montefiore and H. E. W. Turner, eds., *Thomas and the
Evangelists*, London and Naperville 1962, p. 49.
[22]*Parables*, p. 71.
[23]The Hebrew of Isa. 5.2, 'he dug it up', is rendered by the LXX, 'I fenced it round'.
[24]φραγμὸν αὐτῷ περιέθηκεν for Mark's περιέθηκεν φραγμόν and the addition of
ἐν αὐτῷ after ὤρυξεν.

since the main verb ἀπέκτειναν (him they killed and many others) cannot continue to govern πολλούς, of whom 'some they beat, others they killed'.[25] Dodd indeed argued that the whole of v.5 should be excised,[26] leaving the climactic series of three (two servants followed by a son) so congenial to folk-tales. This conjecture has since been strikingly confirmed by the version in Thomas, which has precisely this and must be regarded here as the most original.[27] It explains the developments in the other versions; but not *vice versa*.

Montefiore[28] also notes the absence from Thomas of reference to the καιρός at which the first servant was sent. Since this was a word heavy with theological meaning for the church, it could have been added for allegorical reasons (cf. especially Matthew's ἤγγισεν ὁ καιρός with Luke 21.8). But equally it is quite natural to the story, and allegorical significance need not be attached to it.

The treatment of the servants

In Mark, the first the tenants beat and sent empty away; the second they knocked over the head and dishonoured; the third they killed; and the many others they beat or killed.

In Luke, the first they beat and sent empty away; the second they beat and dishonoured and sent empty away; the third they wounded and threw out.

In Matthew, both sets they beat, killed or stoned.

In Thomas, the first they beat and all but killed; the second they beat also.

The killing is reserved in Luke and Thomas for the son. This seems undoubtedly the more original. Mark spoils the climax, and Matthew again allegorizes from history.[29]

In his only elaboration to the whole story, Thomas adds, after the sending of the first servant: 'the servant came and told his master. His master said, Perhaps they did not know him'.[30] This has no obvious allegorical significance and is not outside the bounds of the story. The recognition theme is however a common feature of gnostic

[25]So Jeremias, *Parables*, p. 71 n. 83, following E. Haenchen.

[26]*Parables of the Kingdom*, p. 129. It is referred to in error as v. 4.

[27]The third servant in Luke is also omitted by Syr[c].

[28]*Thomas*, p. 62.

[29]For the stoning of the prophets cf. II Chron. 24.21; Matt. 23.37; Luke 13.34; Heb. 11.37.

[30]This is an evidently necessary correction, accepted by the editors and commentators, for 'Perhaps he did not know them'.

stories and it may be an addition. On the other hand, it could, as we shall see, point a contrast integral to the original point of the story.

The sending of the son

The simplest form of the story is again that of Thomas: 'Then the master sent his son. He said: Perhaps they will reverence my son.' This is virtually identical with what we have in Matthew ('Afterwards he sent to them his son, saying: They will reverence my son') and must be regarded as the fundamental version. (Luke introduces this new stage with the self-questioning of the lord of the vineyard: τί ποιήσω; but this looks like a further echo of Isaiah (5.4) or a duplication of the τί ποιήσει ὁ κύριος τοῦ ἀμπελῶνος; later on.)

The contrast between servant and son is a common feature of the parables of Jesus. It is in the parable of the prodigal son (Luke 15.19) and in that of the servant and the son in John 8.35.[31] Just because the figure of the son is here clearly intended to be applied to Jesus himself, we are not outside the proper range of parable. Indeed the language which is subsequently allegorized to describe 'the Father' and 'the Son' began life, I am persuaded, in all the gospel traditions (Q, Mark and John) as parabolic, describing the relations of a father to his son.[32] The process of allegorization can in fact be watched in the tradition of this story, as the christological significance is exploited by the addition in Mark and Luke (but *not* in Matthew[33] or Thomas) of the word ἀγαπητόν (Luke τὸν ἀγαπητόν), 'beloved' in the sense of 'only', with its unavoidable echo for the reader of the divine voice at the baptism and transfiguration of Jesus. Mark further emphasizes this by saying 'he had one, an only son'. Moreover, his choice of the word ἔσχατον may betray theological overtones,[34] as in the similar conjunction of ideas in Heb. 1.2: 'At the end of the days he spoke to us in a son, whom he appointed heir of all things'. Of all the versions Mark here appears to be the *most* allegorical and Matthew the least! It looks too as if in Mark the contrast has begun

---

[31]For this as originally a parable, cf. Dodd, *Historical Tradition in the Fourth Gospel*, Cambridge and Toronto 1963, pp. 380–2. Cf. John 15.15.

[32]Cf. my book, *The Human Face of God*, London and Philadelphia 1973, pp. 186–8, citing Jeremias and Dodd.

[33]This oddly is not recognized by Jeremias (op. cit., p. 73) nor by Montefiore, who specifically says: 'All the synoptic versions record that the owner sent last of all his "only son"' (op. cit., p. 63).

[34]But in 12.22 (where it cannot have theological significance) Mark has ἔσχατον. while Matthew and Luke have ὕστερον. So it may be a purely stylistic preference.

to shift from that simply between servant and son to that between the many (12.5) and the one (12.6).

The fact that the son is the only son – and therefore *sole* heir – is relevant to the story only if the point of killing him is that the inheritance would thereby fall to the tenants. But the logic of the transition from 'if son then heir' to 'if killers of the son then heirs' is so crude a calculation (immediately proved wrong by the events) that it has seemed incredible that the farmers could in real life have made it. Much ingenuity has been expended by commentators to show how their action was reasonable. Jeremias in his first edition wrote, 'They evidently have in mind the law that the estate of a proselyte who dies intestate may be regarded as ownerless property'[35] – though why they should have thought he was a proselyte is not evident. This 'law' is taken over by Nineham in his commentary on Mark,[36] but quietly modified by Jeremias in his later edition. In any case, to make the action plausible, we have to assume, without evidence, either that they thought the owner was dead (Jeremias) or that the property had already been made over to the son (as in the parable of the prodigal son) and that he was childless, the father thus reverting to becoming the heir (Bammel[37]). But in this case, as Jeremias says, the father would be the heir, the son the owner. Derrett[38] indeed takes κληρονόμος to *mean* one who has already acquired or been assigned the estate – i.e. they believed he was the owner. But this is unjustified both as an assumption on their behalf and as an interpretation of κληρονόμος in the New Testament. As Montefiore says, 'It is hardly necessary to imagine that the original story turned on a nice point of law. It seems that the labourers in the parable were the kind of people who believed that possession is nine-tenths of the law.'[39]

It is, however, at least worth asking whether this entire calculation (that they would get the vineyard) is not secondary to the story – and with it the emphasis upon the *only* son. For neither feature is present in the Gospel of Thomas, where the point *may* be (though I should not wish to press this) the enormity of so treating him who 'they *knew* was the heir'. In the case of the first servant perhaps, it is said, they did not know him. This time they did. Moreover, the one who

[35]Op. cit.¹, p. 59.

[36]D. E. Nineham, *The Gospel of Mark*, London and New York ²1968, p. 312.

[37]E. Bammel, 'Das Gleichnis von den bösen Winzern (Mk 12.1–9) und das jüdische Erbrecht', *Revue Internationale des Droits de l'Antiquité*, 3ᵐᵉ série, vi, 1959, 14 f.

[38]J. D. M. Derrett, 'The Parable of the Wicked Vinedressers', *Law in the New Testament*, London 1970, p. 306.

[39]*Thomas*, pp. 49 f.

merited the greatest respect received the worst treatment: the first servant they seized, beat and all but killed, the son they seized and killed. What then must the conclusion be? The same as in Luke 12. 47 f.: the servant who knew that he was doing wrong will be punished the more severely. So this generation of Israel's leaders will be visited with final retribution (Matt. 23.32–39).

But this is to anticipate. For we have still to consider the variants in the reception accorded to the son.

The treatment of the son

In Thomas, they seized him and killed him.

In Mark, they seized him and killed him and threw him out of the vineyard.

In Luke, they threw him out of the vineyard and killed him.

In Matthew, they seized him and threw him out of the vineyard and killed him.

Again, Thomas looks the simplest and most original, though Mark's version is entirely natural and is *not* what happened to Jesus. Luke and Matthew reverse the order, and this is generally held to reflect the fact that Jesus was taken out of the city before being crucified. Yet this point is emphasized not in the two gospels concerned but only John 19.17 and Heb. 13.12 f. Nevertheless there must be a suspicion here of allegorical reinterpretation.

The ending of the parable

Thomas closes simply with the words: 'Since they knew he was the heir of the vineyard, they seized him and killed him. He that hath ears, let him hear.' The synoptists all continue with a question: 'What (then) will the lord of the vineyard do?' The further echo of Isa. 5.5 may be as secondary as the previous allusions. This is Jeremias' view, though he is incorrect this time in saying that the reference is not to the Hebrew (where it is not in the form of a question) but to the LXX. For there is not a question in the Greek either.[40] Dodd, writing before the evidence of Thomas, took the view that the question in Mark 12.9a forms the original ending of the parable. Mark and Luke then make Jesus answer his own question – which is quite untypical.[41] In Matthew it is the audience that

[40]His eye may have slipped from Isa. 5.5 to 5.4.
[41]Contrast Luke 7.42; 10.36.

answers. The reply is that 'he will come and destroy the tenants and will give the vineyard to others'. The ἐλεύσεται (Matthew: ὅταν ἔλθη) may echo the church's parousia teaching; and by adding 'Therefore, I tell you the kingdom of God will be taken from you and given to a nation that yields the proper fruit', Matthew completes the allegorization by bringing in the Gentiles. Luke prolongs the conversation further by appending a response from the audience, 'God forbid!'

It looks as if all the additions are secondary, including, of course, Thomas's, 'He that hath ears, let him hear', with which he also ends a number of other parables (8, 21, 63, 96). It is probably best to say simply that Jesus leaves the challenge of the story with its hearers in a form that we cannot now recover, but which they understood well enough.

The addition of the stone saying

This is clearly not an integral part of the story, yet is incorporated into it prior to the audience's final reaction and, in Matthew, prior to its allegorization, which is thus isolated from the parable it interprets. Ps. 118.22 which is quoted was evidently a favourite proof-text in early Christian circles (Acts 4.11; I Peter 2.7) and it supplies the reference to the vindication of Jesus, through exaltation, that the parable lacks. For this reason it must be suspected as an addition of the church. Yet the church's use of it could well have originated here (just as the church's use of Dan. 7.14 could well have started from Jesus' own use of it at his trial – to refer again, before it was reinterpreted of the parousia, to his own vindication by exaltation). It appears to be characteristic of Jesus' polemical use of scripture (as opposed to the evangelists' confirmatory use of testimonia).[42] For the formula, 'or have you not read?', we may compare Mark 2.25 (David and the shewbread) and 12.26 (the passage about the bush),[43] and, with the Lukan version appealing to the meaning of 'what is written', John 10.34 ('I have said, You are gods').[44] But none of these others occurs within a parable, and the fact that the introductory formula to the quotation here differs with each evangelist suggests that the linkage, though already in the tradition they received, is editorial.

Yet the connection with the parable is close. F. F. Bruce[45] has

---

[42]For an expansion of this distinction see ch. 3 below.
[43]Cf. the polemical 'How do the scribes say?' in Mark 12.35–37 (David's son).
[44]Cf. John 8.17: 'In your own law it is written' (the witness of two men is true).
[45]'The Corner Stone', *Exp T* 84, 1973, p. 233.

pointed out that those by whom the Son of Man is rejected in Mark 8.31 ('the elders, the chief priests and the scribes') are precisely those by whom the stone is rejected here and in Acts 4.5, 11. And M. Black[46] notes the well-attested pun on *eben*, stone, and *ben*, son and rightly calls the whole the parable of the Rejected Son (or Stone). The linking of the two by Jesus is therefore very possible, though it could equally have been made by the Palestinian church. The further addition in Luke of another stone-saying from Isa. 8.14 (with which it is also connected in I Peter 2.4–8) is almost certainly evidence of a testimonia collection and of association by catchword. Luke's omission of the second verse of the first quotation (Ps. 118.23) is evidently editorial, so as to bring the two stone references together. The inclusion of the latter in the manuscript tradition of Matt. 21.44 (isolated from the former by the allegorization of the parable!) is surely secondary (despite Jeremias).

The witness of Thomas at this point is interesting. For the stone is the subject of the *next* saying (66). But it is not fused with the parable. This provides confirmation of some association, either in Jesus's own teaching or in some very early collection of it:[47] for the rest of Thomas's order, as Montefiore stresses,[48] is *not* that of the synoptists. But if the stone saying is in the same order it is not in the same context – nor indeed in any context. It is an isolated and obscure *logion*: 'Jesus said, Teach me concerning this stone which the builders rejected; it is the corner-stone.' It is not related as in the New Testament to Jesus' vindication and appears to have some esoteric gnostic significance.[49] Its only contribution to our investigation is that it supplies evidence for a connection of the saying with the parable without a fusion of the two.

To sum up our conclusions so far, we may say:

1. In regard to the context of the parable, the synoptic tradition has strong claims both to originality and reliability. Thomas at this point is worthless.

2. In regard to the form of the parable, the version of Thomas is likely to be the most primitive[50] – except perhaps in the elaboration

[46]'The Christological Use of the Old Testament in the New Testament', *NTS* 18, 1971–2, pp. 11–14.

[47]So, tentatively, R. McL. Wilson, *Studies in the Gospel of Thomas*, London 1960, p. 102.

[48]*Thomas and the Evangelists*, p. 74 f.

[49]R. M. Grant and D. N. Freedman, *The Secret Sayings of Jesus*, New York and London 1960, ad loc., note that the Naasenes too were impressed with this mysterious saying (Hippolytus *Ref.* v. 7.35). Cf. Rev. 2.17?

[50]J. D. Crossan, 'The parable of the wicked husbandmen', *JBL* 40, 1971, pp. 451–65, reaches the same conclusion.

about the first servant, in contrast with the son, not being known, though this could provide the clue to the original conclusion (not the transfer of the vineyard but the inexcusability of the tenants).

3. Within the synoptic tradition Luke is probably nearer to the original version in having no explicit allusion to Isa. 5.2 and in retaining the sending of single servants (albeit three, not two), none of whom gets killed. Matthew's version reveals the highest degree of allegorization (the servants = the former and latter prophets, the vineyard = the kingdom, the others = the Gentiles), *except* in relation to the person of the son, where Mark shows most signs of development (one, beloved, last of all). However, in the treatment accorded to the son, Mark appears the most original.

4. All the conclusions to the parable are suspect.

5. The stone saying is more original in context and interpretation in the synoptists, though Thomas may be right in keeping it distinct from the parable.

We may now move to the inferences to be drawn for the literary relationship between the four different versions.

The first conclusion must be that, at any rate in regard to this story, Thomas is not dependent on any of the synoptic gospels. Nothing in our analysis would require us to question the carefully argued conclusions of both Montefiore and Koester[51] among others that the parabolic material in particular in the Gospel of Thomas rests upon tradition independent of and sometimes (as in this case) superior to that of the canonical gospels. Its relevance to the sifting of the synoptic versions is to provide an independent test, and often a striking confirmation, of the conclusions to which scholars have been driven on form-critical and linguistic grounds.

But if there is no literary connection between Thomas and the synoptists this does nothing to shake but rather, by contrast, reinforces the presumption that there is *some* relationship of literary interdependence between the three synoptists. But before attempting to determine what this is, we must seek in the light of the foregoing analysis to establish what is the basic form of the common *synoptic* tradition, again without pre-judging the priority of any particular gospel.

For this we may use two criteria: (*a*) the sheer fact of common wording, allowing what discount we can for recognizable stylistic

---

[51]J. M. Robinson and H. Koester, *Trajectories through Early Christianity*, Philadelphia 1971, pp. 130–2, 166–87.

alterations; and (b) the tendencies already observed in the transmission which may enable us with greater or less confidence to isolate what is secondary. In other words, we are looking not simply for the highest common factor of shared matter but for its most primitive state.

It is simplest to proceed by underlining the words in the presumed common original and then to comment on the grounds for doing so. It is virtually impossible to *describe* the differences – as one evangelist 'adding', 'omitting', 'rewriting' this or that –without seeming to presuppose some theory of their relationship. All one can do is to indicate which version at any particular point looks to be preserving the nucleus of the tradition and to observe the divergences from that, without implying any pattern of dependence. For instance, Mark might be found to preserve this best and yet stand in a relationship not of priority but of condensation or conflation to one or both of the others. Again, I shall follow the verse-numbering in Mark merely for convenience (if only because in this parable his enumeration happens to begin with 1).

Matt. 21.33–46	Mark 12.1–12	Luke 20.9–19
³³Ἄλλην παραβολὴν ἀκούσατε· ἄνθρωπος ἦν οἰκοδεσπότης ὅστις ἐφύτευσεν ἀμπελῶνα καὶ φραγμὸν αὐτῷ περιέθηκεν καὶ ὤρυξεν ἐν αὐτῷ ληνὸν καὶ ᾠκοδόμησεν πύργον καὶ ἐξέδετο αὐτὸν γεωργοῖς καὶ ἀπεδήμησεν. ³⁴ὅτε δὲ ἤγγισεν ὁ καιρὸς τῶν καρπῶν, ἀπέστειλεν τοὺς δούλους αὐτοῦ πρὸς τοὺς γεωργοὺς λαβεῖν τοὺς καρποὺς αὐτοῦ.	¹Καὶ ἤρξατο αὐτοῖς ἐν παραβολαῖς λαλεῖν· ἀμπελῶνα ἄνθρωπος ἐφύτευσεν καὶ περιέθηκεν φραγμὸν καὶ ὤρυξεν ὑπολήνιον καὶ ᾠκοδόμησεν πύργον καὶ ἐξέδετο αὐτὸν γεωργοῖς καὶ ἀπεδήμησεν. ²καὶ ἀπέστειλεν πρὸς γεωργοὺς τῷ καιρῷ δοῦλον, ἵνα παρὰ τῶν γεωργῶν λάβῃ ἀπὸ τῶν	⁹Ἤρξατο δὲ πρὸς τὸν λαὸν λέγειν τὴν παραβολὴν ταύτην· ἄνθρωπος ἐφύτευσεν ἀμπελῶνα. καὶ ἐξέδετο αὐτὸν γεωργοῖς καὶ ἀπεδήμησεν χρόνους ἱκανούς. ¹⁰καὶ καιρῷ ἀπέστειλεν πρὸς τοὺς γεωργοὺς δοῦλον, ἵνα ἀπὸ τοῦ καρποῦ τοῦ ἀμπελῶνος

Matt. 21.33–46	Mark 12.1–12	Luke 20.9–19

Matt. 21.33–46

³⁵καὶ λαβόντες οἱ γεωργοὶ τοὺς δούλους αὐτοῦ ὃν μὲν ἔδειραν, ὃν δὲ ἀπέκτειναν, ὃν δὲ ἐλιθοβόλησαν.

³⁶πάλιν ἀπέστειλεν ἄλλους δούλους πλείονας τῶν πρώτων, καὶ ἐποίησαν αὐτοῖς ὡσαύτως.

³⁷ὕστερον δὲ ἀπέστειλεν πρὸς αὐτοὺς τὸν υἱὸν αὐτοῦ λέγων· ἐντραπήσονται τὸν υἱόν μου. ³⁸οἱ δὲ γεωργοὶ ἰδόντες τὸν υἱὸν εἶπον ἐν ἑαυτοῖς· οὗτός ἐστιν ὁ κληρονόμος· δεῦτε ἀποκτείνωμεν αὐτὸν καὶ σχῶμεν τὴν κληρονομίαν αὐτοῦ. ³⁹καὶ λαβόντες αὐτὸν ἐξέβαλον ἔξω τοῦ ἀμπελῶνος καὶ ἀπέκτειναν. ⁴⁰ὅταν οὖν ἔλθῃ ὁ κύριος τοῦ ἀμπελῶνος, τί ποιήσει τοῖς γεωργοῖς ἐκείνοις; ⁴¹λέγουσιν αὐτῷ· κακοὺς κακῶς ἀπολέσει αὐτούς, καὶ τὸν ἀμπελῶνα ἐκδώσεται ἄλλοις γεωργοῖς, οἵτινες ἀποδώσουσιν αὐτῷ τοὺς καρποὺς ἐν τοῖς καιροῖς αὐτῶν. ⁴²λέγει αὐτοῖς ὁ Ἰησοῦς· οὐδέποτε ἀνέγνωτε ἐν ταῖς γραφαῖς· λίθον ὃν ἀπεδοκίμασαν οἱ οἰκοδομοῦντες, οὗτος ἐγενήθη εἰς κεφαλὴν γωνίας· παρὰ κυρίου ἐγένετο αὕτη, καὶ ἔστιν θαυμαστὴ ἐν ὀφθαλμοῖς ἡμῶν; ⁴³διὰ τοῦτο λέγω ὑμῖν ὅτι

Mark 12.1–12

καρπῶν τοῦ ἀμπελῶνος· ³καὶ λαβόντες αὐτὸν ἔδειραν καὶ ἀπέστειλαν κενόν. ⁴καὶ πάλιν ἀπέστειλεν πρὸς αὐτοὺς ἄλλον δοῦλον· κἀκεῖνον ἐκεφαλίωσαν καὶ ἠτίμασαν. ⁵καὶ ἄλλον ἀπέστειλεν· κἀκεῖνον ἀπέκτειναν καὶ πολλοὺς ἄλλους, οὓς μὲν δέροντες, οὓς δὲ ἀποκτέννοντες. ⁶ἔτι ἕνα εἶχεν υἱὸν ἀγαπητόν· ἀπέστειλεν αὐτὸν ἔσχατον πρὸς αὐτοὺς λέγων ὅτι ἐντραπήσονται τὸν υἱόν μου. ⁷ἐκεῖνοι δὲ οἱ γεωργοὶ πρὸς ἑαυτοὺς εἶπαν ὅτι οὗτός ἐστιν ὁ κληρονόμος· δεῦτε ἀποκτείνωμεν αὐτόν, καὶ ἡμῶν ἔσται ἡ κληρονομία. ⁸καὶ λαβόντες ἀπέκτειναν αὐτόν, καὶ ἐξέβαλον αὐτὸν ἔξω τοῦ ἀμπελῶνος· ⁹τί ποιήσει ὁ κύριος τοῦ ἀμπελῶνος; ἐλεύσεται καὶ ἀπολέσει τοὺς γεωργοὺς καὶ δώσει τὸν ἀμπελῶνα ἄλλοις. ¹⁰οὐδὲ τὴν γραφὴν ταύτην ἀνέγνωτε· λίθον ὃν ἀπεδοκίμασαν οἱ οἰκοδομοῦντες, οὗτος ἐγενήθη εἰς κεφαλὴν γωνίας· ¹¹παρὰ κυρίου ἐγένετο αὕτη, καὶ ἔστιν θαυμαστὴ ἐν ὀφθαλμοῖς ἡμῶν;

Luke 20.9–19

³καὶ δώσουσιν αὐτῷ· οἱ δὲ γεωργοὶ ἐξαπέστειλαν αὐτὸν δείραντες κενόν. ¹¹καὶ προσέθετο ἕτερον πέμψαι δοῦλον· οἱ δὲ κἀκεῖνον δείραντες καὶ ἀτιμάσαντες ἐξαπέστειλαν κενόν. ¹²καὶ προσέθετο τρίτον πέμψαι· οἱ δὲ καὶ τοῦτον τραυματίσαντες ἐξέβαλον. ¹³εἶπεν δὲ ὁ κύριος τοῦ ἀμπελῶνος· τί ποιήσω; πέμψω τὸν υἱόν μου τὸν ἀγαπητόν· ἴσως τοῦτον ἐντραπήσονται. ¹⁴ἰδόντες δὲ αὐτὸν οἱ γεωργοὶ διελογίζοντο πρὸς ἀλλήλους λέγοντες· οὗτός ἐστιν ὁ κληρονόμος· ἀποκτείνωμεν αὐτόν, ἵνα ἡμῶν γένηται ἡ κληρονομία. ¹⁵καὶ ἐκβαλόντες αὐτὸν ἔξω τοῦ ἀμπελῶνος ἀπέκτειναν. τί οὖν ποιήσει αὐτοῖς ὁ κύριος τοῦ ἀμπελῶνος; ¹⁶ἐλεύσεται καὶ ἀπολέσει τοὺς γεωργοὺς τούτους, καὶ δώσει τὸν ἀμπελῶνα ἄλλοις. ἀκούσαντες δὲ εἶπαν· μὴ γένοιτο. ¹⁷ὁ δὲ ἐμβλέψας αὐτοῖς εἶπεν· τί οὖν ἐστιν τὸ γεγραμμένον τοῦτο· λίθον ὃν ἀπεδοκίμασαν οἱ οἰκοδομοῦντες, οὗτος ἐγενήθη εἰς κεφαλὴν γωνίας;

Matt. 21.33–46	Mark 12.1–12	Luke 20.9–19

ἀρθήσεται ἀφ᾽ ὑμῶν ἡ βασιλεία τοῦ θεοῦ καὶ δοθήσεται ἔθνει ποιοῦντι τοὺς καρποὺς αὐτῆς.[44]

[18]πᾶς ὁ πεσὼν ἐπ᾽ ἐκεῖνον τὸν λίθον συνθλασθήσεται· ἐφ᾽ ὃν δ᾽ ἂν πέσῃ, λικμήσει αὐτόν.

[45]ἀκούσαντες δὲ οἱ ἀρχιερεῖς καὶ οἱ Φαρισαῖοι τὰς παραβολὰς αὐτοῦ ἔγνωσαν ὅτι περὶ αὐτῶν λέγει· [46]καὶ ζητοῦντες αὐτὸν κρατῆσαι ἐφοβήθησαν τοὺς ὄχλους, ἐπεὶ εἰς προφήτην αὐτὸν εἶχον.

[12]καὶ ἐζήτουν αὐτὸν κρατῆσαι καὶ ἐφοβήθησαν τὸν ὄχλον· ἔγνωσαν γὰρ ὅτι πρὸς αὐτοὺς τὴν παραβολὴν εἶπεν.

[19]καὶ ἐζήτησαν οἱ γραμματεῖς καὶ οἱ ἀρχιερεῖς ἐπιβαλεῖν ἐπ᾽ αὐτὸν τὰς χεῖρας ἐν αὐτῇ τῇ ὥρᾳ, καὶ ἐφοβήθησαν τὸν λαόν· ἔγνωσαν γὰρ ὅτι πρὸς αὐτοὺς εἶπεν τὴν παραβολὴν ταύτην.

v.1. The introductory formula is evidently in each case redactional. The subsequent variations in Matthew (οἰκοδεσπότης) and Luke (χρόνους ἱκανούς) have already been noted as secondary. But was the allusion to Isa. 5 already in the *synoptic* version? In other words, has Luke omitted it or have Matthew and Mark added it? Luke may have thought the details irrelevant (as they are) and inadvertently shown himself more primitive. But the evidence of Thomas must add weight to the supposition that one of the evangelists has added them. If so, it looks like Mark, with Matthew bringing them more closely into line with the LXX text. A final judgment on this must, however, depend on how the wider pattern of dependence is assessed, and I have therefore used dotted lines. 2–4. Mark appears the most basic. Luke's variations show characteristics of his style.[52] Matthew regroups the servants (in the plural), apparently for allegorical reasons. 5. It looks as though a third single servant (? who was killed) may have been part of the common *synoptic* tradition, with Luke continuing to rewrite. As it is impossible to be sure, I have again used dotted lines. There is every reason to regard Mark 5b as secondary, whether or not there is

[52]Cf. Jeremias, *Parables*, p. 72 n. 84.

further interdependence (either way) with Matthew. 6. Here Matthew clearly seems to have the most basic version, with Mark and Luke each supplying his own introduction and drawing out the christological implications. 7. Mark and Matthew seem to preserve the common tradition, with Matthew perhaps improving the style at the end (with two imperatives) and Luke again doing some rewriting. 8. Mark is here likely to represent the original, with Matthew and Luke reversing the killing and the expulsion. 9. Mark and (with variations) Luke appear to be basic (except for Luke's additional response from the audience), with Matthew this time doing the most rewriting. 10 f. The introductions to the scriptural quotation are evidently editorial, contrasting with verbatim agreement in the citation itself. Luke's omission of the second half is clearly determined by his added quotation, while Matthew's explicit allegorization of the parable is equally secondary. 12. Mark presents the common matter, with Matthew and Luke exhibiting different variations.

If now we look at the material underlined, it is evident that much the highest proportion of it occurs in Mark, who has also much the lowest proportion of that which is not underlined. If the criterion for distinguishing these two were simply the extent of common wording, then all this would show is that Mark is the middle-term: his version could just as plausibly have been conflated from the matter common to Matthew and Luke. But since the criterion has also been what presents itself on independent critical grounds to be the most primitive state of the tradition, it amounts to a fairly powerful argument for Markan priority. Particularly is this so in regard to the material which is _not_ underlined. It is not merely that so much of the common wording appears in Mark: it is that so much of what is evidently secondary does not. Unless therefore Mark the evangelist is viewed as a sort of Jeremias before his time, peeling off the accretions theological and stylistic and reconstituting the most primitive text, it appears that we must conclude that he stands closest to source.

Moreover, on the evidence of this parable, there is really no other competitor for first place. Luke scores at a number of points over Mark – the omission of the details from Isaiah, the refusal to collectivize the servants or see any of them killed. But there is too much distinctive writing in the Lukan idiom to make it credible that we are here at source. Nor is it easy to see how the versions in Mark or Matthew could have been derived from him. Matthew too has too much material, particularly of an allegorizing character, which by any critical standards must be regarded as secondary, to be the starting-point of the other two versions. In particular it is difficult to see how Luke could have derived directly from Matthew his set of three separate servants none of whom gets killed. It is much easier to view Mark at this point as the basis of the other two. Kümmel indeed concluded his survey by saying: 'There are no certain arguments for reconstructing a text more primitive than our Mark.'[53] But this was before the evidence provided by Thomas, and it also ignores some of that within the synoptic tradition itself.

For there are still powerful objections to the priority of Mark in the generally accepted sense that his gospel *as it stands* is the source for Matthew and Luke. Apart from the uncertainty represented by the words underlined with dotted lines, there is the crucial verse at the climax of the story relating to the sending of the son. Here on the same critical criteria, vindicated now by the Gospel of Thomas, Matthew has the least allegorized version, precisely at the point where one would have expected this tendency to be most operative –and Mark has christologically the most developed. Though he does not list this passage as having been noted by scholars, it must, I think, be added to the considerable list of 'suggested exceptions to the priority of Mark' compiled by E. P. Sanders.[54] In particular, it is remarkably parallel to the situation which we find at the reply of Jesus to the high priest in Mark 14.62 and parallels. There too Mark has the most explicit christological claim (with an unambiguous 'I am') and Matthew the least, and there are other factors to indicate that Matthew may be closest to the original version.[55]

I believe that at this point the conclusion must be faced that none of our existing gospels as it stands is the source of the written tradition they have in common. In other words, we are back at some *Grundschrift* or Ur-gospel that lies behind them all.

The reaction to this of anyone with any knowledge of the history of the synoptic problem is likely to be one of dismay. First, it will be said, why introduce a hypothetical document at all? And secondly, why this one? Has not its ghost been well and truly laid?

The great asset, says Farmer, of the Griesbach hypothesis he advocates is that it explains the literary agreements between the gospels 'without an appeal to hypothetical sources'.[56] In other

[53]Op cit., (n. 17 above), p. 126.

[54]*The Tendencies of the Synoptic Tradition*, Cambridge 1969, Appendix II, pp. 290–3.

[55]Cf. my *Jesus and His Coming*, London and New York 1957, pp. 43–50. I there argued, on the basis of the priority of Mark, for a subsequent alteration in the Markan *text*. But there is very little evidence for this, and none in Mark 12.6 (except *possibly* for the omission of ἐσχατον).

[56]*Synoptic Problem*, p. 8.

words, by abandoning the priority of Mark, one can dispense with Q. Yet, ironically, on the evidence of the material before us the only plausible candidate for priority is Mark *unless* we can appeal to a hypothetical source. But in fact there is no virtue in refusing recourse to a hypothetical document if it is demanded by the data.[57] No one is suggesting that we should *begin* by inventing documents. That we have not done. It is only because we have apparently been driven to it by the evidence that we have been forced to go behind Mark.

But has not Ur-Marcus been disposed of more effectively even than Q? Turner and Streeter thought they had buried him once and for all.

> One more nail has been driven into the coffin of that old acquaintance of our youth Ur-Marcus. He did enough harm in his time, but he is dead and gone; let no attempts be made to disinter his skeleton.[58]

> Renounce once and for all the chase of the phantom Ur-Marcus.[59]

But Farmer, who quotes these passages, has called attention to what he calls Streeter's 'fatal omission' (traceable to Burkitt) in dismissing Ur-Marcus solely because it was unnecessary to explain the *agreements* between Matthew and Luke against Mark. These agreements, wrote Streeter, are 'the only valid objection to the theory that the document used by Matthew and Luke was our Mark'.[60] As Farmer rightly says, 'There was no consideration of the very significant evidence for Ur-Marcus from passages where all three have material in common, but where there are differences between their accounts which cannot be explained on the assumption that Matthew and/or Luke copied Mark'.[61] Yet Farmer too concentrates his whole attack on Streeter on his failure to explain the agreements, adding[62] that for conscientious adherents of the two-document hypothesis the only escape from Ur-Marcus in passages where Mark appears secondary to

---

[57]Farmer himself fully concedes this: 'There is nothing wrong in hypothecating the existence of an otherwise unknown source or sources if there exists evidence that is best explained thereby. . . . But a critic should not posit the existence of hypothetical sources until he has made an attempt to solve the problem without appeal to such sources.' ('How material common to Matthew and Luke is viewed on the Griesbach hypothesis: Prolegomenon to further discussion'. As yet unpublished.)

[58]C. H. Turner, 'Marcan usage, part VI', *JTS* 26, 1924–5, p. 346.

[59]B. H. Streeter, *The Four Gospels*, London and New York 1924; [4]1930, p. 331. Farmer's isolation of this clause obscures the fact that in its context it is not jussive but concessive.

[60]Ibid. Earlier he mentioned, only to refute, the arguments for Ur-Marcus from what Mark, Matthew and Luke *omit*(pp.168—81). But this is in any case irrelevant to our passage.

[61]Op. cit., p. 93.   [62]Ibid., p. 94.

Matthew or Luke is an appeal to Mark's use of Q (which Streeter rejected). Yet in our parable it is not the agreements between Matthew and Luke that raise the issue, which are indeed so minor as to be negligible[63] (none is even mentioned by Streeter). Nor is the use of Q remotely relevant. It is that neither Mark nor any one of the other gospels can throughout be regarded as the prototype of the common tradition.[64]

The fact that Mark is nearest to it makes it natural to call this underlying document Ur-Marcus. Yet that would be to prejudge the issue. All that we can logically infer is that less subsequent development, whether of a communal or an editorial nature, took place upon it in the Markan than in the Matthean or Lukan traditions. We could equally well call it Ur-Matthaeus if we place the *Grundschrift* relatively further back in the process. In fact the hypothesis we are urging requires no more than that the processes described by the form-and redaction-critics were operative upon, and not simply prior to, the first written documents. The assumption that there was a period of oral transmission *followed by* a fixing of the tradition in literary form, which then *superseded* the oral process, is in any case being shown to be much too simple. At the further end of the so-called tunnel-period it is now clear that oral tradition retained its vitality and authority well after the writing of the finished gospels.[65] At the beginning too it is arbitrary to assume that summaries of Jesus' works and words for kerygmatic and catechetical purposes were not written down quite early. This has always indeed been accepted by advocates of the Q hypothesis in relation to the teaching material: the original written document or documents are not likely to be reproduced without modification in either Matthew or Luke, and the evidence for translation-variants suggests indeed a source that goes back behind the Greek-speaking church. All that is here being suggested is that evidence from the triple tradition likewise indicates that the basic document (or documents) is prior in written form to any of the three synoptic gospels. One important advantage of the Q hypothesis (in contrast to the view that Luke drew on Matthew for his common material or *vice versa*) is that it does not compel us to say that one

---

[63] οἱ γεωργοί in Matt. 21.35 and Luke 20.10; ἰδόντες in Matt. 21.38 and Luke 20.14; and οὖν in Matt. 21.40 and Luke 20.14. The only agreement of substance, though not of verbal identity, is the reversal of the order of the killing and the throwing out in Matt. 21.39 and Luke 20.15.

[64] J. A. Fitzmyer dares to say: 'To my way of thinking, the possibility of Ur-Markus is still admissible', 'The priority of Mark and the "Q" source in Luke' in D. G. Miller, ed., *Jesus and Man's Hope*, I, Pittsburgh 1970, 147.

[65] Cf. H. Koester, *Synoptische Überlieferung bei den apostolischen Vätern*, Berlin 1957. This is also borne out by the Gospel of Thomas.

gospel or the other must consistently preserve this material in its most primitive state: we can judge the version of each saying on its merits. So with the triple tradition. On the view we are urging, the most original form of the material may at any given point be found in any one (or two) of the three gospels. We do not have to force it to fit a theory of over-all priority. We can test it at its several points, as we have been doing with this sample, and judge accordingly.[66]

Two questions, however, remain. Can we say anything more specific about the *Grundschrift* behind the triple tradition, or does it remain simply an 'x'? And what is the subsequent interrelationship, if any, between the distinctively Matthaean, Markan and Lukan developments of it? Are our gospels as such dependent on each other? Did any use the others' finished material?

Any answer to the first question must at once take us beyond the very limited sample we have selected. For this story is but part of a large amount of material which stands in a fairly consistent order. Indeed, the argument from order for a single underlying document is much stronger than in the case of Q. The inference from this order to the priority of Mark *without* postulating an original document to which he was the most faithful has been shown to rest on a fallacy.[67] The fact that Mark almost invariably keeps the common order when Matthew or Luke departs from it merely proves him to have been a middle-term (he could come first, second or third). Even if one introduces an Ur-document, as the argument from order originally did, this logically implies no conclusion about the priority of our Mark. It simply shows that, as in the case of other developments (allegorical, literary, theological etc.), Matthew and Luke reflect more subsequent workings (though these could indeed be expected to create more disturbance to the original order).[68] Nor does the fact

[66]This approach is very much in line with the openness urged by Sanders at the conclusion of his careful study of the tendencies of the synoptic tradition (op. cit., pp. 278 f.). For its wider implications, cf. my *Redating the New Testament*, London and Philadelphia 1976, pp. 93 f.

[67]This is agreed between B. C. Butler, *The Originality of St Matthew*, Cambridge and New York 1951, pp. 62–71; G. M. Styler, 'The Priority of Mark' in C. F. D. Moule, ed., *The Birth of the New Testament*, Cambridge and New York 1962, pp. 224f., [3]1981, p. 290; and Farmer, op. cit., pp. 66, 212–5.

[68]Farmer raises the question: 'Since both Matthew and Luke deviated from the Ur-gospel, and since neither had knowledge of the action of the other, why do not their deviations from the order of the Ur-gospel coincide more often? Why are there not more instances where neither Matthew nor Luke supports the order found in Mark?' (op. cit., p. 214). An answer might be that neither has *that* much occasion to diverge from the original order (any more than does Mark) and that when either does so it is for reasons of redactional rearrangement that the other does not share. A conspiracy theory is out of place.

that in the triple tradition the Ur-gospel always looks most like Mark prove anything about its extent or content, since, as Farmer says, 'any source reconstructed primarily from passages found in all three Synoptics, *ipso facto*, will be conformed in extent and content to the shortest of the three'.[69]

Yet against these logical non-sequiturs from the internal evidence must be weighed the external tradition preserved by Papias[70] that behind Mark lies a summary of apostolic preaching associated with the name of Peter, parallel to his other tradition of a collection of λόγια (in Hebrew) associated with the name of Matthew. Just as the latter cannot simply be identified with our Gospel of Matthew, so Mark's record of Peter's preaching may bear a less direct relation to the second gospel than Papias would suggest. But that some written account of what Jesus proclaimed and did and suffered circulated early and that it was *more like* what became incorporated in the Gospel of Mark than any other would certainly fit what is suggested, though not demonstrated, by the internal evidence. And again it seems plausible that a version of this document was combined with a translation of a sayings-collection or collections, plus other preaching[71] and teaching[72] matter, to form, probably in several stages,[73] the Gospels of Matthew and Luke. In other words, we are back at the earlier form of the two-document hypothesis, whether we choose to designate these proto-documents (which after all are not purely hypothetical) Aleph and Beta (with Marsh), Aleph and Lambda (with Holtzmann), or P and Q (with Armitage Robinson).[74]

The subsequent work of the form-and redaction-critics has thrown much light on the processes through which both these kinds of material passed in the life and preaching and liturgy of the church before and after it reached written forms. But it has not, I think, affected the basic truth of the pattern. What it has done is to shake

[69]Op. cit., p. 41.

[70]Eusebius, *HE* III. 39.15 f.

[71]Here one should almost certainly include an independent version of the passion narrative incorporated in Luke. John has yet another.

[72]Particularly the catechetical and disciplinary matter characteristic of Matthew, also to be found, independently as I believe, in that Christian 'manual of discipline', the Didache.

[73]We are not here concerned with the evidence that the Gospels of Mark, Luke and Matthew (like that of John) may themselves have gone through several states or recensions. For evidence of this even in Mark, cf. my *Jesus and His Coming*, pp. 128–36.

[74]For the positions of Marsh and Holtzmann, cf. Farmer, op. cit., pp. 11–15, 40–5. For Armitage Robinson's usage cf. R. H. Lightfoot, *History and Interpretation in the Gospels*, London and New York 1935, p. 27.

the confidence of the source-critics that the solution to the synoptic problem can be found simply in 'the literary relationships between Matthew, Mark and Luke' as we now have them. The quotation is from the sub-title of Farmer's book and in this regard he is even more confident than Streeter, since he does not think it necessary to invoke *any* underlying document: our Luke can be explained from our Matthew, and our Mark from both. Whereas Streeter held that in their common material Mark was always more primitive than Matthew and Luke, while in the Q material either Matthew or Luke might preserve the earlier form, Farmer is committed to saying that in their common matter[75] Matthew is always more primitive than Luke and Matthew and Luke always more primitive than Mark. I should wish to reserve freedom in both cases. Yet the basic truth of the two-document hypothesis is reinforced by the fact that more often than not (as in the sample we have been studying) it is Mark that seems nearest to source, whereas in the non-Markan material the instances of apparent priority are much more evenly balanced between Matthew and Luke. But there is no ground for arguing, with Streeter, that a form of the tradition is prior *because* it is in Mark, nor, with Farmer, that it is excluded from so being *for that reason*.

Finally, I come to the question of the relationship of our present synoptic gospels not to the traditions behind them but to each other. When every allowance has been made for their common material, did Matthew, Mark and Luke develop in mutual isolation or did any one use either or both of the others? Again the question cannot be answered without going far beyond the sample we have taken. But employing that as a test can we draw any conclusions?

We here come back to the words tentatively underscored with a dotted line. There was doubt – and the doubt must remain – whether they ever belonged to the basic common synoptic tradition. *If* Luke did not exclude them, then the details from Isa. 5.2 in Mark 12.1 and Matt. 21.33 will have been introduced by one evangelist (or his community) and taken over by the other. We have indicated that Matthew shows further signs of alignment to the LXX. This would then be an argument (albeit weak) that Matthew knew and used Mark.

In Mark 12.5 and parallels there is a more complex situation. The

---

[75]He would not deny that there was *parallel* material in Luke not directly derived from Matthew (e.g. the parables of the Pounds, the Great Feast and the Lost Sheep, and parts of the eschatological discourse in Luke 17), where the priority of each version must be assessed on its merits.

third individual servant is paralleled in Luke 20.12, but there he is not killed. The probability, I think, is that (as in the context generally) Luke is rewriting what is already in the common document, with Mark (perhaps) introducing the killing. In 5b we have a generalized statement about 'other servants' for which there is no parallel in Luke and which there is every reason (grammatical as well as allegorical) to regard as secondary. But Matthew has a close but further elaborated parallel to this (with the addition of 'stoning'), which he has substituted for any account of individual servants. This seems a clear instance of Matthew having known and used our Mark – though the conclusion still stands that he also went *behind* our Mark in the next verse (relating to the son).

None of Luke's rewriting appears to show the influence of Mark or *vice versa*, unless the common use of ἀγαπητόν betrays assimilation. But in Luke it is a title (with the article), whereas in Mark it is not; and it is as likely to have come in from the baptism and transfiguration narratives (or the common Christian tradition of Jesus as God's only son) as from copying between the evangelists. Luke's additional stone-saying evidently comes from this stock rather than from either of the other gospels.

As we have seen, the only evidence in this passage, apart from insignificant stylistic details, of secondary agreement between Matthew and Luke is in their reversal of the order (against Mark) of the killing and expulsion of the son. If this is motivated by allegorical considerations, then it could denote interdependence, but equally again it may reflect the wider Christian tradition (as found in John and Hebrews). The passion narratives of Matthew and Luke do not suggest that they attached any editorial significance to it.

Finally, *if* Matthew 21.44 is part of the true text, it would argue for assimilation at the redactional and not merely the scribal stage. But this must remain very dubious.

On this second question, then, the only substantial evidence *within this passage* for literary connection between the gospels themselves is for the use of Mark by Matthew. This would favour a modified version of the hypothesis of Streeter rather than of Augustine or Griesbach, both of which put Matthew before Mark. But the sample is obviously much too small for any extended conclusion. In any case, such interrelationship assumes far less importance if we are not, as on each of these three hypotheses, concerned with fundamental dependence for tradition but with the subsequent mutual influence of parallel developments within the common life of the church of the earliest Christian *paradosis*.[76]

[76]I have not been able to take into account the recent monograph by K. Snodgrass, *The Parable of the Wicked Tenants*, Tübingen 1983. He argues that the version in the Gospel of Thomas stems from a post-synoptic stage and that Matthew's version is the earliest we possess. The stone-quotation from Ps. 118.22 belonged with the parable from its origin, providing the key to the original understanding of the parable. There is good reason to suppose that the parable stems from Jesus himself and that the allegorical element is fundamental to it.

3

Did Jesus Have a Distinctive Use of Scripture?[1]

One of the most succinct summaries of the issues involved in the relation of the historical Jesus to the Christ of the church's faith is Harvey K. McArthur's 'From the Historical Jesus to Christology,'[2] originally delivered as an address to C. F. D. Moule's New Testament seminar at Cambridge when I, alas, was away being Bishop of Woolwich. It states with great clarity the various positions one can take, although I would incline more to what McArthur calls 'the historical risk school,' while he would lean toward 'the immune from historical risk school.'

In this I am an unashamed follower of C. H. Dodd, who surprisingly gets no mention in the work, rather than of the German-American tradition that runs through Kähler and Bultmann to Tillich and Knox. Indeed, one of the moments that has seared itself upon my memory was when I was taken as a young teacher of the New Testament by my friend and host John Knox to the weekly faculty luncheon in the halcyon days of Union Theological Seminary. I had no idea that I was to be more than a guest sitting at the feet of the great. When suddenly at the end of lunch Knox turned to me with the indication that I was now 'on' and was to address the assembled company, it was like a nighmare. I rapidly decided that attack was the best and indeed only form of defence and, greatly daring, took the initiative by continuing the friendly riposte I had been making to Knox about his position and Tillich's and why I found it untenable.

I now realize that this was but continuing a classic conversation held there between Tillich and Dodd some years earlier, in 1950, described by Langdon Gilkey in the appendix to F. W. Dillistone's life of Dodd. In it Tillich is recorded as saying to Dodd:

[1]First published in *Christological Perspectives : Essays in Honor of Harvey K. McArthur*, ed. R. F. Berkey and S. A. Edwards, New York 1982, pp. 49–57.
[2]In *Interpretation* 23, 1969, pp. 190–206.

Then there are *two* risks, a double risk involved for the Christian: one that the witness of the New Testament refers to an actual historical figure, and the second that the figure so described is the Christ. 'Yes,' said Dodd, 'there are two risks, one historical and the other religious – and a historical faith cannot escape either one.' Tillich said he could not tolerate such a double indemnity, so to speak, and stuck to his 'single risk' theory. . . .

Dodd then went on to maintain – and I don't think Tillich agreed with him – that the preliminary, historical risk was really not all that great. He clearly felt relatively comfortable with the 'high level' of probability that was entailed in the assertions, via historical inquiry, that there was a historical Jesus and that the main characteristics of his life, relevant to his role as the Christ, could be known with great probability.[3]

For myself, I want to side with Dodd on each count. I do not believe it is possible to ensure immunity against historical risk. There comes a point, reached perhaps only after a thousand qualifications, when the credibility gap gets too great; other candidates come into view when the question 'Lord, to whom else should we go?' is asked. But equally I believe, and the belief grows stronger rather than weaker the longer I spend on New Testament work, that the gospels afford good confidence that we can reach down to bedrock tradition about the historical Jesus. This is increasingly so in relation to the Fourth Gospel. But here I would like to fasten on one relatively small clue, to be found in all the gospels, which I am not aware has been noticed by those who have worked on the criterion of 'dissimilarity'. Indeed, although Dodd himself in his highly suggestive contribution *According to the Scriptures* believed that the church's 'most original and fruitful process of rethinking the Old Testament' must have originated in the creative mind of the Master himself,[4] he never raised the question whether Jesus' own use of Scripture might at any point be so distinctive as to provide a test of authenticity. It is this that I would like to explore as a tribute to the stimulus that Harvey McArthur's unflagging zeal for 'the quest' has afforded to one of its distant pursuers.

I start with a simple – and innocent – question: Why do people quote Scripture? The reasons run into one another, but confining myself for the purposes of this essay simply to the evidence of the

---

[3]*C. H. Dodd: Interpreter of the New Testament*, London and Grand Rapids, Michigan 1977, pp. 242f.
[4]*According to the Scriptures*, London 1952, p. 110.

gospels, I would discern four:

1. The *allusive use* is the most common use in all ages. Consciously or unconsciously people put their thoughts into the words of Scripture because it seems to say what they want to say better than they themselves could, for the extra aura of authority that its words convey, or for overtones or echoes of meaning which its associations introduce. This is the most common reason for quotation of any kind, and in the gospels it is found constantly on the lips of Jesus, of other speakers, and of the evangelists. Often in this allusive use it is difficult if not impossible to tell whether a quotation is actually intended at all (e.g., in the ransom saying of Mark 10.45), and for now I shall confine myself to sentences or phrases printed in boldface in Kurt Aland's United Bible Societies' Greek text.[5] But, especially in apocalyptic, half the art of the allusive use of Scripture is precisely the release of images and associations that depend on *not* being tied down to precise or pedestrian quotation. It is well known that the book of Revelation, while soaked in the Old Testament (particularly Daniel and Ezekiel), never once quotes a specific text. And this is characteristic of other apocalyptic passages, for example II Thess. 2, Did. 16, and, within the gospels, Mark 13.24–27, all of which contain a pastiche of allusive phrases.

It is not necessary to give detailed instances of the allusive use, but quick and obvious examples would be:

The echo of Isa. 5.1–7 in the parable of the wicked tenants (Mark 12.1–12 and pars.), whether this is made explicit, as in Mark and Matthew, or not, as in Luke and the Gospel of Thomas.

The echo of Jer. 22.5 in Matt. 23.38 = Luke 13.35: 'Your house shall be left to you,' whether or not the quotation is completed by what is probably the scribal addition of 'desolate'.

The use of Ps. 22.1, the cry of dereliction, by Jesus on the cross (Matt. 27.46 = Mark 15.34), or Ps. 22.7 by the evangelists to describe the passers-by 'wagging their heads' (Matt. 27.39 = Mark 15.29).

The evident allusion to Isa. 35 and 61 in Jesus' answer to the disciples of John the Baptist (Matt. 11.5 = Luke 7.22) or to Ps. 110.1 and Dan. 7.13 in his reply to the high priest (Mark 14.62 and

[5]K. Aland et al., eds., *The Greek New Testament*, London and New York 1966. I have used for this purpose the first edition (1966) in preference to the third (1975), since the latter uses boldface type only for direct quotations. In only one case (John 7.42), however, where the quotation was evidently regarded as too free to count, does this affect any but the first, allusive use.

pars.) or to Jacob's ladder (Gen. 28.12) in John 1.51.

This recourse to Scripture is clearly no test of whether the words are dominical or reflect the theology of the church, for it occurs indiscriminately. For example, in John 1.23 the reference to Isa. 40.3 is placed on the lips of John the Baptist, while in the synoptics (Mark 1.3 and par.) the same quotation forms part of the evangelists' comment. Echoes of Scripture are found in many contexts: on the lips of the crowds at the triumphal entry. 'Blessed is he that comes in the name of the Lord' (Ps. 118.26) in Mark 11.10 and parallels and John 12.13; on the lips of Jesus' enemies at the cross, 'He trusted in God; let him deliver him if he will have him' (Ps. 22.8) in Matt. 27.43; in hymns of the church (e.g., the Magnificat and Benedictus in Luke 1); and in the evangelists' descriptions, for instance, of the weighing out of the thirty pieces of silver (Zech. 11.12) in Matt. 26.15 and of the division of Jesus' garments by lot (Ps. 22.18) in Mark 15.24 and pars.

2. The second use of Scripture, into which the first soon flows, is what might be called the *confirmatory use*. It is to show how the events of the life of Jesus fulfil the Old Testament. It is often difficult to decide where allusion passes over into claims for fulfilment. Thus the partition of Jesus' clothes which in the synoptics (Mark 15.24 and pars.) is described allusively is in John (19.24) seen as confirming the Old Testament. Or again, the citation of Isa. 6.9 ('that seeing they may not see', etc.), which in Mark (4.12) and Luke (8.10) is a clear allusion, in Matthew (13.13) and John (9.39) is first introduced more indirectly (not in boldface type) and is later followed up by a fulfilment formula (Matt. 13.14f.; John 12.38–40). This second usage is especially characteristic of Matthew, with fourteen instances (although Matthew has more actual examples of the first usage). But it is surprisingly rare in Mark and Luke, where the allusive use is far more common, especially in Luke. Mark has only three examples of fulfilment quotations, and in each case they are introduced by 'as is written': the double citation of Mal. 3.1 and Isa. 40.3 with reference to John the Baptist in 1.2f.; the citation of Isa. 29.13 ('This people honours me with their lips but their heart is far from me') in 7.6; and that of Zech. 13.7 ('Strike the shepherd and the sheep shall be scattered') in 14.27. Of these, Luke retains only one, expanding the quotation from Isa. 40 (3.4–6), but, like Matthew (11.10), reserving that from Mal. 3.1 for its use on Jesus' lips after the departure of John's disciples (7.27). Luke adds only three fulfilment quotations of his own: a double one (Exod. 13.2, 12; Lev. 12.8) to show how the presentation of Jesus in the temple complied with the Levitical law

(2.23f.); the citation of Isa. 61.1f. in Jesus' sermon at Nazareth (4.17–19); and the reference, again on Jesus' lips, to Isa. 53.12 ('He shall be numbered with the wicked') in 22.37.

In John the fulfilment quotations outnumber all the other uses put together, but this merely indicates that when John actually quotes Scripture it is more often than not for this purpose. Non-specific echoes of Jewish ways of thinking and speaking are much more numerous. Most of the fulfilment quotations, as in Matthew, are comments of the evangelist: 2.17 (on the cleansing of the temple); 12.15 (on the triumphal entry); 12.38, 40 (on the unbelief of the Jews); and 19.24, 36f., (on details of the crucifixion). But there are two, from the last discourses, on Jesus' lips: 13.18 ('He who eats bread with me has turned against me,' from Ps. 41.9) and 15.25 ('They hated me without reason,' from Ps. 69.4). And there is one, in 7.38, referring to an unidentifiable γλαφή, 'Streams of living water shall flow out from within him,' where whether one attributes it to Jesus (with the RSV) or, more probably, to the evangelist (with the NEB) depends on how one punctuates. In any case, this confirmatory use of Scripture certainly provides no criterion for distinguishing the usage of Jesus from that of the early church, and the strong probability must be that the claim to fulfilment (e.g. especially of the 'suffering servant' in Luke 22.37) is read back on to his lips rather than the other way around.

3. Third, there is what might be called the *argumentative use* of Scripture – either contesting the meaning or interpretation of a passage or using it to prove one's point. The two naturally flow into each other, since the point usually depends on the interpretation. Sometimes both sides quote Scripture to argue their case. Obvious examples are the devil and Jesus in the temptation narrative (Matt. 4.7–10 = Luke 4.4–12) or the Sadducees and Jesus in the dispute about resurrection (Mark 12.18–27 and pars.). In Matthew (22.37, 39) and Mark (12.29–31) it is Jesus who cites the summary of the law, and in Luke (10.27) it is the lawyer, while in the case of the rich young ruler it is Jesus who quotes the ten commandments in all three versions (Mark 10.19 and pars.). It is surprising that these four examples are the only clear instances of this usage of Scripture in Luke. Mark (7.10; 10.4, 6–8) and Matthew (15.4; 19.4f., 7) also record Jesus' arguments with the Jews over *korban* and divorce, which turn on the true interpretation and intention of Scripture, while Matthew twice (9.13; 12.7) makes him refer his opponents to the real meaning of the text 'I desire mercy and not sacrifice' (Hos. 6.6), and also has the five antitheses of the Sermon on the Mount

(5.21, 31, 33, 38, 43), where Jesus deepens and corrects what was said to them of old, and in the case of oaths (5.34f.) himself quotes Scripture in his retort. There is only one specific example of this third use in John (7.42), where the crowds refer to the fact that according to the scriptures the Messiah is to be of the family of David and to come from his village Bethlehem (cf. II Sam. 7.12; Ps. 89.3f.; Micah 5.2). Yet in a real sense the whole central section of the Fourth Gospel is one long argument with the Jews about the meaning of Scripture, focusing on the comment 'You study the scriptures diligently, supposing that in having them you have eternal life; yet, although their testimony points to me, you refuse to come to me for that life' (5.39f.). Yet it is figures like Abraham, Moses, and Isaiah who are adduced as witnesses, rather than texts about them or from them. It is largely accidental, too, that appeals to principle, like the precedence of circumcision over the sabbath (7.22) or the requirement in law of at least two witnesses (8.17), are not grounded in actual quotations, as the latter is by Matthew (18.16) and Paul (II Cor. 13.1; cf. I Tim. 5.19) by allusion to Deut. 19.15.

All the instances of this argumentative use of Scripture occur within the gospels in conversations rather than in the evangelists' own comments. This is what one would expect, though clearly it is no test of whether they go back to the original interlocutors. Argument over the interpretation of Scripture is as old as Scripture itself; 'the Bible to prove' has ever been one of the church's most ready weapons. The interpretations of texts at Qumran and the argumentative use of Scripture by Paul, to go no further, show that the appearance in the gospels of this form of apologetic is nothing distinctive.

4. There is a rarer and subtly different use, which could be called the *challenging use* of Scripture. It also occurs, by definition, in polemical contexts and is an extension of the last usage. But it is not so much contending about the interpretation of Scripture or arguing one's case from Scripture as delivering a challenge by asking a question, using the Bible to pose rather than to prove. It is set in the interrogative mood and throws down a gauntlet: 'What do you make of the text or passage in which . . . ?' It is characteristically introduced by a formula such as 'Have you not read?' (Mark 2.25; 12.10, 26; Matt. 12.3, 5; 19.4; 21.16, 42; 22.31; Luke 6.3) or by a question beginning with πῶς, 'how' (Mark 9.12; 12.35; Matt. 22.43; Luke 20.41), or 'What do you think?' (Matt. 22.42). There is always an element of παραπροσδοκία, or turning the tables on opponents, of going over on to the initiative with them – not

continuing the argument about agreed texts but tossing something at them to compel them to rethink their presuppositions.

A good example of the difference is in the debate with the Sadducees already mentioned (Mark 12.18–27 and pars.) They cite scripture to try to entangle Jesus in its interpretation. He, though saying they err in not knowing the scriptures or the power of God, answers their question, 'Whose wife will she be?' not by citing a contrary scripture passage but on his own authority. But then he turns on them for their disbelief in the resurrection and throws at them a text from the book of Moses, 'at the [passage about the] bush,' which appears to have nothing to do with the case, challenging them to see that it implies that God is the God not of the dead but of the living. There is no further argument; they must either see or not see.

Mark has two other instances from the same chapter, all three being used also by Matthew and Luke. The first comes at the close of the parable of the wicked tenants (Mark 12.10f. and pars.). When the story seems to be over, Jesus comes back at his opponents with the words 'Or can it be that you have never read this text: 'The stone which the builders rejected has become the main corner-stone. This is the Lord's doing and it is wonderful in our eyes'?' (Ps. 118.22f.). There is, and is meant to be, no reply.

Later on (Mark 12.35–37 and pars.), Jesus once more takes the initiative when, according to Matthew (22.41), Jesus asked the assembled Pharisees, 'What is your opinion about the Messiah? Whose son is he?' The Pharisees replied, 'The son of David.' The debate seems to be proceeding within familiar parameters. Then comes the unexpected use of scripture (Ps. 110.1) to challenge their accepted assumptions:

> 'How then is it,' [Jesus] asked, 'that David by inspiration calls him "Lord"? For he says, "The Lord said to my Lord, 'Sit at my right hand until I put your enemies under your feet.'" If David calls him "Lord" how can he be David's son?'

And again, 'Not a man could say a word in reply.'

Mark introduces this last incident with the words 'How do the scribes say . . . ?' (12.35), which is similar to the puzzled question of the disciples in 9.11: 'Why do the scribes say that Elijah must come first?' Jesus replies that not only must Elijah come but that he has come. Then in a confused passage, which Matthew smooths out (17.12), Jesus turns on them with an apparently unrelated counter-question: 'How is it that the scripture says of the Son of Man

that he is to endure great sufferings and be treated with contempt?'
(9.12). Again we have the same posing use of scripture, although this
time without reference to a specific text.

With this must be considered the appeal to scripture in an earlier
polemical passage, Mark 2.24–28 and parallels. Here again there is
no actual citation, but the form is the same. In answer to the
Pharisees' objection to the plucking of grain on the sabbath, Jesus
replies not with a text but with a story: 'Have you never read what
David did when he and his men were hungry and had nothing to eat?
How he went into the house of God . . . ?' (cf. I Sam. 21.1–6). He is
not arguing the interpretation of scripture, and it does not logically
demonstrate that "the Son of Man is sovereign even over the
sabbath." The biblical example is flung down as a challenge and a
scandal.

There are no independent examples of this use of scripture in
Luke, but Matthew has another that must be placed in this category.
To the indignant question of the chief priests and scribes at the
triumphal entry, 'Do you hear what they are saying?' ('Hosanna to
the son of David'), Jesus replied with a counter-question, citing Ps.
8.2: 'I do; have you never read that text, "Thou hast made children
and babes at the breast sound aloud thy praises"?' (21.15–16). Such
ripostes are not invitations to argue the meaning of a text or attempts
to prove anything. They are intended to pose and to stump – and they
do.

Finally, there is a further example from John (10.33–36). The Jews
accuse Jesus of blasphemy: 'You, a mere man, claim to be a god.' He
comes back at them with a question drawing on Ps. 82.6: 'It is not
written in your own law, "I said: You are gods"? Those are called
gods to whom the word of God was delivered – and Scripture cannot
be set aside. Then why do you charge me with blasphemy because I,
consecrated and sent into the world by the Father, said, "I am God's
son"?' This comes near to the argumentative use of scripture, yet it is
not primarily an argument about the interpretation of texts,
countering or inviting other interpretations. As in the other cases, it
stops the argument altogether, merely provoking one more attempt
at arrest (10.39). Nor is it used to demonstrate Jesus's sonship: the
consonance of his deeds with the Father's will can alone do that
(10.37f.) It is a challenge to deeper discernment, to stop and think
again.

The nearest parallel in the gospel material to this is that of parables
to pose a challenge: 'What do you think about this, Simon? From
whom do earthly monarchs collect tax or toll? From their own

citizens, or from aliens?' (Matt. 17.25); 'What do you think? Suppose a man has a hundred sheep . . . ' (Matt. 18.12f.); 'But what do you think about this? A man had two sons . . . ' (Matt. 21.28–32); 'Now, which will love him most?' (Luke 7.42); 'Which of these three do you think was neighbour to the man who fell into the hands of robbers?' (Luke 10.36).

It is widely agreed that in the parables and in the questions Jesus put, as distinct from the answers frequently supplied to these questions, there are some of the most characteristic and identifiable features of Jesus' teaching. In this fourth use of Scripture, I suggest, there is a similar mark of distinctiveness. In one instance, that of the wicked tenants, it is intimately associated with a parable, and Matthew Black[6] has argued convincingly that the connection between the story and the scriptural quotation is original, depending on a pun, lying behind the Greek, on *ben* ('son') and *eben* ('stone'), which is attested elsewhere (e.g., in the saying of John the Baptist, 'God can make children for Abraham out of these stones' (Matt. 3.9 = Luke 3.8). In any case, this use of Scripture, though the occurrences are insufficient for statistical confidence, has three marks that pass the same tests of authenticity as the phrase 'the Son of Man': (*a*) it alone of all the uses, or titles, occurs always on the lips of Jesus and of no others; (*b*) it has multiple attestation of synoptic and Johannine usage; and (c) it has no similarity, to my knowledge, to the usage either of Qumran and the rabbis or of subsequent Christian writers in the Epistles and Acts. The other three uses – to allude, to confirm, and to argue – are so common both before and after that one must at least ask if this is not a point to be added to those listed by Joachim Jeremias[7] at which we could be in touch with the *ipsissima vox*. That is not to say, any more than with the occurrences of the Son of Man, that every one goes back to Jesus. The example peculiar to Matthew (21.16) must be suspect; and Matthew also seems to have added the introduction 'Have you not read?' in 12.5 and 19.4. But the question presents itself whether this should not be included as one of the remembered forms of Jesus' teaching, like his distinctive use of *amēn*, which for his contemporaries marked off its originality and authority from that of their scribes.

[6]'The Christological Use of the Old Testament in the New Testament', *NTS* 18, 1971–72, pp. 11–14.

[7]*New Testament Theology* I, London and New York 1971, pp. 29–37.

4

The Lord's Prayer

This piece was prepared not so much as a contribution to original research but rather as part of a working model to try to show theological students at Cambridge that gospel 'criticism' can be thoroughly constructive and not the threat that it appears to so many laymen. The samples I selected covered different genres of material – narrative, parable, prayer, theology – as well as being taken from different strands of the gospel traditions, the double (or 'Q') tradition, the triple (or 'Markan'), the Johannine, or all four together. The other passages I chose, the parable of the Wicked Husbandmen, the prologue to the Fourth Gospel, the accounts of the Empty Tomb, are treated in different ways elsewhere in this collection (chs. 2, 5, 7). But the Lord's Prayer focuses particularly sharply the tension which so often seems to exist between faith and scholarship, devotional reverence and academic rigour. Of course, scholarship will not of itself lead to faith, nor is using one's critical faculties a recipe for praying. But they need not be antithetical either. On the contrary, to take a parallel example, musical criticism should enable one to enter more deeply and appreciatively into the music. Similarly, to analyse historically and critically the formation and development of the prayer that lies at the very heart of the Christian life may enable one to pray it, as Paul says, not with the spirit only but with the understanding also, by catching all kinds of overtones and resonances, instead of being content to remain simply at the level of parrot-like recitation.

Yet merely to raise the question of the prayer's wording, let alone to appear to tamper with it by retranslation, is regarded as almost blasphemous. 'They're even changing the Lord's Prayer' has been a popular reaction (aided and abetted by the press) to the revised liturgies. No one stops to ask 'Changing from what?' It is of course the version that people have been brought up to, which Englishmen assume, here as elsewhere, is 'the Authorized Version' (though it would surprise them to learn that it has never actually been authorized: the Americans are more accurate in calling it the King James Version). But, as we shall see, in this case it is not the Authorized Version which has been regarded as the base-line. It is what they have learnt at their mothers' knee from the Book of Common Prayer; and it is this that the revisers have had the effrontery to 'alter' – as if it had actually been written by the Lord himself.

Similarly, in the wake of the publication of the New English Bible, I was constantly asked, Why did you change this or that? The answer was, We didn't 'change' anything. We did not start from, nor even have to hand, the Authorized Version, or for that matter any other version. Naturally it lay at the back of our minds, although the translating panels were made up of men who for years had probably *used* it less than any other comparable group of educated people. Indeed, even finding a copy of it in my study has often presented me with problems. For the meaning, and above all for the true text, we went straight to the original Greek (or, in the case of the Old Testament, the Hebrew); and, as will become apparent, the text to be translated is particularly important in the case of the Lord's Prayer. For by constant use over the centuries in very varying Christian communities and cultures different versions have grown up and have then become assimilated to each other. So far from there being a simple unchanging norm which it is sacrilegious to touch, the church (and not merely its scribes who copied the manuscripts) has freely adapted to its own situations the Prayer by which it has lived, and continues to live. Otherwise it would have become fossilized and its constant recitation the very thing against which Jesus warned, 'vain repetition'.

Permutations of textual and translational variants apart, the Lord's Prayer has come down to us in three different versions from the earliest days of the church. I reproduce them in the Revised Standard Version and in a correspondingly literal translation of that early Christian manual of discipline known as the Didache or 'the Teaching of the Twelve Apostles'.

Luke 11.2–4	*Matt. 6.9–13*	*Didache 8*
Father,	Our Father who art in heaven (τοῖς οὐρανοῖς)	Our Father who art in heaven (τῷ οὐρανῷ),
Hallowed be thy name.	Hallowed be thy name.	Hallowed be thy name.
Thy kingdom come.	Thy kingdom come	Thy kingdom come,
	Thy will be done,	Thy will be done,
	On earth as it is in heaven.	On earth as it is in heaven.

Give (δίδου) us each day our daily bread;	Give (δός) us this day our daily bread;	Give (δός) us this day our daily bread;
and forgive us our sins,	and forgive us our debts (τὰ ὀφειλήματα),	and forgive us our debt (τὴν ὀφειλήν),
as we ourselves forgive everyone who is indebted to us;	as we also have forgiven our debtors;	as we also forgive our debtors;
and lead us not into temptation.	and lead us not into temptation; but deliver us from evil.	and lead us not into temptation; but deliver us from evil
	[For thine is the kingdom and the power and the glory, forever. Amen.]	For thine is the power and the glory for ever.

Suprisingly the Lord's Prayer is not to be found in the Gospels of Mark or John – though it is unquestionably presupposed by both. There are echoes of it in Mark 14.36, 'Abba, Father . . . not what I will, but what thou wilt', and v. 38, 'Pray that you may not enter into temptation'; also in John 17.11, 'Holy Father, keep them in thy name' and v. 15, 'Keep them from the evil one'. Indeed Christopher Evans in his book *The Lord's Prayer*[1] has seen John 17 as a prolonged meditation on this prayer.

Yet its absence from the other two gospels is not altogether so astonishing. For the Lord's Prayer is not something that you write down, you learn it – and then pass it on orally. And the version you know is the version you have been taught, not read. If you have been brought up in England you have learnt to say 'trespasses', if in Scotland 'debts'. Yet 'trespasses' is not in the Authorized Version at all (nor for that matter in the Greek of Matthew or Luke). But most people I am sure have no idea of this, nor could they repeat the text of either Matthew or Luke in the AV.

Moreover in this version Matthew and Luke are almost identical in length (the only real difference being the absence of the doxology in Luke). Now contrast the length of the two as they appear in the RSV or NEB. This is a warning against using the AV as a scholarly tool – for it is based on manuscripts which have already assimilated the text of Luke to that of Matthew, so that they come out looking much more similar than they really are.

This raises the question of the relation of the versions of Matthew and Luke to each other. Clearly there is no simple *literary* relationship, of one copying the other or even of both using a common source. If the Prayer stood in the document known as 'Q' (the material shared by Matthew and Luke), then it was in different

[1] C. F. Evans, *The Lord's Prayer*, London 1963, pp. 76f.

editions of Q. But more probably the two versions represent parallel material deriving from the liturgical tradition of different churches. The differences here would be less likely to be due simply to the editorial work of the individual evangelists, who would have hesitated to take personal liberties with so sacred a text. Yet both must go back to a common *Greek* version. None of the differences can be put down to translation variants of the Aramaic, as is possibly the case in other parts of the 'Q' material. Decisive is the common use of the very rare Greek word ἐπιούσιος ('daily').

Before comparing the two canonical versions, a word on the third from the Didache. The Didache was discovered only just over a hundred years ago and was first published in 1883. As a document it is still something of a joker in the pack. There has been wild variation in the dating of it – from the first century AD to the second, third or fourth. The latest massive French commentary on the Didache by J.-P. Audet[2] daringly puts it between 50 and 70, which by usual dating standards is very early indeed. My reaction is to believe that this is still too late, and I have given reasons in my *Redating the New Testament*[3] for thinking that it should be between 40 and 60. But even if it is genuinely primitive (rather than a document made to look primitive), is its version of the Prayer independent of the other two?

In the Didache it is introduced by the words 'as the Lord commanded in his gospel'. Other references to 'the gospel' in the Didache, in 11.3 and especially 15.3 ('as you have it in the gospel'), suggest that this may already be a written document to which the readers are being referred as familiar. The obvious inference is that this is the Gospel of Matthew, to whose version indeed it stands very close. Yet other quotations cannot demonstrate that the Didache presupposes Matthew in its present form. It may well refer, as I have argued, to a proto-Matthew and could throw light on the preliterary history of the Matthean tradition. At any rate I believe that we should be open to this, rather than dismiss its evidence as secondary from the beginning. Yet clearly it is from the same liturgical tradition as that represented by Matthew – probably, as B. H. Streeter thought, that of the church of Antioch.

Let us then turn to a comparison of the texts. For this I shall draw on Jeremias' classic monograph;[4] for he has done much of the work for us.

[2] J.-P. Audet, *La Didache: Instructions des Apôtres*, Paris 1958.
[3] *Op. cit.*, p. 322–7.
[4] ET, *The Lord's Prayer*, Philadelphia 1964; reprinted as 'The Lord's Prayer in the Light of Recent Research' in *The Prayers of Jesus*, London and Philadelphia 1967, pp. 82–107, to which the page-references will be given.

Before looking at the content of the Prayer we should first note, as he points out, the contexts in which it occurs in the different versions.

In *Matthew* it is in the Sermon on the Mount, in the section on almsgiving, prayer and fasting (6.1–18). The teaching on prayer is introduced by two negatives: Don't be like the hypocrites (the Jews) – showing off in public (6.5f.); and Don't be like heathen (the Gentiles) – babbling on with long prayers (6.7f.). Rather, 'This is how you should pray.' Then at the end of the prayer its teaching on forgiveness is taken up and elaborated (6.14f.).

In *Luke* it is not in his parallel 'Sermon on the Plain' but in the distinctive travel-narrative between Galilee and Jerusalem which forms the middle section of his gospel. It is introduced by a reference which is as vague in time and place as all the rest in this section: 'Once, in a certain place, Jesus was at prayer. When he ceased, one of his disciples said, "Lord, teach us to pray, as John taught his disciples." He answered "When you pray, say. . . . "' The prayer is then followed by two parables on the subject, the story of the friend at midnight, teaching persistence in prayer (11.5–10), and the saying 'Is there a father among you who will offer his son a snake when he asks for a fish. . . . ? How much more will the heavenly Father give the Holy Spirit to those who ask him!', teaching trust in the providential goodness of God (11.11–13).

In *the Didache* the context is comparable with Matthew, but the Prayer is placed in the setting of church order and catechesis: 'Let not your fastings be with the hypocrites, for they fast on the second and fifth day of the week; but you keep your fast on the fourth and the sixth. Neither pray as the hypocrites, but, as the Lord commanded in his gospel, pray like this:'. And it ends: 'Three times in the day pray so', thus deliberately putting it in the place occupied by the statutory prayers of Judaism. It is then followed by the teaching on the Eucharist, as it has been preceded by instruction on Baptism. This suggests that it is part of the instruction of new converts, as in the order of the church catechism: the Creed, the Lord's Prayer, the Ten Commandments.

Clearly none of these contexts is a reliable indication of how Jesus himself gave the Prayer. In Matthew it is assimilated to a block of ethical and religious instruction. In the Didache it forms part of a series of liturgical and disciplinary regulations. In Luke it is related to Jesus' example and teaching on prayer – the context most likely no doubt to be nearest to source. All of them presuppose communities held together by a common discipline of prayer like those of Qumran, the rabbinic schools, and, as Luke says, the disciples of

John. Jeremias makes an interesting distinction between Matthew and Luke:

> The Matthaean catechism on prayer is addressed to people who have learned to pray in childhood but whose prayer stands in danger of becoming a routine. The Lucan catechism on prayer, on the other hand, is addressed to people who must for the first time learn to pray and whose courage to pray must be roused. It is clear that Matthew is transmitting to us instruction on prayer directed at Jewish-Christians, Luke at Gentile-Christians. . . . Each of the evangelists transmits to us the wording of the Lord's Prayer as it was prayed in his church at that time.[5]

Jeremias says this means about AD 75. I believe, as I argued in my *Redating*, that it points rather to the 50s or early 60s.

When we come to a comparison of the texts themselves, the first thing that strikes us, when textual assimilations and accretions are eliminated, is how much more succinct is the Lukan version in comparison with that of Matthew and the Didache. The presumption of originality must be in favour of the shorter. Liturgical tradition always tends to gather moss and grow more fulsome. It is difficult to believe that words attributed to the Lord should be cut, but every reason why they should be garnered and expanded. Moreover the extra length really adds nothing of substance. It occurs at four places, each time at the end of clauses:

1. To 'Father' Matthew adds 'who is in the heavens' (ἐν τοῖς οὐρανοῖς – a characteristically Matthaean phrase), the Didache 'who is in heaven'. This brings the daring and unadorned address to God as *abba* into line with Jewish piety.

2. To 'Hallowed be they name' and 'Thy kingdom come' Matthew and the Didache add: 'Thy will be done, as in heaven so on earth', providing an interpretation of the preceding words. Yet 'Thy will be done' is echoed in Mark 14.36 and, even if not part of the original prayer, it certainly reflects a memory of Jesus.

3. To 'lead us not into temptation' Matthew and the Didache add: 'but deliver us from evil', thus interpreting it in the sense of 'do not let us succumb to temptation'. We shall return to this when considering the meaning of this difficult clause.

4. The doxology. Many manuscripts of Matthew, but not the most ancient, add 'For thine is the kingdom, and the power and the glory'. The Didache has 'For thine is the power and the glory for ever'.

---

[5]Op. cit., pp. 88f.

Clearly this formed no part even of the original text of Matthew. The only manuscript of the Didache we possess is itself very late (AD 1056), and in all probability it may also have been added to that from later liturgical practice. It is a typical Jewish pious doxology, modelled on I Chron. 29.11. There is much variation in it in the textual tradition of Matthew, as well as between Matthew and the Didache.

We can therefore with confidence strip off all this extra padding as likely to be secondary – though we certainly cannot rule out that Jesus gave his prayer in different forms and contexts, himself elaborating and expanding its meaning.

What now of what is left at the points where the texts themselves diverge?

First, Matthew and the Didache have 'give us' (δός, the aorist imperative, implying a single action) today (σήμερον) our daily bread': Luke, 'give us (δίδου, the present imperative, implying constant action) each day (τὸ καθ᾽ ἡμέραν) our daily bread'.

There is general agreement here that Luke, as his custom is, is generalizing, making the clause applicable to the continuing Christian life, exactly as in 9.23, 'Let him take up his cross *daily*'. καθ᾽ ἡμέραν is a phrase that occurs once in Matthew and Mark (in the same passage), never in John, and twelve times in Luke–Acts. We may therefore say with confidence that this wording belongs to Luke or his community. As we shall see when we come to its probable meaning, the temporal contrast between σήμερον, 'today', and ἐπιούσιον, 'coming', which is preserved by Matthew but lost in Luke, is almost certainly part of the original meaning. Also all the other imperatives in the Prayer are in the aorist tense, denoting single rather than repeated action. So here Matthew's text clearly looks the most original.

Secondly, Matthew has 'Forgive us our debts as we too have forgiven (ἀφήκαμεν) those who are indebted to us'; Luke, 'Forgive us our sins (ἁμαρτίας), for we ourselves forgive (καὶ γὰρ αὐτοὶ ἀφίομεν) everyone who is indebted to us'; and Didache, 'Forgive us our debt (ὀφειλήν) as we forgive (ἀφίεμεν) those who are indebted to us'.

One thing is certain and that is that Luke's ἁμαρτίας (sins) is interpretative and secondary. In Aramaic the word used for sin means literally 'debt' – hence the parables of the two debtors (Luke 7.41f.) and of the unmerciful servant (Matt. 18.23–35) used by Jesus to illustrate forgiveness. Luke has retained this background in his second clause ('everyone who is indebted to us'); but in his first interprets its meaning for non-Palestinians in terms of the regular

New Testament word for 'sins'. Matthew also does this in terms of 'trespasses' (παραπτώματα), but only in the explicatory verses that *follow* the Prayer (6.14f.).

Matthew and the Didache have a minor and perhaps insignificant variation at this point – 'debts' (ὀφειλήματα) and 'debt' (ὀφειλήν), the latter being a Hellenistic Greek form found in the secular papyri and also in Paul (of conjugal debt, in I Cor. 7.3). The singular, meaning our whole load of guilt, could well be more original – as in 'the Lamb of God who takes away the sin of the world' (John 1.29), rather than 'sins' as in the later liturgical tradition of the Agnus Dei. The tendency of liturgy is always to generalize and multiply so as to make sure that one has left nothing out (observe the frequent use of 'all' in informal prayers and litanies, as in 'all prisoners and captives'). Luke also does this in his second clause 'for we ourselves forgive *everyone* who is indebted to us'. But certainly I should not want to press this point in favour of the originality of the Didache text.

There is much more variation in the second clause. It is interesting that the version we have been brought up on, 'as we forgive those who trespass against us' is not represented in either Matthew or Luke but in the Didache (unknown to all till a hundred years ago!). But is this version right in thus interpreting the meaning?

I think basically, Yes. According to the teaching of Jesus, readiness to forgive is a condition of being able to receive forgiveness (Matt. 6.14f.; 18.35; Mark 11.25). But the divine forgiveness is unconditional and prevenient. It goes out freely and spontaneously to the sinner; it does not wait upon the servant to *have forgiven* his fellow-servant, so that he thereby proves himself worthy of forgiveness. Where misunderstanding starts is when our attitude is made a precondition of forgiveness – so that the action of God comes only as a *response* to our forgiveness of others and is made dependent upon it. Instead of being a sign of capacity to receive forgiveness, it becomes a condition of earning it.[6] There is a similar confusion in the Lukan story of the anointing of Jesus (Luke 7.36–50), which leads into the parable of the two debtors, one of whom is owed five hundred silver pieces, the other fifty. Both are forgiven, unconditionally. The exchange that follows, 'Which of the two will love him most?': 'I should think the one that was let off most', makes it clear

[6]Cf. C. F. D. Moule, '"As we forgive". A note on the Distinction between Deserts and Capacity in the Understanding of Forgiveness', in E. Bammel, C. K. Barrett and W. D. Davies, eds., *Donum Gentilicum: New Testament Studies in Honour of David Daube*, Oxford and New York 1978, pp. 68–77; reprinted in Moule's *Essays in New Testament Interpretation*, Cambridge 1982, pp. 278–86, to which page-references will be given.

that Jesus' conclusion must be intended to mean, as the NEB takes it: 'Her great love shows the many sins she has been forgiven; for where little has been forgiven, little love is shown'. The love is the consequence, not the ground, of the forgiveness. But the Greek is usually translated, as in the RSV, 'Her many sins are forgiven, for she loved much'. This would imply that her great love was the cause rather than the corollary of her being forgiven.[7]

It looks on the face of it as though Matthew's 'Forgive us our debts as we also *have forgiven* our debtors' is again making our worthiness a precondition of God's action. If so, it is undoubtedly a misinterpretation in a legalistic direction, of which there is other evidence in the Jewish-Christian circles for which this gospel was written. But Jeremias here argues that behind Matthew's past tense lies what is called in Semitic grammar a *perfectum praesens*, a perfect with a present sense, referring to an action occurring here and now. 'The correct translation of the Matthaean form', he says, 'would therefore run, "as we also herewith forgive our debtors."' Not being an Aramaic scholar, I forbear to judge. But if this is the meaning, then *in Greek* the Didache gets it right ('Forgive us our debt as we forgive those who are indebted to us') and could be the original form of the prayer in the church at Antioch which Matthew or his community has misunderstood. For the interpretation he appends, 'For *if* you forgive men their trespasses your Father in heaven *will* forgive you' (but not apparently otherwise), implies that forgiveness on our part is a *pre*condition of the divine action. So once more the Didache may preserve the true sense which the church's liturgical tradition has retained, interestingly *against* the biblical evidence!

Finally, limiting ourselves at this point to the variants relevant to establishing the true text of the Prayer, one should mention a variant in the text of Luke that is *not*, like the others, a change or addition to assimilate his text to that of Matthew, which soon established itself as the ecclesiastical norm. Instead of the clause 'Thy kingdom come' (or, according to Marcion, instead of 'Hallowed be thy name'), there is weak manuscript support for 'May thy Holy Spirit come upon us and cleanse us'. The evidence is certainly not strong enough for supposing it to be part of the Prayer as it left the lips of Jesus, but it may, as Jeremias points out, indicate its adaptation as a prayer for

---

[7]Cf. Moule, op. cit., pp. 283f: 'The essential question is . . . upon which verb the ὅτι, the "because", depends. Why not recognize that the offending ὅτι, the "because", can depend as easily on the λέγω, the 'I tell you', as on the ἀφέωνται? "The reason", Jesus is saying, "why I [am able to] tell you that her many sins are forgiven is the fact that she is showing so much love."'

the coming of the Spirit when used at Christian initiation.[8] In the same way Marcion's version of the following clause, 'Give us *thy* bread', could be an adaptation for its use at the Eucharist. We should recall that the instruction about the Lord's Prayer in the Didache comes between that for Baptism and the Eucharist and indicates contexts in which it was used in the primitive church. In the same way I Peter 1.17, 'If you say "Our Father"' (NEB), *could* relate, like other pointers, to this epistle being originally a homily at Christian initiation. But all this tells us more about the use of the Lord's Prayer in the early church[9] than about the teaching of Jesus himself.

So, what, having sifted the additions and variations in the text, may we conclude on critical grounds is the version likely to take us nearest to source? Jeremias sums up the situation by saying: 'The Lucan version has preserved the oldest form with respect to *length*, but the Matthaean text is more original with regard to *wording*'. I would agree, though *possibly* the Didache text may have something to offer in giving us the form used in the Antiochene church *underlying* that of Matthew. This is also relevant, especially if it does take us back to the 40s and 50s, for how Paul, who as we shall see also echoes it, would have learnt to pray it as a missionary of that church.

Thus we are sent back to some such text as:

> Father
> Hallowed by thy name;
> Thy kingdom come;
> Give us today our daily bread,
> And forgive us our debt (or load of sin),
>   as we also forgive our debtors;
> And lead us not into temptation.

The rest is commentary – though that does not mean that it is false comentary, only that it is interpretation, such as every translation ancient or recent must also be. But what is the most likely interpretation, as opposed to the most probable text, must now engage us. So with this in mind let us return to examine it clause by clause.

[8]Cf. the parable which follows in Luke 11.13: 'How much more will your heavenly Father give the Holy Spirit to those who ask him?'

[9]For this cf. F. H. Chase, *The Lord's Prayer in the Early Church*, Texts and Studies I. 3, ed. J. Armitage Robinson, Cambridge 1891; T. W. Manson, 'The Lord's Prayer', *BJRL* 38, 1955–6, pp. 99–113, 436–8.

1. 'Father'

For this term one must refer once more to Jeremias, not only on the Lord's Prayer, but on *Abba*.[10] – a classic study, though his conclusions have been challenged and require to be reconsidered at points.

The address of God as *abba*, Father, is unique and distinctive to Jesus. If anything is part of what Jeremias calls the *ipsissima vox*,[11] this is. Other Jews never used such familiarity in prayer to God; Jesus always did, except when quoting Ps. 22.1 on the cross. As Jeremias puts it, 'Jesus' use of *abba* in addressing God reveals the heart of his relationship to God': it is the core of the 'revelation' granted him by the Father (Matt. 11.27). In E. Lohmeyer's words:[12] 'If Tertullian called the Lord's Prayer a *breviarium totius evangelii*, this address is the *breviarium breviarii*'. *Abba* is preserved in the Aramaic at Mark 14.36. More significantly it is retained in Aramaic by Paul in Gal. 4.6: 'To prove that you are really children of God, God has sent the Spirit of his Son into our hearts crying "Abba! Father!"', and Rom. 8.15f. (of saying the Lord's Prayer): 'When we cry "Abba! Father!" it is the Spirit himself bearing witness with our spirit that we are children of God.' This is the very heart of the gospel, that we, as Christians, share Jesus' unique relationship to God; and the daring thing about the Lord's Prayer, is that he tells his disciples to take upon *their* lips *his* address to God as 'Dear Father', or *liebe Vater*, as Jeremias renders it. *Abba* and *imma* ('daddy' and 'mummy') were the first words that the child learned to use[13] and the believer has to become as a little child (Matt. 18.3). In Jesus' time *abba* was not confined to small children, but it was always used in intimacy. The calling of God '*abba*' is the privilege of those who can stand in this relationship. The awareness of this persists in the Western liturgical tradition, 'We are bold to say', and even more in the Eastern. Though God is father to all, not all men are his children or can thus presume to address him. 'The right to become the children of God' is, as the Johannine prologue says 'given' (John 1.12). However much traditional material there may be in the Lord's Prayer, its first word sets it apart as distinctively Christian. This impact is lost by the ecclesiastical expansion '*Our* Father, *who art in heaven*', which is based on Jewish models.[14]

[10]ET in *The Prayers of Jesus*, pp. 11–65.
[11]For this, in distinction from the *ipsissima verba*, cf. ibid., pp. 108–15.
[12]*The Lord's Prayer*, ET London 1965, New York 1966, p. 297.
[13]b. *Ber.* 40a; b. *Sanh.* 70b.
[14]Cf. C. W. Dugmore, *The Influence of the Synagogue upon the Divine Office*, Oxford and New York 1944, pp. 114–27; Lohmeyer, *The Lord's Prayer*, pp. 302–4.

2. *Hallowed be thy name,*
   Thy kingdom come.

We may begin with the comment by Christopher Evans:

> In these first words of the Prayer, 'Abba, Hallowed be thy name',
> there are juxtaposed with extreme compression, nearness and
> farness, familiarity and distance, likeness and unlikeness, the
> closest possible analogy and the greatest possible distinction, the
> simplicity and directness of an intimate earthly approach and awe
> and reverence before what is totally other. This juxtaposition is
> the very mainspring of true prayer'.[15]

One gets it again in John 17.11, 'Holy Father', which, as we saw,
Evans regards as a reflection on the Prayer.[16]

The double petition, 'Hallowed be thy name, Thy kingdom come',
represents, as Jeremias shows, the *most* traditional part of the
Prayer. It recalls the ancient *Aramaic* prayer (rather than Hebrew
like the more formal liturgy), the *Kaddish* (or 'Holy'), which
concluded the synagogue service and with which Jesus would have
been familiar from childhood. Jeremias reconstructs what he regards
as probably its oldest form:

> Exalted and hallowed be his great name
> in the world which he created according to his will.
> May he let his kingdom rule
> in your lifetime and in your days and in the lifetime
> of the whole house of Israel, speedily and soon.
> And to this, say: amen.[17]

We may note in comparison the brevity of Jesus' prayer, which was
not a characteristic of Jewish prayers any more than of Gentile. It is
not surprising that the clause was filled out. It was simply too direct
and succinct.

The heart of the Prayer is eschatological, asking for the coming of
God's kingdom and the final vindication of his name. R. E. Brown[18]
argues strongly that the word 'hallowed' ($\dot{\alpha}\gamma\iota\alpha\sigma\theta\acute{\eta}\tau\omega$) here is a
'divine passive', asking God to sanctify his own name, and that the
once-and-for-all aorist subjunctive points to the culminating hour:
'Vindicate your holiness' (cf. Ezek. 36.22f.). We get the same in John
12.28, 'Father, glorify thy name' (for 'sanctify' and 'glorify' are

---

[15] *The Lord's Prayer*, p. 29.   [16] Ibid., p. 76.
[17] *The Prayers of Jesus*, p. 98.
[18] 'The Pater Noster as an Eschatological Prayer', *Theological Studies* 22, 1961, pp.
175–208; reprinted in his *New Testament Essays*, Milwaukee 1965, pp. 217–53 (and
especially 228–32), to which references will be given.

virtually synonymous), and the answer comes: 'I have glorified it, and I will glorify it again', the future having reference to the ultimate vindication of God's holiness *as Father*. The same applies to the coming of the kingdom, and its meaning here must be determined by the centrality of this category to the whole teaching of Jesus. Its being 'at hand' or 'upon you', was the heart of his message and thus the core of his prayer. God was in the process of completing his glorious work. This it is that must be 'prayed down'. Matthew's community in filling out the petition by 'Thy will be done, as in heaven so on earth', replaces the temporal contrast with a spatial one and weakens the sense of eschatological urgency, 'speedily and soon'. Yet the note of urgency is still retained when Jesus himself comes to be seen by the early church as the focus of the kingdom, as in the Aramaic prayer '*Marana tha*' (I Cor. 16.22), reflected in Rev. 22.20, 'Amen. Come, Lord Jesus', and Did. 10.6, 'Let grace come and let this world pass away. . . . *Marana tha*. Amen'. This petition for the coming of the kingdom in the hallowing of God's name conditions the interpretation of the rest of the prayer. The loss of the eschatological perspective, already evident in the church's adaptations (Matthew's in this clause and Luke's omission of 'today' in the next), makes it strange for us — though, as we shall see, this can be exaggerated.

3. *Give us today our daily bread.*

This is apparently the simplest of all the clauses. Yet it is the one whose meaning is most in doubt. Everything turns on the meaning of the Greek word ἐπιούσιος. It occurs nowhere else for certain outside the three versions of the Lord's Prayer, which, as I said, shows that they all go back to a common Greek translation. Parallels have been claimed in an inscription (which turns out to be a doubtful emendation) and in an uncertain reading in a papyrus (lent to a friend at University College, London, who never returned it!).[19] Origen (*De Orat.* 27) thought the evangelists had invented it (which is very doubtful) and he simply guessed at its derivation and meaning. Even the knowledge of his own language did not help him and in fact he almost certainly got it wrong, allowing his predilection for Platonic philosophy to overcome his semantics.

There are two issues (*a*) the derivation, (*b*) the meaning.

(*a*) It could come from (i) ἐπί + εἰμί εἶναι (to be), with its noun οὐσία

[19]For the state of affairs on this question, cf. B. M. Metzger, 'How Many Times does "*epiousios*" occur outside the Lord's Prayer?', *ExpT* 69, 1957–8, pp. 52–4.

or (ii) ἐπί + εἶμι, ἰέναι (to come or go), from which we get the familiar present participle ἡ ἐπιοῦσα ἡμέρα, the coming or next day.

On purely philological grounds (despite Origen), the latter is more probable. J. B. Lightfoot[20] insists that ἐπί οὐσία would become ἐπούσιος. But this cannot be dogmatically stated in the *Koinē* Greek of the New Testament as opposed to classical usage. Nevertheless the parallel with the participle ἐπιοῦσα, from which the adjective ἐπιούσιος could be formed, makes this look the more probable.

(b) Whatever the derivation, its meaning can be understood at two possible levels.

(i) If it comes from ἐπί and οὐσία (being) it could mean what is sufficient for existence, what we need to keep alive. Yet οὐσία would not normally be used for 'existence'. Hence those who take it this way (e.g. Origen and Jerome) refer it to the real or essential bread, and make the prayer not one for material subsistence but for spiritual being. In the Vulgate Jerome translated it in Matthew *supersubstantialem*, while, from 'indecision, scruple or carelessness',[21] retaining *quotidianum* from the old Latin version in Luke. Later when the original Greek had been forgotten this difference was debated, for instance by St Bernard and Abelard, as a highly significant one for the intention of the two evangelists.[22] *Quotidianum* has always maintained itself in the liturgical tradition of the West (hence our 'daily'), despite the ecclesiastical dominance of Matthew. *Supersubstantialem* is probably just translation-Latin (ἐπί = *super*, οὐσία = *substantia*). There is no such Latin word. Lewis and Short in their Latin dictionary, quoting only this occurrence, take it to mean 'necessary to support life'; but for Jerome it probably signified something much more like 'supernatural'.

(ii) If it comes from ἐπιέναι, coming, then it can be taken quite literally as bread for the coming day. If the Prayer was prayed in the morning then it would be for the day ahead, if in the evening then for the next day about to start at 6 p.m. But it could mean the bread that comes to the day or belongs to it: hence daily allowance or ration (cf. Matt. 20.1–16 for daily payment, and Luke 12.42, where the function of the steward is to 'give' the household τὸ σιτομέτριον ἐν καιρῷ, its 'daily dollop'). But this would more naturally be

---

[20] *On a Fresh Revision of the English New Testament*, London 1871, Appendix on ἐπιούσιος.

[21] Lightfoot, op. cit., p. 225.

[22] Cf. Lightfoot, op. cit., p. 225–9.

rendered by ἐφήμερος, as in James 2.15 of those who lack their 'daily food'. It has been conjectured that behind it may stand no more than a simple Aramaic phrase, 'bread of the day',²³ but a reference to the future seems more likely and makes point of the contrast with 'today', which is otherwise redundant.

Jeremias argues that the decisive factor is that Jerome in his commentary on Matthew 6.11 says that in the Gospel according to the Hebrews²⁴ is to be found at this point the Aramaic *mahar*, which Jerome says means *crastinum* (belonging to tomorrow), so that the sense is 'Our bread for tomorrow, give us today'. Jeremias maintains that the Lord's Prayer would have been prayed uninterruptedly in Palestine in the first century and that someone using the Gospel of Matthew (as this apocryphal Gospel appears to do) would not have *translated* the Lord's Prayer as he did the rest of the text. 'He simply wrote down the holy words in the form in which he prayed them.' He thus argues that this represents unbroken usage from the days of Jesus and must be decisive for its meaning. But other scholars are not so persuaded.²⁵

Yet it still would not settle what the petition means. Many have pointed to the background of the manna in Exod. 16. The Israelites are told to gather only enough for the day ahead and 'those who had gathered more had not too much and those who had gathered less had not too little. Each had just as much as he could eat' (16.18; cf. Prov. 30.8, 'Provide me only with the food I need'; i.e, not too much or too little). It had been argued that ἐπιούσιος is an indication not of time but of measure: 'the food we need' (*Good News Bible*). This is certainly in line with Jesus' teaching: Don't worry about what you are to eat or drink. Pray for it trustingly and it will be given you; for your heavenly Father knows your need (Matt. 6.25–34).²⁶

Yet the analogy with the manna, specific in John 6, could equally suggest that the reference is to the bread of the *coming age*, what

---

²³The τὸ καθ᾽ ἡμέραν of Luke 11.3, rather than simply καθ᾽ ἡμέραν, may suggest that he is understanding it as epexegetic of ἐπιούσιον, i.e., the bread that belongs to each day.

²⁴The text will be found under the Gospel of the Nazaraeans in *NTApoc* I, p. 147.

²⁵P. Vielhauer in *NTApoc* I, p. 142, strongly disagrees, as does Lohmeyer. But W. Förster in his balanced article on ἐπιούσιος in G. Kittel, ed., *Theological Dictionary of the New Testament* II, ET Grand Rapids, Michigan 1964, p. 595, says that the point must be taken seriously without closing the discussion.

²⁶B. Orchard, 'The Meaning of the *Ton Epiousion* (Matt. 6.11 = Luke 11.3)', *Biblical Theology Bulletin* 3, 1973, pp. 274–82, takes it to mean 'the bread that comes to us' or 'what we come upon'. That is to say: Be like the birds, rather than try to store up or make provision for the future. Cf. Luke 15.12, which incidentally he does not quote: δός μοι τὸ ἐπιβάλλον μέρος τῆς οὐσίας, 'the share that is coming to me'.

Jeremias calls 'the great tomorrow'. This eschatological reference is justified also by the associations of eating bread with the kingdom of God (Luke 14.15; etc). Ἐπιούσιος ἄρτος would then be more or less the equivalent of αἰώνιος ἄρτος, becoming a petition for the immanent realization of the age to come – praying it down now. This fits the contrast with Matthew's 'today', lost in Luke's clearly secondary καθ᾽ ἡμέραν,[27] and provides a link with the bread of the Eucharist, at which it was prayed (cf. Marcion's 'thy bread'). Brown points out that to 'give bread' is a surprisingly rare phrase in the New Testament. Apart from the Lord's Prayer, it occurs only at the Last Supper, 'He took the bread . . . and gave' (Mark 14.22 and pars.); in the desert feeding (Mark 6.41 and 8.6 and pars.; John 6.11), which in all the evangelists has eucharistic as well as eschatological overtones; and in the theological reflection of John 6.32, 'My Father gives you the real bread from heaven'. Yet this cannot be decisive for how Jesus, as distinct from the church, saw the prayer.

To sum up, all turns on how 'eschatologically' we interpret the whole. We cannot *demonstrate* anything beyond 'the bread we need for the morrow'. Lohmeyer thinks that the very rarity of the word ἐπιούσιος points to a pregnant combination of all the different levels: 'The bread . . . is earthly bread, the bread of the poor and needy, and at the same time, because of the eschatological hour in which it is prayed for and eaten, it is the future bread in this today, the bread of the elect and the blessed', and he stresses the 'us', 'the eschatological communion of the children of God who today eat "our bread", their Father's gift, as they will soon eat it in their Father's house'.[28]

4. *Forgive us our debt(s), as we also forgive our debtors.*

We have already gone into this clause in some detail in order to establish the original text. Jeremias argues, as we saw, that Matthew's 'have forgiven' means 'as we forthwith forgive' – like Zacchaeus in Luke 19.8: 'Here and now I give half my possessions to charity.' But whether we press the *perfectum praestans* or translate with the Didache 'as we also forgive our debtors', the sense is the same: 'Forgive us – with the implication that we also forgive' (as a consequence rather than as a condition): Freely have you received, freely give.

[27]So Jeremias strongly, and many others: e.g., A. Schweitzer, *The Mysticism of Paul the Apostle*, ET London and New York 1931, pp. 239–41; Brown, 'The Pater Noster as an Eschatological Prayer', pp. 238–43.

[28]*The Lord's Prayer*, p. 157.

But what is the meaning of the clause as a whole?

Jeremias argues again that it is invoking, praying down, the messianic era of salvation, the age of forgiveness. That the Son of Man has power 'on earth' to forgive sins, 'before the time', is seen by the New Testament writers as a sign of the inbreaking of the kingdom. And this is in line with the Didache's 'Let grace come: let this world pass away.' The forgiveness of sins is essentially eschatological, a feature of the coming kingdom. This was the heart of the apostolic preaching, in what may be its earliest and very Jewish form: 'Repent . . . and turn to God, so that your sins may be wiped out. Then the Lord may grant you a time of recovery and send you the Messiah he has already appointed' (Acts 3.19).[29] It was embodied in the distinctively Christian offer: 'Be baptized . . . in the name of Jesus the Messiah for the forgiveness of sins; and you will receive the gift of the Holy Spirit' (Acts 2.38). This is the sacrament of realized eschatology, and the Lord's Prayer is praying again for the realization of the age to come within this age.

Yet once more the eschatological dimension can be exaggerated. 'Forgive as you have been forgiven' is the mark of the new life however conceived. The prayer makes perfectly good sense as: Give us the freedom of the new world, release us from the burden of indebtedness, the chain of *karma*, so that forgiven we can forgive, reconciled we can reconcile, liberated we can liberate.

5. *Lead us not into temptation.*[30]

Our idea of temptation is of something delectable to be resisted (cf. Oscar Wilde, 'I couldn't help it. I can resist everything except temptation'); the biblical idea of temptation is of something searing to be rescued from. To grasp this distinction is the first necessity for understanding this clause.

The biblical understanding is typically reflected in I Peter 1.6, 'Even though you smart for a little while, if need be under trials (πειρασμοί, temptations) of many kinds', and 4.12, 'The fiery ordeal that is upon you (τῇ πυρώσει πρὸς πειρασμόν)'. The basic idea is of testing, as metal is assayed in the fire (1.7). πειρασμός is associated with suffering and endurance. It is often said to refer to the final ordeal, the ultimate eschatological test which is 'to come upon all who dwell on the face of the whole earth' (Luke 21.35), the 'great tribulation' from which had it not been shortened no human being

---

[29] Cf. my article 'The Most Primitive Christology of All?', reprinted in *Twelve New Testament Studies*, p. 139–53.

[30] On this clause, cf. C. F. D. Moule, 'An Unsolved Problem in the Temptation Clause in the Lord's Prayer,' *Reformed Theological Review* 33, 1974, pp. 65–75.

would be saved (Matt. 24.21f.; cf. Dan. 12.1). Yet this, as in Daniel, is characteristically called θλῖψις (tribulation) not πειρασμός. Those who stress the eschatological character of the Prayer as a whole naturally see the clause as originally having specific allusion to this. But this would require reference to '*the* test', and in fact only once in the New Testament is πειρασμός used with the article, in Rev. 3.10: 'I will keep you from the hour of the ordeal which is to come upon the whole inhabited world.' But 'lead us not into temptation' has no such clearly limited application. In fact all the other references to temptation in the New Testament (often in the plural) are against such a restriction.

Two in particular are worth looking at, as they are commentaries, if not on the Lord's Prayer or popular misunderstanding of it, at least on Jewish presuppositions about temptation.

The Epistle of James, I have argued in my *Redating the New Testament*, may be the earliest finished piece of Christian writing, and it contains many apparent echoes of, though not quotations from, the teaching of the Sermon on the Mount. In 1.12–14 James writes:

> Happy is the man who remains steadfast under trial (πειρασμόν) for having passed that test he will receive for his prize the gift of life promised to those who love God. No one under trial (πειραζόμενος) should say 'I am being tempted by God'; for God is untouched (ἀπείραστος) by evil, and does not himself tempt anyone. Temptation arises when a man is enticed and lured away by his own lust.

We may observe that this comes near to what we usually mean when *we* say a thing is 'tempting', i.e., desirable: there is no absolute distinction, only a matter of emphasis (cf. also I Tim. 6.9, 'temptations and snares and many foolish harmful desires'). This comment of James could be correcting a false inference from the Prayer that it is God who leads us into temptation. God does indeed test men in the Old Testament (e.g., Abraham); and the Psalmist prays 'Test me, O Lord, and try me; put my heart and mind to the proof, (Ps. 26.2). Yet it is not with intent to entice or pervert, but to prove and purify, as in Ps. 66.10f.: 'For thou, O God, has tested us: thou hast tried us as silver is tried. Thou didst bring (εἰσήγαγες) us into the net; thou didst lay affliction on our loins.'

The other passage is I Cor. 10.13: 'God keeps faith, and he will not allow you to be tested above your powers, but when the test comes he will at the same time provide a way out, by enabling you to sustain it' (or, perhaps, ensure that the outcome, τὴν ἔκβασιν, is that you are able to sustain it).[31] This is not, be it noted, a prayer or promise to escape being tempted, but being tempted not to fall, to be kept or rescued from evil or the power of the evil one (cf. John 17.15; II Peter 2.9; Rev. 3.10).

These two passages suggest the following reflections. As always, the Hebrew way of thinking does not distinguish as clearly as we do what God wills and what God permits. 'Do not lead us into temptation' does not necessarily imply that God tempts us. In the New Testament it is always Satan who is the source or agent of temptation (cf. e.g., I Cor. 7.5, 'that Satan may not tempt you'). Yet God may allow his servants, like Job, to be put to the test, exactly as his own Son 'was *led up by the Spirit* into the wilderness to be *tempted by the Devil*' (Matt. 4.1; Luke 4.1). Jeremias aptly quotes what he calls 'a very ancient Jewish evening prayer,[32] which Jesus could have known and with which he perhaps makes a direct point of contact':

> Lead my foot not into the power of sin
> And bring me not into the power of iniquity,
> And not into the power of temptation,
> And not into the power of anything shameful.

He comments:

> The juxtaposition of 'sin', 'iniquity', 'temptation' and 'anything shameful', as well as the expression 'bring into the power of', show that this Jewish evening prayer has in view not an unmediated action of God but his permission which allows something to happen.

In other words, it means: Do not allow me to fall into the grip of all these things, to succumb to them. So 'Lead us not into temptation' must mean: Do not allow us to be enmeshed or caught up in temptation. Similarly in Gethsemane, another commentary on the Lord's Prayer, 'Pray that you do not *enter into* temptation' (Mark 14.38) does not mean 'Pray that you are not put to the test' but 'Pray that you are not engulfed by it',[33] or as Paul expresses it: 'Pray that there may be a way out, so that you are not sucked in or submerged by

---

[31] For ἔκβασις as 'outcome' cf. Wisd. 2.17; 11.14; Heb. 13.7 – the only other occurrences of the word in biblical Greek.

[32] b. *Ber.* 60b; *The Prayers of Jesus*, p. 105

[33] So, strongly J. Carmignac, *Recherches sur le 'Notre Père'*, Paris 1969, ch. 12. But Moule, 'An Unsolved Problem in the Temptation Clause', shows how hypothetical this is, really requiring ἐμπίπτειν, as in I Tim. 3.6, rather than εἰσενεγκεῖν. Yet he agrees that 'psychologically if not logically' this is what the petition must mean.

it.' Rather, as the Matthaean addition here rightly interprets it, it is a petition 'Rescue us from evil'.

This last phrase is more likely from other New Testament usage to refer to the masculine 'the evil one' (i.e., what we should call the power of evil), as in John 17.15, 'Keep them from the evil one.' This was strongly argued by Lightfoot.[34] Yet not all the evidence favours the masculine. Cf. Did. 10.5, 'Remember, O Lord, thy church to rescue it from all evil', where it must be neuter.

This clause may again have reference, with Jeremias, to the last ordeal, the final apostasy, as Jeremias argues: Preserve us from falling away at the last. But there is no reason to limit it to this. There have been attempts in recent liturgical experiment to find alternative translations. But the final revision of the Church of England's Alternative Services Book returns to 'Lead us not into temptation', which is probably as good as one can hope to achieve. In fact much can still be made of the simple piety offered in the anonymous paraphrase: 'If the occasion of sinning presents itself, grant that the desire may not be found in me: if the desire is there, grant that the occasion may not present itself.'

6. Finally, a word on the *doxology*.

Almost certainly, as we saw, this is not part of the new prayer taught by Jesus. 'But', as Jeremias rightly adds,

> it would be a completely erroneous conclusion to suppose that the Lord's Prayer was ever prayed without some closing words of praise to God; in Palestinian practice it was completely unthinkable that a prayer would end with the word 'temptation'. Now, in Judaism prayers were often concluded with a 'seal', a sentence of praise freely formulated by the man who was praying. This was doubtless also what Jesus intended with the Lord's Prayer, and what the congregation did in the earliest period.[35]

A doxology would be improvised *ex tempore*. The one which has become established is formulated, as we saw, on traditional models (cf. I Chron. 29.11) and is found in various forms in the Didache and the later manuscripts of Matthew. It is clearly secondary – yet as

---

[34] *On a Fresh Revision of the English New Testament*, [3]1891, Appendix 2 (it only appears in the third edition). He got the change through the RV, but the RSV reverted to the neuter. The appendix is however still worth reading, if only for its invective, as a sledge-hammer with which to crack a nut (in this case the unfortunate Canon Cook of Exeter who is demolished with utmost courtesy and devastating scholarship). Cf. Lightfoot's description of the Gothic version of the Gospels as a work of 'highly questionable date and wholly questionable ignorance' (op. cit., p. 301).

[35] *The Prayers of Jesus*, p. 106.

natural to the pious Jew as such interjected blessings as 'The Holy One: Blessed be He!'. It is part of the Prayer's necessary assimilation to Jewish culture; and it is noticeable that it is absent from Luke, who reflects Gentile conditions.

To sum up, we have always to be aware of the eschatological context and overtones of the Prayer for a Jew. Yet this does not mean that Jesus was confined to the apocalyptic outlook of many of his contemporaries, thus narrowing down the reference of each clause. There was a wide a spectrum in first-century Judaism as in the twentieth-century Christian church: not all, or even most, were adventists. The prayer could be prayed by all sorts in the early Christian communities, and drawn out and developed in different directions, both Jewish and Gentile. Having tried to listen to the *ipsissima vox*, we are not tied to the *ipsissima verba*; we have each to pray it, as we have each to hear the gospel, τῇ ἰδίᾳ διαλέκτῳ (Acts 2.6), in our own idiom and culture. And this is what the changing liturgical tradition of the church, so far from being a threat, has in fact made possible. We are not bound to the first century – or even to Jesus.

5

The Relation of the Prologue to the Gospel of St John[1]

The Gospel according to St John has been compared in its composition with everything from a seamless robe to a thing of shreds and patches. Here, as in virtually every aspect of the study of the gospel, critics can come away with apparently diametrically opposite conclusions. Indeed, the effect of reading too much on the Fourth Gospel is to make one feel either that everything has been said about it that conceivably could be said or that it really does not matter what one says, for one is just as likely to be right as anyone else. And both of these feelings are particularly strong as one approaches the Prologue.

I do not intend in this article to become involved in the vexed question of the integrity of the Gospel as a whole. But as the relation of the Prologue to the body of the Gospel is simply one part of this larger question, I will state, without argument, the position on it which I shall presuppose.

(1) On purely stylistic grounds I believe the Gospel must be judged to be a literary unity. Whatever the slight variations from the average in word-count in certain passages, I accept the view that the whole is the work of a single hand, including the Prologue and the Epilogue. The attempt to isolate sources on literary grounds cannot be said to have succeeded.[2] 'It looks as though', to quote Professor Pierson Parker, 'if the author of the Fourth Gospel used documentary sources, he wrote them all himself.'[3]

(2) But if it is the work of a single hand, it was certainly not written at a single sitting. The seaminess of the 'seamless robe' is only too apparent. At many points there are signs of suture and disorder. I am

---

[1] First published in *NTS* 9, 1962–3, pp. 120–9.
[2] Cf. the references in my article, 'The New Look on the Fourth Gospel', *Twelve New Testament Studies*, p. 97.
[3] 'Two Editions of John', *JBL* 75, 1956, p. 304.

not convinced by any elaborate theory of dislocation from a presumed perfect order. On the other hand, it seems to me probable that the Gospel has been composed from material called forth in the first instance by different occasions and that the whole has been left without the final tidying up which it requires. As any teacher knows, the final co-ordination of material which he has used at different times or composed originally for different contexts is the most tedious process in the preparation of a book. If death supervened before the author had found the time or the inclination for this last task of revision, his work would in this respect have anticipated the fate of many of the commentaries upon it.[4] Yet substantially the Gospel is an ordered whole, which might have circulated in its present state for some time before its author's death. And this indeed is, I believe, what happened, with the exception of the additions which I now go on to discuss.

Evidence for two editions or recensions within the body of the Gospel itself[5] must remain somewhat subjective. Yet there are two isolable problems, at the beginning and the end, which are in a class by themselves, the Prologue in chapter 1 and the Epilogue of chapter 21.

On the Epilogue, again, I will do no more than summarize my conclusions. This I believe to have been written by the same hand, but at a later date. I have suggested elsewhere[6] that the last chapter of the Gospel was added at about the time when the Epistles were written, and that these were separated from the first draft of the Gospel by an interval of at least a decade, and probably more. In the Epistles we are nearer the end than 'the beginning' (I John 2.24): it is already 'the last hour' (I John 2.18). And of this there is no hint in the Gospel – except in the 'waiting till I come' of the Epilogue (John 21.22), where alone we find a conception of the parousia comparable with that of the first Epistle (I John 2.28). The Epilogue, moreover, is clearly the work of an old man, of whom some thought that he would never die (John 21.23).[7] It reflects the same preoccupation with the pastoral authority of the church's ministry (John

---

[4]To go no further than the English-speaking world, this is true of J. H. Bernard, E. C. Hoskyns, R. H. Lightfoot and, alas, most recently of J. N. Sanders. We have fragments only on St John from J. B. Lightfoot, F. J. A. Hort and H. Scott Holland – and B. F. Westcott's commentary on the Greek text was also left unfinished.

[5]Cf. Parker, op. cit. pp. 303–14.

[6]'The Destination and Purpose of the Johannine Epistles', *NTS* 7, 1960–1, pp. 57–9, reprinted in *Twelve New Testament Studies*, pp. 127–30.

[7]For a modification of this judgment, cf. my *Redating the New Testament*, pp. 279–82.

21.15–17) as do the Epistles; and the 'we know that his witness is true' of John 21.24 echoes both the 'we' of the first Epistle and the 'you know that our witness is true' of III John 12.

But if the Epilogue is an addition, it is related to the whole as a simple annexe to an existing structure, built on in the same style and marked off from it by a clean line. The Prologue, however, presents a more complex situation. It is like a porch to the house, designed and executed by the same architect but in a grander and more elevated style. Moreover, there is no clear line demarcating it from the main building. There is no agreement even as to exactly where the Prologue ends. Liturgically we have become accustomed to thinking of it closing with v. 14, which is on any reckoning its climax. But on inspection it clearly continues down to the end of v. 18. The reason for stopping at v. 14 is because v. 15 seems to begin a new line of thought. But if that verse were not there there would be no suggestion of a break, since without it v. 14 runs directly into v. 16:

[14]And the Word became flesh and dwelt among us; we have beheld his glory, glory as of the only Son from the Father, full of grace and truth.
[16]And from his fullness have we all received, grace upon grace. [17]For the law was given through Moses; grace and truth came through Jesus Christ. [18]No one has ever seen God; the only Son, who is in the bosom of the Father, he has made him known.

Moreover, though v. 15 is the most rude interruption in the Prologue, it is not the only one. The change of subject at v. 6 is equally unexpected, where the historical appearance of John the Baptist breaks without warning into a series of timeless statements about the Logos.

Furthermore, as has often been observed, there are within the Prologue alternations not only of subject but of rhythm. It may be an exaggeration to speak of 'poetry' interrupted by 'prose', but if we put these words in inverted commas they can serve to designate a real difference of level and of 'feel'. This difference has prompted numerous reconstructions from these verses of what has been called a 'Wisdom hymn' or 'Logos ode'. This has generally been assumed to be pre-Johannine and even non-Christian in origin, and to have been taken over from the Mandaeans or the Alexandrians or the Gnostics. I find little evidence for this, and much presumption against. Nor does it even fit the facts to presuppose an independent Logos poem previously composed by the same author and then forced into uneasy union with the narrative of his Gospel. It is more as though in the Prologue the themes of the Gospel are played over beforehand, as in the overture to an opera.

Even if we exclude the narrative connexions with John the Baptist, the list of themes common to the Prologue and the rest of the Gospel is impressive.

	Prologue	*Gospel*
The pre-existence of the Logos or Son	1. 1f.	17.5
In him was life	1.4	5.26
Life is light	1.4	8.12
Light rejected by darkness	1.5	3.19
Yet not quenched by it	1.5	12.35
Light coming into the world	1.9	3.19 12.46[8]
Christ not received by his own	1.11	4.44
Being born of God and not of flesh	1.13	3.6; 8.41f.
Seeing his glory	1.14	12.41
The only-begotten Son	1.14, 18	3.16
Truth in Jesus Christ	1.17	14.6
No one has seen God, except the one who comes from God's side	1.18	6.46

Furthermore, it may be that there is a deliberate correspondence between the *structure* of the Prologue and that of the Gospel.[9]

	Prologue	*Gospel*
Christ as the agent of creation both old and new	1.3	1.35–4.42
Christ as the life of the world	1.4	4.43–6.71
Christ as the light of the world	1.4f.	7.1–9.41
He came to his own and his own received him not	1.10f.	10.1–12.50
But to all who believed in his name he gave power to become children of God	1.12f.	13.1–20.29

Yet for all this parallelism the Prologue is not simply constructed out of material from the Gospel, nor does the theology of the

---

[8]These parallels would appear decisive for taking ἐρχόμενον in 1.9 with φῶς and not ἄνθρωπον.

[9]I owe this suggestion to B. T. D. Smith's essay, 'The Johannine Theology', in *The Parting of the Roads: Studies in the Development of Judaism and Early Christianity*, ed. F. J. Foakes-Jackson, London 1912, p. 256 n. 1.

Prologue wholly control the narrative that follows. It has been said by no less a Johannine scholar than E. F. Scott that 'in the Fourth Gospel the Messianic idea is replaced by that of the Logos'.[10] But this is precisely what does not happen. The word λόγος never recurs as a title, and the dominant christology of the Gospel is expressed rather in terms of 'the Christ, the Son of God' (20.21). Moreover, there are connections missing precisely where we might most expect them. Thus, the most markedly 'metaphysical' language of the Gospel – of the pre-existent Son of Man who descends from heaven to return thither (3.13) – finds no echo in the Prologue, nor is the distinction, which some have seen as Platonic, between τὰ ἄνω and τὰ κάτω (3.31) taken up in it. Indeed, of the three theological 'meditations' in chapter 3 – vv. 6–15, 16–21 and 31–6 – it is the central and least philosophical one which alone has any close affinities with the Prologue.

Above all, in the central affirmation of the Prologue, that 'the Word became flesh' (1.14), the usage of the key terms is subtly different from that of the Gospel as a whole. The contrast is focused in 6.63, where Jesus says, 'It is the spirit that gives life, the flesh is of no avail; the words that I have spoken to you are spirit and life'. Here Jesus is no longer the Word who is made flesh, but the one who speaks words which are not flesh but spirit – for 'that which is born of the flesh is flesh, and that which is born of the Spirit is spirit' (3.6). It is true that in the Prologue there is the same antithesis between being born 'of the will of the flesh' and being born 'of God' (1.13) and in ch. 6 it is the 'flesh' of the Son of Man that gives 'life' (6.51–8). Nevertheless, for anything like a parallel to the terminology of John 1.14 we have to go not to the Gospel but to the Epistles – to the formula 'Jesus Christ come in the flesh' of I John 4.2 and II John 7 and to the phrase 'the word of life' in I John 1.1.

This last reference, to the exordium of the first Epistle, brings us to the very close relationship between this and the Prologue to the Gospel. The parallels are obvious and striking:

I John 1.1	ὃ ἦν ἀπ᾽ ἀρχῆς	John 1.1	ἐν ἀρχῇ ἦν ὁ λόγος
	ἐθεασάμεθα	14	ἐθεασάμεθα
	τοῦ λόγου τῆς ζωῆς	4	ἐν [τῷ λόγῳ] ζωὴ ἦν
2	ἡ ζωὴ ἐφανερώθη	4	ἡ ζωὴ ἦν τὸ φῶς
	ἦν πρὸς τὸν πατέρα	2	ἦν πρὸς τὸν θεόν

The only question is, Which is modelled on which? I have argued in general for the priority of the Gospel over the Epistles;[11] but I am not convinced that this applies to the Prologue. Indeed, though certainty must always fall short of proof, there is much to be said for supposing that here the relationship is the other way round, and that the opening of the first Epistle represents the first sketch for the Prologue, which, no one can doubt, is in every way the richer and profounder. While the Epistles presuppose the main body of the Gospel, they seem to provide the bridge between the Gospel and the Prologue. In particular is this true of the central category of the Logos. The phrase 'the word of life' in I John 1.4, which may or may not have a personal reference, appears to stand mid-way between the early Christian use of λόγος for 'the message' and the fully hypostatized usage of the Prologue. Moreover, the pregnant phrase σὰρξ ἐγένετο in John 1.14 looks like a development of the expression ἐν σαρκὶ ἐληλυθότα (I John 4.2) rather than the other way round.

We have already noted signs that the Epilogue belongs to the period which called forth the Epistles and there are not lacking indications that the Prologue also belongs to this period rather than to that of the Gospel as a whole.

I have argued elsewhere[12] that the Gospel was primarily written from an evangelistic rather than an apologetic motive and that whereas the Epistles contain clear anti-docetic polemic this is not true of the Gospel. At least, it is not true of the body of the Gospel; but traces of it have often been suspected in the Prologue. Thus, there is, above all, the stark assertion of the Word *become flesh*, which is even more uncompromising than the anti-docetic watchword of the Epistles, 'come in the flesh'. Moreover, we again find here the 'we' of the Johannine community with its insistent stress on the veracity of its eyewitness. We may compare:

John 1.14   We have beheld his glory.
I John 1.1   That . . . which we have heard, which we have seen with our eyes, which we have looked upon and touched with our hands.
John 21.24   We know that his testimony is true.
III John 12   We bear witness, and you know that our testimony is true.

The only verse in the body of the Gospel with the same ring is 19.35: 'He who saw it has borne witness—his testimony is true and he

---

[11]*Twelve New Testament Studies*, pp. 127–30.
[12]'The Destination and Purpose of St John's Gospel', *NTS* 6, 1959–60, pp. 117–31; reprinted in *Twelve New Testament Studies*, pp. 107–25.

knows that he tells the truth – that you also may believe.' It is possible that this verse may have been added at the same time, to underline the Evangelist's eyewitness testimony to the physical fact of the death of Christ ('with the water and the blood') which was only later to be called in question (I John 5.6). Hitherto, it had been sufficient to assert the historical facts: now it was necessary to do battle for them.

Our conclusion so far is that the order of the Johannine writings is (1) the body of the Gospel, (2) the Epistles, (3) the Epilogue and Prologue. The Prologue is, on this view, not simply, like most prefaces, written after the work it introduces, drawing its themes together. It is a definite addition – more like a preface to a second edition – setting the original work in a new context.

If this conclusion is accepted, then it must follow that the Gospel once began – as it ended – differently. Its original ending is still there for all to see, at 20.31. But its original beginning cannot be reconstructed with certainty, because – to use our previous metaphor – the porch has not merely been added on to the front of the house but built into it. To take away the porch now leaves the masonry disturbed.

Nevertheless, there are, as we have seen, obvious joins in the brickwork of the porch itself. It is an oversimplification merely to separate the strata of 'poetry' and 'prose'. But if for the moment we allow this way of putting it, our thesis will be not (as has usually been suggested) that the Prologue of St John's Gospel consists of a poem with prose additions, but the other way round. We shall argue the case for an original narrative opening around which a poetic structure (with its own prose commentary) has subsequently been built.

The place from which to begin is again the 'fault' in v. 15: 'John bore witness to him, and cried, "This was he of whom I said, 'He who comes after me ranks before me, for he was before me'"'.' It is not easy to account for the presence of this verse in the Prologue at all unless it was there already as part of the original building. It is hard to see it being added as an explanation, because (unlike other verses to be considered) it explains nothing in the context: it merely interrupts.

There there is the other break at v. 6, with the introduction of the words: 'There was a man sent from God, whose name was John. . . .' This is abrupt, if not incongruous, as an addition; but as part of an original structure it is entirely explicable. Indeed, unless we posit some brief introduction to the Gospel, corresponding to Mark 1.1,

Luke 1.1–4 or (on the assumption that it was the original opening) 3.1–2a, it may well have stood as its first verse. The parallels with the synoptists show how natural this would be:

> John 1.6   ἐγένετο ἄνθρωπος, . . . ὄνομα αὐτῷ Ἰωάνης[13]
> Mark 1.4   ἐγένετο Ἰωάνης ὁ βαπτίζων
> Luke 1.5   ἐγένετο . . . ἱερεύς τις ὀνόματι Ζαχαρίας
> Luke 3.2   ἐγένετο ῥῆμα θεοῦ ἐπὶ Ἰωάνην

Exactly how this opening would have continued we shall never know, as the verses immediately following v. 6 have evidently been affected by the theme of 'the light' in vv. 4f., and this theme, though integral to the Gospel as a whole, seems hardly likely to have been introduced without explanation in its second verse (v. 7). Nor is it quite clear (as it is in the case of the single v. 15) where this section ends and the new material again takes over.

But let us turn now to this latter work. There have been numerous attempts on grounds of rhythm and diction to discover and isolate in the Prologue an underlying poetic structure. The very variety of the solutions suggests that this may be a hopeless task. That there is something in it is however confirmed by the persistence of the attempts.[14] And for all the difference in detail there is a wide measure of agreement that the following verses *at least*, marked as they are by strong signs of Hebraic parallelism, both climactic and antithetical, form some kind of ode or rhythmic meditation:

1   In the beginning was the Word,
And the Word was with God,
And the Word was God
3   All things were made through him.
And without him was not anything made that was made.
4   In him was life,
And the life was the light of men.
5   The light shines in the darkness,
And the darkness has not overcome it.
10   He was in the world,
And the world was made through him,
Yet the world knew him not.

[13]M. E. Boismard, *St John's Prologue*, London and Westminster, Maryland, 1957, pp. 24f., draws attention to the Old Testament parallels – e.g. I Sam 1.1 ('There was a certain man . . . whose name was Elkanah'), Judges 13.2, etc.
[14]For the most recent survey, cf. P. H. Menoud, 'Les Études Johanniques de Bultmann à Barrett', in *L'Évangile de Jean*, ed. F. M. Braun, Paris 1958, pp. 16–18.

11 He came to his own home,
    And his own people received him not.
14 And the Word became flesh
    And dwelt among us.

This represents the irreducible minimum of common material in the reconstructions of J. Weiss,[15] C. Cryer,[16] C. F. Burney,[17] J. H. Bernard,[18] H. C. Green[19] and R. Schnackenburg.[20] The uncertainty attending any such reconstruction is occasioned by the fact that there are other verses which, though not poetic in structure (or not so obviously so), are yet clearly dependent theologically on the rhythmic meditation. These other verses are:

[2]He was in the beginning with God.
[12]But to all who received him, who believed in his name, he gave power to become children of God; [13]who were born, not of blood nor of the will of the flesh nor of the will of man, but of God.
[14b]We have beheld his glory, glory as of the only Son from the Father, full of grace and truth.
[16]And from his fullness have we all received, grace upon grace.
[17]For the law was given through Moses; grace and truth came through Jesus Christ. [18]No one has ever seen God; the only Son, who is in the bosom of the Father, he has made him known.

Some of these verses may properly belong to the poetic meditation rather than to the theological commentary upon it.[21] But for our purposes a precise differentiation between the two is unimportant. For both can be regarded as belonging to the later structure. But if we detach this second layer *in toto*, we are then left with the following as constituting possibly the original opening to the Gospel:

[6]There was a man sent from God, whose name was John.
[7]He came for testimony, to bear witness to the light, that all

[15]*The History of Primitive Christianity*, ET New York and London 1937, p. 790.
[16]'The Prologue to the Fourth Gospel', *ExpT* 32, 1920–21, pp. 440–3.
[17]*The Aramaic Origin of the Fourth Gospel*, Oxford and New York 1922, pp. 40f.
[18]*St John* (ICC), London 1928, New York 1929, pp. 144f.
[19]'The Composition of St John's Prologue', *ExpT* 66, 1955, pp. 291–4.
[20]'Logos-Hymnus and johanneischer Prolog', *Biblische Zeitschrift* n.s. 1, 1957, pp. 69–109.
[21]For R. E. Brown, *The Gospel according to John*, New York 1966–70, London 1971, p. 22, the original hymn consists of vv. 1—2, 3—5, 10—12b, 14, 16

might believe through him. [8]He was not the light, but came to bear witness to the light. [9]The true light that enlightens every man was coming into the world. [15]John bore witness to him, and cried, 'This was he of whom I said, "He who comes after me ranks before me, for he was before me"'. [19]And this is the testimony of John, when the Jews sent priests and Levites from Jerusalem to ask him, 'Who are you?', etc.

The language of vv. 7–9 has doubtless been affected by the Prologue subsequently built around it; but at least we have here a more or less continuous piece of prose narrative, leading without a break into the heart of the Gospel story.

If this admittedly tentative investigation into the original opening of the Gospel were of purely archaeological interest it would not perhaps matter very much whether it were true or not. But if the hypothesis we have been advancing is at all probable – and the supposition that the Prologue (unlike the Epilogue) was written *with* the Gospel and before the Epistles, is equally hypothetical and I think more difficult – then two consequences of importance follow, one for the historical setting, and the other for the theology, of the Gospel.

The first consequence is that the Logos theology belongs to the *environment* of the Gospel rather than to its *background*. These two are not usually sufficiently distinguished. I have argued in my article on 'The Destination and Purpose of St John's Gospel' quoted above that the environment in and for which the Gospel was published was one of Greek-speaking Diaspora Judaism, but that the background of the author and his tradition was Aramaic-speaking Palestinian Judaism. I should certainly not wish to be dogmatic and say that the Logos-hymn could not be the product of Palestinian Judaism – Bultmann attributes it (however improbably) to an Aramaic-speaking Mandaean community. If however it does belong to the latest stage of the composition of the Gospel, and already reflects the conditions of its reception, then it can very naturally be attributed to the world of thought of Hellenistic Judaism. But if it is separable from the main body of the Gospel tradition, then we have even less reason for supposing that the thought-forms which mould this tradition must be Hellenistic and must be late. Already the Dead Sea Scrolls have questioned earlier dogmatism in this matter in regard to other categories. But it could still be argued that the Logos theology (for which they provide no parallel) locates the Gospel both in place and time at a considerable remove from the Palestinian scene which it purports to describe. Even here it would be wise not to be too confident; for one of the most interesting correspondences in the Qumran literature is in fact with John 1.3: 'By his knowledge everything has been brought into being. And everything that is, he established by his purpose; and apart from him nothing is done' (1QS xi.11). The equation Knowledge = Wisdom = Logos would not be hard to make, and it suggests that we need not range very far even into the world of Diaspora Judaism to account for the Prologue. But even if the Logos terminology of the Prologue were still judged to be Hellenistic and late, it cannot be used, if our thesis is correct, to impugn the Palestinian background of the main body of the Johannine tradition, if on other grounds this were considered plausible.

Secondly, the stage of composition of the Prologue is important for our assessment of the Johannine theology of history. If the Prologue shaped and controlled the composition of the material that follows it, then it is possible to read the Fourth Gospel as though John were primarily interested in timeless truths of mystical or philosophical speculation which are subsequently *illustrated* in the history, in much the same way that Hegel saw the Christian stories as picture-book presentations of what is eternally valid in the realm of ideas. In this case the factual accuracy of the narratives would largely be a matter of indifference. The Lazarus story, for instance, could illustrate the truth that Jesus is the resurrection and the life equally well if it were simply a parable, like that of Dives and Lazarus, cast into the form of a miracle for dramatic effect. The details of the narrative, moreover, would be determined as much by their symbolic significance as by any relation to fact. In particulars, if not in principle, historicity then becomes expendable, and the stories could be spun out of the theology.

But if the Gospel was composed as we have suggested, then this interpretation must be ruled out. (It is hardly one that fits the facts in any case, since the Gospel abounds in historical and geographical detail for which no plausible symbolic significance can be found.) If we are right, the timeless truths were not the matrix of the Gospel, but the fruit of meditation upon it. On this view the Gospel is no less theological. But the history has its own primacy, the facts are sacred – and the theology is given only in, with and under it. This is made crystal clear in the opening verses of the first Epistle, and the Prologue restates it by insisting upon the centrality of the Word made flesh. It simply reaffirms what without the Prologue would be inescapable, namely, that for this Gospel the history – as the locus of the revelation — is everything. The narrative cannot be read merely as illustration, for the pictorially minded, of the metaphysics. For it was not so written. The metaphysics came later — to place the narrative in a cosmic setting; not to detract one whit from its factuality, but to allow this to be seen in its ultimate depth and significance.

6

The Significance of the Foot-Washing[1]

The story of the washing of the disciples' feet in John 13.1–17 is a test-passage for the exegesis of the Fourth Gospel. It has divided commentators from the earliest times[2] into those who see in this incident simply a lesson in humility and those who view it as but thinly veiled instruction about the meaning of the Christian sacraments.

The former view, which was that of Chrysostom, is upheld in a recent study of the passage by J. Michl.[3] But in the latter camp Professor O. Cullmann[4] (following in the tradition of A. Loisy[5] and W. Bauer[6]) interprets the words of Jesus to Peter, 'He who has bathed does not need to wash, except for his feet, but he is clean all over' (v. 10), to mean that he who has been baptized needs only the Eucharist for post-baptismal sin.

On one point, I believe, it is possible to be reasonably certain, and that is that there is no reference to the Eucharist in the words εἰ μὴ τοὺς πόδας. As R. Bultmann justly comments,[7] 'It is grotesque that the Lord's supper should be represented by the foot-washing, especially when the setting of the incident is already that of a meal.' There is, however, no a priori reason why Jesus should not have been alluding to Christian baptism – he was after all more than alluding to

[1]First published in *Neotestamentica et Patristica: Eine Freundesgabe Herrn Professor Dr Oscar Cullmann zu seinem 60. Geburtstag überreicht*, Leiden 1962, pp. 144–7.
[2]See E. C. Hoskyns and F. M. Davey, *The Fourth Gospel*, London and Chicago 1940, ad loc.
[3]'Der Sinn Der Fusswaschung', *Bibl* 40, 1959, pp. 697–708.
[4]*Early Christian Worship*, ET London and Chicago 1953, pp. 105–10. He is followed by A. J. B. Higgins, *The Lord's Supper in the New Testament*, London and Chicago 1952, pp. 84f.
[5]*Le quatrième évangile*, Paris 1903, ²1921, ad loc.
[6]*Das Johannesevangelium*, Tübingen ²1925, ad loc.
[7]*The Gospel of John*, ET Oxford and Philadelphia 1971, ad loc.

the Eucharist in the same context. I have myself suggested in an earlier article[8] that, if there is any sacramental reference, the 'bathing' is to be seen as the act of universal baptism[9] that Jesus is about to accomplish in his death, which in turn is to be the ground of the church's sacramental action (the 'washing') and will make it sufficient for salvation. I would certainly not rule out this meaning as an overtone (and an important overtone) of the passage. Nevertheless, it is not by any means what on the surface the passage is about, and no sacramental teaching is drawn from the incident in Jesus' subsequent comment in vv. 12–17 (in marked contrast with the eucharistic discourse of ch. 6).

Indeed, one suspects that the sacramental reference would not have been found necessary were it not that the purely exemplary explanation offered in v. 15 ('I have given you an example [ὑπόδειγμα], that you also should do as I have done') seems such a weak point after the momentous introduction to the story in vv. 1– 3. Nor does it apparently account in any way for the mysterious conversation with Peter in vv. 6–10, and in particular for the *necessity* of the washing if he is to have any part or lot with Jesus.

My own view is that the primary explanation of the incident *is* to be found within the context of Jesus' ministry rather than in that of the church's life, but that to see it as purely exemplary, as an object lesson in humility, is to miss its deepest significance. The clue, I suggest, lies in recognizing this passage as the Johannine equivalent of Mark 10.32–45.

Jesus is trying to show the disciples what his going up to Jerusalem, his going to the Father, really means. They suppose that he is going to glory, and so he is. They call him 'Teacher' and 'Lord', and they do well. But if they are to have any part with him it can be only as they are prepared to drink the cup that he drinks and be baptized with his baptism. The disciple cannot be greater than his master; he must follow in his path of humiliation: only so can he hope to share in the blessedness of the coming age (John 13.15–17). For Jesus' glory means the glory of the servant, the δοῦλος: the world's notions of κυριότης (John 13.14; Mark 10.42) and ἐξουσία (John 13.3; Mark 10.42) must be turned completely upside down. Can the disciples accept and themselves share in this reversal? That is the question posed by the conversation of Mark 10 and, more dramatically, by the symbolic action of John 13.

    [8]'The One Baptism', *SJT* 6, 1953, p. 264.
    [9]Excellently brought out by Cullmann in his *Baptism in the New Testament*, ET London 1950, Chicago 1951.

That this comparison between the two passages is not arbitrary is borne out by the fact that Luke also has his parallel to Mark 10.41–5 at the Last Supper, in 22.24–7. The whole passage, Luke 22.14–38, contained much independent and apparently old tradition and supports the supposition that some such discussion took place in the Upper Room. Indeed, Luke 22.27,

> For which is the greater, one who sits at table or one who serves? Is not the one who sits at table? But I am among you as one who serves,

might have been specifically written as commentary on the foot-washing,[10] and Luke's narrative contains other echoes of Johannine themes.

In particular, it helps to throw light on the conversation with Peter, which occurs at this point in both gospels, whereas in Matthew and Mark it takes place in Gethsemane. Peter first protests strongly (as at Caesarea Philippi[11]), and then offers to go the whole way. His reply in John 13.9, 'Lord, not my feet only but also my hands and my head', is to be interpreted in line with 13.37, 'Lord, why cannot I follow you now? I will lay down my life for you', and Luke 22.33, 'Lord, I am ready to go with you to prison and to death.' Jesus' answer in v. 10, 'He who has bathed does not need to wash, except for his feet,[12] but is clean all over', is a dissuasive couched in the perfectly straightforward observation that the man who has had a bath before he goes out to dinner needs only, as we should say, to wash his hands. In other words, Jesus is saying to Peter, I am not asking you to follow me to death (cf. 18.8f.); for where I am going you cannot follow me now – though you shall follow afterwards (13.36; cf. 21.18f.). I am asking only that you

---

[10]It has led to the (to me quite improbable) suggestion that the whole incident of the foot-washing is a Johannine construction spun out of this synoptic saying (e.g. C. K. Barrett, *The Gospel According to St John.*, London and New York 1955, p. 363). If the story had occurred in Luke and the saying in John, priority would undoubtedly have been given to the story, and the saying taken as evidence that John used Luke. In fact I am convinced that there is no literary dependence in either direction.

[11]Mark 8.31–8 is in its turn closely parallel to Mark 10.32–45.

[12]The shorter reading, which omits εἰ μὴ τοὺς πόδας, is, I am inclined to think, simply a mistake. If τοὺς πόδας alone were missing it would make sense to say that 'he who has had a bath only needs to wash', but to say that 'he has no need to wash' cannot be squared in the context with Jesus' insistence on the absolute necessity of the washing (v. 8). The longer reading has now the further support of p⁶⁶ (which makes the point even more strongly by adding μόνον, with D). It is evidence of the wishful thinking of those in the Bultmann tradition (who would like to excise all sacramental references in the Fourth Gospel) that E. Lohse, 'Wort and Sakrament im Johannesevangelium', *NTS* 7, 1961, p. 113, can actually write, 'The addition εἰ μὴ τοὺς πόδας is also missing from p⁶⁶!'.

should all identify yourselves with me in the cup I must drink and the baptism I must undergo. And just as he presses upon them the cup at supper (Mark 14.23; Matt. 26.27; Luke 22.17), so he asks them all to submit to the washing.

But in particular he makes a bid for Simon's faith. Hence the strange alternation of singular and plural in Luke 22.31, 'Simon, Simon, behold Satan demanded to have you [plural] that he might sift you like wheat, but I have prayed for you [singular] that your faith may not fail', and in Mark 14.37, 'And he came forward and found them sleeping, and he said to Peter, "Simon, are you asleep [singular]? Could you not watch one hour? Watch [plural] and pray that you may not enter into temptation"'. So in John 13 the unspoken challenge to all the disciples is focused upon Peter (v. 6). Jesus knows that his faith and knowledge are bound to fail in the immediate instance; but in each tradition there is the promise that he will come through to a different and a deeper understanding: 'What I am doing you do not know now, but afterward you will understand' (John 13.7); 'When you have turned again, strengthen your brethren' (Luke 22.32).

Jesus' washing of the disciples' feet is therefore to be interpreted as a bid for their solidarity with him as he goes to his death, putting to them, and to Peter in particular, the challenge, 'Are you able to be baptized with the baptism with which I am baptized?' For without that they can have no part with him, no share in his glory. Unless they are prepared to bear his cross – which is the same as to bear his love – they cannot be his disciples. And they can prove this only by themselves accepting the role of the servant: 'By this all men will know that you are my disciples, if you have love for one another' (John 13.35). The foot-washing is the ὑπόδειγμα of this love – to the uttermost – by virtue of the fact that it is also the ὑπόδειγμα of the one, final baptism of the Cross (cf. the εἰς τέλος of 13.1 with the τετέλεσται of 19.30). There is for the disciple no share in Christ without it, just as later there is to be no incorporation without the washing of the church's sacramental act.

7

The Shroud and the New Testament[1]

One of the things that shook my natural predisposition to scepticism about the Turin Shroud was precisely that it could not at all easily be harmonized with the New Testament accounts of the grave-clothes. I am not saying that it is incompatible with them but simply that no forger starting, as he inevitably would, from the gospel narratives, and especially that of the fourth, would have created the shroud we have. Yet *if* it is genuine, it must make us look again at the biblical evidence. The gospels are notoriously difficult to harmonize with themselves, let alone with what has been called this 'fifth gospel'. Nevertheless it may, I believe, help us to reconstruct the situation in a manner which I, at any rate, would never have arrived at, unless I had been prepared to take account of this extra-canonical witness.[2]

Let us begin with the burial of Jesus. This incidentally is one of the best attested of all historical facts about him. That Christ not only died and rose but was 'buried' is part of our earliest summary of the Christian faith in a letter written within twenty-five years of the crucifixion, where Paul is appealing to tradition which he himself received from the Jerusalem church (I Cor. 15.3–4), probably within five years of it (cf. Gal. 1.18). The burial is also narrated in all four gospels (Matt. 27.57–61; Mark 15.42–47; Luke 23.50–56; John 19.38–42), with John's account almost

[1]First published in *Face to Face with the Turin Shroud*, ed. P. Jennings, Great Wakering, Essex, and Oxford 1978, pp. 69–80.
[2]I have deliberately not cluttered this chapter with footnotes to authorities ancient or modern for the positions I have adopted. Suffice it to mention three treatments which refer to a wealth of other evidence: Edward A. Wuenschel, 'The Shroud of Turin and the Burial of Christ', *CBQ* 7, 1945, pp. 405–37, and 8, 1946, pp. 135–78; Ceslas Lavergne, OP, 'La preuve de la resurrection de Jésus d'apres Jean 20, 7', 'Le sudarium et la position des linges après la resurrection', and 'Le corps glorieux et la preuve que Jésus est ressuscité', Σινδών 3, 1961, nos. 5 and 6; and André Feuillet, 'La découverte du tombeau vide en Jean 20, 3–10 et la foi au Christ ressuscité', *Ésprit et Vie* 87, 1977, nos. 18 and 19, pp. 257–66, 273–84.

certainly independent of the others, and it is mentioned in a sermon summary in Acts, 'they took him down from the gibbet and laid him in a tomb' (Acts 13.29), which from the word ξύλον (wood or tree) almost certainly goes back to pre-Lukan sources (cf. Acts 5.30; 10.39; Gal. 3.13; I Peter 2.24). The view that we can know nothing about the body of Jesus, because as the corpse of a condemned criminal it would have been dissolved in a lime- pit, is sheer dogmatic scepticism, flying in the face of all the evidence that it met no such fate. In fact, under Jewish law (cf. Deuteronomy 21.23), it should have been buried before sun-down in one of the two plots in Jerusalem specifically reserved for criminals (Mishnah, *Sanh.* 6.5), and desire to remedy the concession of the pagan governor (especially to a non-relative in the case of a man condemned for high treason) *could* have supplied a motive for fanatical Jewish patriots, zealous for the law, to raid the tomb and transfer the body.

Following, therefore, the evidence we have, which is factual and circumstantial and not obviously subject to doctrinal motivation or suspicious alignment, there is multiple testimony for the tradition that the body of Jesus, released by Pilate at the request of Joseph of Arimathea, was taken from the cross late on the Friday afternoon (Matt. 27.57; Mark 15.42) and laid in a rock-tomb (Matt. 27.60; Mark 15.46; Luke 23.53) hitherto unused (Matt. 27.60; Luke 23.53; John 19.41). By then, despite the proximity of the grave (John 19.42), Luke tells us in an odd but graphic phrase (ἐπέφωσκεν [23.54]) it was already starting to be what we should call 'lighting-up time', i.e. when the lamps were lit or, more probably, when the first stars became visible which marked the beginning of the Sabbath. Clearly there was no time, before further work became illegal and darkness set in, for more than the most preliminary attention to the corpse. According to Mark (15.46) Joseph had already bought a linen cloth (σινδών) and in this he wrapped (ἐνείλησεν) or according to Matthew (27.59) and Luke (23.53) folded (ἐνετύλιξεν) the body of Jesus. According to John (19.39f.) Joseph and Nicodemus 'bound' it (ἔδησαν; though one uncial manuscript has 'wrapped', perhaps by assimilation to Mark) in ὀθόνια. This last is a word of uncertain meaning but it is best regarded not, with many modern versions, on a false analogy from its diminutive form, as strips but as a generic plural for grave-clothes of unspecified material, though presumably linen. At any rate Luke, or his scribe (in 24.12), uses ὀθόνια to cover what he had previously described as the σινδών.

John adds that a substantial mixture of myrrh and aloes, evidently a dry preparation in powdered or granule form like incense,[3] was brought by Nicodemus and put 'with' the clothing, presumably to serve as a temporary agent to arrest the effects of putrefaction until further attention could be given. One of the things specifically allowed by the Mishnah (*Shab.* 23.5) to be done for a corpse if need be on the Sabbath was to 'let it lie on sand that it may be the longer preserved'. The enormous quantity of material (100 lbs, though the Roman pound was only about three-quarters of ours) could be an exaggerated figure to bring out the generosity of the gesture, like the stress, in the earlier story of the anointing, on the vastly expensive flask of oil which the woman broke into (Matt. 26.6, 9; Mark 14.3, 5; John 12.3, 5; cf. Luke 7.47). But there are parallels for such quantities at the funerals of important personages, and if the mixture were packed under and around the body a good deal would have been needed. It is perfectly credible as a rich man's last tribute (cf. Matt. 27.57 and Isa. 53.9).

Finally, all the evangelists agree, a stone was 'rolled across' the mouth of the tomb (Matt. 27.60; Mark 15.46; and by implication Luke 24.2 and John 20.1) for protection until the women could return some thirty-six hours later at first light on Sunday. Meanwhile, according to Mark (16.1), the women purchased aromatic oils when the Sabbath ended at nightfall on Saturday, precisely as the Mishnah lays down (*Shab.* 23.4). (Luke 23.56 has them prepare spices and perfumes early on the Friday evening before resting on the Sabbath.) These were evidently in liquid form to 'anoint' the body of Jesus (Mark 16.1), just as before his death the woman had anointed it (Luke 7.38, 46; John 12.3; cf. 11.2) by 'pouring' (Matt. 26.7; Mark 14.3) perfumed oil from her flask. The purpose of these unguents was different from that of the Johannine mixture. It was, after the obligatory washing of the corpse (cf. Acts 9.37), for which elementary act it is clear from the silence of all the canonical witnesses (in contrast with the later apocryphal Gospel of Peter, 24) there had been no time on the Friday, to clean it up and leave it in a decorous and fragrant condition. Normally of course this would have been done in preparation for entombment (cf. Matt. 26.12; Mark 14.8; John 12.7) rather than after it.

So far there is no difficulty in correlating the biblical evidence with that of the Shroud. Any presumption that the body was wrapped *round* in a winding sheet (contrast the swaddling cloths of Luke 2.7 or swathed in 'strips of linen cloth' (John 19, 40, NEB), rather like an

---

[3]Cf. Prov. 7.17, 'I have sprinkled my bed with myrrh, my clothes with aloes and cassia', which hardly suggests anything wet!

Egyptian mummy, is read into the texts (there is no compound in the Greek beginning with περί, round) and has no support in Palestine burial customs, which the fourth evangelist insists were followed (John 19.40). That the corpse of Jesus was enfolded in a single linen cloth passing lengthwise over the head and covering the whole body back and front, as the Shroud would indicate, is not, I submit, what any forger with medieval or modern presuppositions would have thought of; but it makes complete sense of the texts and fully comports with what other ancient evidence we have.

It is when we come to the accounts of what was discovered on Easter morning that the problems begin. According to Luke 24.12, if it is part of the original text, as with a growing number of scholars I am now persuaded that it is (it is omitted by only one Greek manuscript), what Peter saw peering in was the ὀθόνια, which must, as I said, mean or at least include the σινδών Luke has mentioned earlier (Luke 23.53). According to John (20.5–8) 'the other disciple' similarly 'peers in and sees the ὀθόνια lying', but then Peter, followed subsequently by his companion, enters the tomb and we are given a more detailed description. 'He sees the ὀθόνια lying and the napkin (σουδάριον) which had been over the head (ἐπὶ τῆς κεφαλῆς; not 'about his head' as in the Authorized Version) not lying with the ὀθόνια but folded or rolled (ἐντετυλιγμένον; the same word used earlier by Matthew and Luke of the enshrouded body) in a place by itself (χωρὶς . . . εἰς ἕνα τόπον)'. The Greek is in fact extraordinarily elusive, considering the significance that the evangelist evidently attaches to the details. His expressions are so loose that it *could* mean that the clothes were lying strewn about with the napkin that had been over the head rolled up or bundled *into* a heap by itself. This would be entirely *compatible* with Mary Magdalene's inference from the same evidence (John 20.11) that the grave had been tampered with: 'they have taken my Lord away, and I do not know where they have laid him' (John 20.13). So we should not expect the evidence of the eyes to be of unambiguous interpretation. It was only the faith of one man that put two and two together.

But what does the evangelist intend his readers to suppose that the disciples did see? This cannot be decided without taking into account his earlier description of the raising of Lazarus. His tomb was a cave with a stone placed against it, ἐπ' αὐτῷ (John 11.38), and he 'came out' from it 'bound (δεδεμένος) hand and foot with bands (κειρίαι) and his face bound round (περιεδέδετο) with a napkin (σουδάριον)' (John 11.44). The NEB translation 'his hands and feet swathed in linen bands' is again a paraphrase. There is nothing to say what the χειρία were made of – the only ancient evidence (the scholiast on Aristophanes' *Birds*, 816) tells us that a χειρία was 'a kind of binder made of twisted rushes, somewhat like a thong, with which bedsteads were strung' – more like cords or ropes. All we know is that they restricted, though evidently not totally, the movement of the man's hands and feet. On the assumption (too obvious to mention) that Lazarus had also been placed in a shroud, it would seem likely that the thongs had been tied loosely round the outside of it to hold it in place, functioning in this respect in lieu of a box which the Jews did not use – (cf. II. Kings 13.21) until the body decomposed and the bones were put together in an ossuary (contrast the Egyptian practice of embalming Joseph and putting him in a coffin). This is presumably what the women would have done to the body of Jesus after they had finished their work. The fact that they had not finished would explain the absence of any mention of χειρίαι in his case.

But what of the σουδάριον which was 'round the face' of Lazarus and 'over the head' of Jesus? Σουδάριον is a loan word from the Latin and defines the object not by its material (though clearly it was cloth of some kind) but by its function, namely to remove sweat, like a handkerchief or neckerchief – and so it is used elsewhere in the New Testament (Luke 19.20; Acts 19.12). It seems in the highest degree improbable that a cloth for this purpose would have been big enough to cover the length of a man twice. It is clearly distinguished by John from the main body of the ὀθόνια, which Luke equates with the σινδών. The only reason for supposing, as some have, that the σουδάριον is itself the Shroud is that the latter evidently did go over the head and face, as well of course as over the whole body.[4] Yet neither in the case of Lazarus nor in that of Jesus does it say that the σουδάριον *covered* the face. We are told that it was round the face of the former and over the head of the latter. The only position, I submit, which fits both these descriptions, assuming as we surely must that they are referring to the same burial custom, is of something tied across the top of the head round the face and under the chin. In other words it describes a jaw-band, which would have been functionally necessary to keep the mouth shut and, together with the closing of the eyes (cf. Gen. 46.4), would have been required before *rigor mortis* set in. Refer-

---

[4]Confusingly too in the Latin languages the word for 'shroud' is *sudario* (Italian and Spanish) or *suaire* (French), thus making for equation of the two.

ence is specifically made to these customs again in the Mishnah
(*Shab.* 23.5), and the chin could be bound (though not the eyes
closed) on the Sabbath, providing it was 'not in order to raise it but
to prevent it sinking' (for movement of any sort was 'work'). The
band was evidently constructed by folding or rolling diagonally a
large handkerchief or neck-cloth, rather like our triangular ban-
dage.

I began by assuming that the only trace that the σουδάριον could
possibly have left on the enveloping σινδών was at the top of the
head, where I took the white strip in a negative image of the Turin
Shroud to be the space for it. But with the realization from the
three-dimensionality of the image revealed by the computer that the
white spots are the high spots, I can now see that this is more likely
to be a protruding ridge formed by the σουδάριον itself. Conversely
the dark band immediately under the chin, especially when seen in
'3-D', looks as if it is where the jaw-band has retracted a portion of
the beard which would otherwise show up. The vertical dark strips
on either side of the face between the cheeks and the locks,
otherwise so odd, could similarly be caused by the band holding
back the intervening hair. The band would then continue up in
front of the ears, behind the hair growing from the forward part of
the head, and be knotted over the crown. So if I am right, the line of
the jaw-band would be reflected on the Shroud, not only by where
it directly touches it, but still more by what it retracts and thus does
not allow to show up.

That the σουδάριον was a jaw-band has been recognized by a
number of commentators from the New Testament material alone
(e.g., J. N. Sanders and R. E. Brown) and would seem to me almost
certain. It is an altogether more likely interpretation of the Johannine evidence than that it refers to some purely hypothetical
turban-like object collapsed in upon itself such as Henry Latham
supposed in the famous chapter on the witness of the grave-clothes
in his influential book *The Risen Master* (1901). This would be
described as going 'round the head', which John does not say of
Jesus (despite the Authorized Version), and could not be said to go
'round the face', as he does of Lazarus. But though the Turin
Shroud is not itself required to establish this point, it has certainly
helped me to envisage more clearly what the function and position
of the σουδάριον must have been. This again is not, I suggest, how
any forger would have thought. He would have imagined it lying
over the face, rather like the bogus St Veronica's veil and incorporated its image on a separate piece of material.

But in what position are we to suppose that the σουδάριον was subsequently found? This depends on what picture the fourth evangelist is intending to present. That he means us to conclude that the grave had been rifled and the body removed from the clothes (as his expressions would *allow*) is clearly impossible: this first and most natural explanation is firmly corrected. Does he intend us to suppose that the grave-clothes had been left behind undisturbed in their original positions, the body having passed through and out of them, as Latham argued? Like most people, I find today, I had always assumed that this was his intention; but I am not so sure. He *could* of course have imagined the body passing through the clothes as later it did through closed doors (John 20.19, 26) – though why then had the stone been removed (John 20.1)? But dematerialization is, I suspect, a distinctively twentieth- century way of envisaging the relationship between flesh and spirit, matter and energy. How a first-century Jew would naturally have envis- aged resurrection would have been as a corpse 'awaking from sleep', like Tabitha in Acts (9.40), as indeed Jesus predicts of Lazarus (John 11.11), and then like Lazarus 'coming out' of the tomb. The difference was that whereas Lazarus, returning to the weakness of a flesh-body, had to have the stone taken away and the bands untied, Jesus would have been conceived as divesting himself and 'walking out' on death. Something like this seems to have been imagined by the apocryphal Gospel according to the Hebrews, where Jesus hands the σινδών to the servant of the (high?) priest, a story which, however legendary, reflects the presuppositions of the ancient world.

The same assumption seems to have been true of almost all exegetes until recent times. Thus Chrysostom makes the point that the arrangement of the grave-clothes argues not that they had not been moved but that it could not have been the work of robbers, who would either have taken them with the body or left them in disarray. Bengel, the great eighteenth-century commentator, says that it means that they were not 'thrown off in a disorderly manner: the angels doubtless ministered to the rising man, one of them composing the linen cloths, the other the napkin'! Godet at the end of the nineteenth century says, 'the napkin especially, wrapped together carefully put aside, attested not a precipitate removal, but a calm and holy awakening'; and Westcott takes the same line.

One is bound to admit that the tidiness of the arrangement lies more in the eye of the beholder than in the Greek. But, if the clothes had been left undisturbed, the jaw-band would *not* have been separated from the rest in a place apart, but have been *between* the two layers of the σινδών. To attempt, with Lavergne (and, with modifications, Feuillet) to make the Greek mean that the σουδάριον was 'on the contrary wrapped (in the shroud) in its (original) position' is a desperate expedient. If this is what the evangelist meant to say, his language is not merely loose but positively misleading. I think indeed that he intends us to infer that, while the ὀθόνια were lying flat, the σουδάριον was still in its twisted oval shape (as it could have been, however removed). But that the latter was found *inside* the former is an impossible deduction. If, as Latham surmised, the σουδάριον was a separate head-piece (for which there is no evidence in Jewish burial customs of the time) and if the ὀθόνια were strips of linen that covered only the body, then undisturbed the two could have been separated by the distance of the neck. But if, as all the evidence suggests, the σουδάριον was a jaw-band and the ὀθόνια corresponded to the σινδών, and to the Shroud we have, then I think the conclusion must follow that, for the two to be found lying apart, movement of some sort would have been involved, (as εἰς ἕνα τόπον, 'into one place', would strictly suggest though not, in this Greek, necessarily imply).

None of this is of course to say anything about what actually occurred. On this a reverent agnosticism alone is appropriate. The canonical gospels are silent, in contrast again with the Gospel of Peter (35–44) which describes Jesus rising from the tomb supported and held by the hand by two men whose heads reached to heaven, with the cross following! All the Shroud can do is to confirm, as I believe it does, the presuppositions of first-century as opposed to twentieth-century readers. But finally what *difference* would it make to us if it were genuine?

First let me stress the 'if'. There will never be final proof that this is the actual cloth that wrapped the body of Jesus of Nazareth. Even if all the tests proved positive there would only be a very strong possibility that it was the burial cloth of this man. If the date of the linen were to come out correct, then there is a pretty powerful concurrence of evidence that would point to this conclusion. Clearly it carries the image of a man, almost certainly a Jew, of the right age, who suffered death by crucifixion. Though most of the marks of this barbarous punishment would not point distinctively to this one man, the evidence of severe injury to the scalp by a 'crown of thorns' surely cannot reasonably be posited of any usual victim: it was a mock coronation as King of the Jews. There is also the fact that, unlike any other shroud, it did not disintegrate with the corpse it covered. For some reason it became separated from its body prior to decomposition and was regarded by a long series of people in most hazardous circumstances, and against all Jewish tabus about anything in contact with a corpse, as too precious not to preserve. If then everything else were to prove positive, there must be a strong presumption that it belonged to this man. We cannot say more, but neither, I think, can we say less. If then it were this very cloth, what difference would it make?

In the first place it would be bound to make us take the evidence that comports with it much more seriously. There is, as we have seen, the evidence from the Mishnah which agrees at points very well, and which for the first time would be confirmed as valid for Judaea prior to the war of AD 66–70. Then there is the archaeological evidence from the skeleton found in Jerusalem in 1968 of a Jew named Jehohanan, crucified at this same period, which confirms (apparently) that the nails did not, as Christian tradition has depicted and a forger would have assumed, go through the palms, which medical tests have shown in any case could not support the weight of the body. But it is the bearing out of the New Testament evidence that is much the most significant. It does not of course prove the gospels are, or set out to be, exact historical records. The well-known differences between them remain, though these mainly relate to the appearances; but I am convinced that the light thrown by the Shroud can help us to understand how apparently discrepant accounts e.g., of the grave-cloths, are in fact compatible.

The first thing that the genuineness of the Shroud would shake is the theory that the whole story of the empty tomb is an invention of the early church. Despite its advocacy by Bultmann and other distinguished scholars I have never regarded this in any case as in the least degree probable. The story is firmly entrenched in all the strands of the gospel tradition, and I believe that Paul's statement of the common apostolic teaching, received after his conversion, that Christ 'was buried . . . and was raised to life on the third day' points to a connection between the Resurrection and the tomb (not merely the appearances, which could in I Corinthians have taken place anywhere) taking us back to the very first years of the Christian movement. The survival of the shroud would simply add weight to the very strong presumption that the tomb of Jesus *was* found empty – though how it became empty neither the gospels nor, I believe, the Shroud tell us. But somehow the body disappeared. The traditional challenge, that the authorities had only to produce the body to discredit the whole message that Jesus was risen, must, I think, be taken more seriously than I have tended to suppose. The argument certainly does not hold the other way round. The mere fact that it was not produced can never prove it could not have been produced, any more than the absence of Hitler's corpse to this day proves that he rose from the dead. But if a lifeless cadaver had been produced which could irrefutably have been identified with Jesus of Nazareth, then the proclamation that he was not dead but alive would have seemed as unconvincing to Jewish as to modern presuppositions. The Christian church would never have got off the ground. Positively this proves nothing about the mode or meaning of 'resurrection'. But the Shroud would unquestionably add weight to the universal witness of the New Testament that there was a physical and not merely a spiritual aspect to this event.

If genuine, the Shroud would also constrain us to take more seriously many details in the record which its image had confirmed. This applies especially to the Fourth Gospel – a conclusion which does not surprise me in the least, since I have become convinced that it contains some of the best history in the New Testament. But it should shake a good many current scholarly presuppositions that it tells us much of the Christ of faith but little of the Jesus of history.

First, in regard to the death of Jesus, the Shroud bears out the reports in all the gospels of multiple buffetings and Roman scourgings (far exceeding the Jewish thirty-nine strokes) and confirms how brutal these were. It supports a cap, and not merely as traditional art would have suggested, a circlet of thorns. The additional abrasions on the back of one shoulder could also bear out the tradition which John records (19.17), though not the synoptists, that Jesus was compelled to carry his own cross at least part of the way. Again, the attachment of the body to the cross by nails, and not ropes, attested by John (20.25) and implicitly by Luke (24.39) and which is clearly true of Jehohanan is of course also confirmed by the Shroud. So are two important details strongly insisted upon by John on the evidence of eyewitness. The first is that the legs of Jesus were not broken, unlike those of the two crucified with him (John 19.32f.), a practice now confirmed by the shattered skeleton to which I have referred. The second is the lance-stab in the side with its effusion of blood and water which is clearly traceable on the Shroud (John 19.34).

With regard to the burial and grave-clothes, we have already seen that the gospel evidence, though most unlikely to have suggested the Shroud we have, both illumines and is illuminated by it at a large number of detailed points, not least in regard to the σουδάριον of which again John alone speaks.

Finally, though this is inevitably a subjective judgment, the image of the Shroud reveals a visage, like that of Hamlet's father, altogether 'most majestical'. It is surely a face that could credibly have commanded the loyalty and faith which the gospels describe. The image might have been terribly disillusioning. But no one, I think, since its full photographic likeness became revealed, from the agnostic Delage onwards, could say that it was out of keeping with the man of supreme inner authority whom the gospel records present.

Yet the face on the Shroud, we should never forget, is the face of a dead man. Its exclusive picture is a last testimony to the past. It is the imprint of the old body of flesh and blood, not of the risen Christ, nor even apparently, from its closed eyes, of some moment of awakening. Even if the cloth is authentic, it could still have been removed from the corpse by human agency after the image had been formed. Yet, on what looks at present[5] to be the most promising hypothesis, it does appear to record some moment, some burst perhaps of low-energy non-ionizing radiation, lasting but a fraction of a second. Otherwise it would have penetrated further than the surface of the fibres, which is what the microscope tests disclose.

What then was this moment or this energy? No one can say – or perhaps ever will. We may, however, rule out dematerialization in the crudely literal sense that the entire mass of matter composing the body was changed, according to the formula $E = Mc^2$, into an equivalent amount of energy. That would have destroyed the Shroud, Jerusalem, and everything else one can think of. Matthew's 'violent earthquake' (28.2) would have been nothing! We are not here in the realm of transforming physical matter into physical energy according to the rules of repeatable experiment. If we can say anything at all, it seems that we are moving much more in the shadowy realm of paranormal physics and psychology associated with exceptionally intense spiritual states. The gospel narratives – and we must do them the justice of starting by taking them seriously – speak of some other body, of spirit, *not* of flesh (like the resuscitated body of Lazarus and the others), which could nevertheless appear to 'materialize'. What relation, if any, it bore to the 'astral' or other bodies of which parapsychology speaks, we

[5] See the additional paragraph at the end.

cannot say. In the language of the men of the New Testament it would be a body of 'glory' or 'light' or 'spirit', such as that of the angels at the tomb, perceptible only to the eye of faith and vision. (Compare especially the description of the angel in Matt. 28.3 with that of the risen Christ in Rev. 1.14.) In other words, if we are to use any term at all, it would be one more like 'trans-materialization'. The New Testament accounts of the appearances differ considerably – though the degree of materialization and the difference of location seem to me neither here nor there and, like any other phenomena in this field, would depend greatly on the experiencing subject. In any case this is *not* the body whose image the Shroud shows us. What it *could* show us might be, so to speak, a side-effect of its generation, a brief but intense discharge of some sort of physical radiation sufficient to have left marks of thermal discolouration on the cloth. It would be the last trace, the final footprint, as it were, of the old body – corresponding more to the skin sloughed off by the snake, except of course that it was nothing substantial but only an image. For on the assumption of some kind of physical transformation, of which science as yet can say nothing, then all the material of the old appears to have been 'used up' in the creation of the new. There was nothing left over, not even hair and finger-nails, as in the parallels of Buddhist holy men quite literally 'absorbed into the light' which I quoted in my book *The Human Face of God* (p. 139). Of Jesus we must say unequivocally with the angelic messengers, 'he is not here' (Mark 16.6; Matt. 28.6): it is vain to 'search among the dead for one who lives' (Luke 24.5) – even in the Shroud.

The Turin Shroud can provide no knock-down proof of Resurrection, and faith would surely not wish to have it so. We cannot even, in my judgment, usefully say whether it presupposes, let alone catches, some 'moment of resurrection'. For that is to compare one unknown (the process of the image-formation) with another (what we mean by 'resurrection'). It would not, if authentic, put anything beyond either faith or doubt. But it ought surely to make us less dismissive. We shall have to come to terms with the new evidence, however disturbing to our presuppositions, scientific or religious. Indeed it should help to teach us, like any other advance in knowledge, that the more we know the more we do not know. It may humble us to confess that, in the words of my great Puritan namesake, John Robinson, 'God hath yet more truth to break forth' from his holy Shroud. It would not affect my faith, but it could affect my unbelief. For if in the recognition of the face and the hands and the feet and all the other wounds we, like those who knew him best, are led to say, 'It is the Lord!' (John 21.7), then perhaps we shall have to learn to count ourselves also among those who have '*seen* and believed'. But that, as St John makes clear, brings with it no special blessing (John 20.29), but rather special responsibility (John 17.18–21).

*   *   *

Since this was written the results of the 1978 tests have been published. But unfortunately they have settled little. The scientists have disagreed among themselves; and it has become apparent that important experts, with their questions, were unrepresented on the team, particularly from the decisive field of textile archaeology. The formation of the image, which, unlike the bloodstains, was confirmed as limited to the surface of the fibres, remains as mysterious as ever. But I would agree with the tendency to discount the explanation of some moment of radiation, and in particular the analogies this has suggested to the popular mind. I should be inclined to look more in the direction of parallels to which attention was drawn by Volckringer[6] many years ago from the images left by plants in herbaria (formed admittedly over a much longer period; though there is no reason why that on the Shroud should have 'come out' immediately – in other words, by degradation of the cellulose in the cloth rather than by the addition of any kind of substance or by some dramatic molecular transformation. Above all in the 1978 tests permission was not granted, and has still been withheld, for Carbon-14 dating tests, although the small samples snipped off the edges of the cloth some ten years earlier would now be more than adequate for several such tests. Until we know whether we are dealing with a cloth dating from the first century AD or from the middle ages (the most likely period for a forgery; and its historical pedigree takes us back over 600 years at least), it is really pointless to speculate on the *process* of the image-formation. Meanwhile I have vowed silence. But nothing has shaken my conviction that the burden of proof still lies with those who believe it was an artefact to show how it was done. But even if it does turn out to be a forgery (like every other such relic known to me), I shall remain grateful for the study into which it has forced me of Jewish burial-customs and

[6]Cf. P. Barbet, *A Doctor at Calvary*, ET New York 1953 = *The Passion of Our Lord Jesus Christ*, London and Dublin 1954, pp. 38f., and the illustrations.

the interpretation of the gospel evidence. I feel a great deal more certain than I did about the meaning of certain key terms, like σουδάριον and ὀθόνια, and the presuppositions lying behind the narrative. If it *were* genuine, then its implications for the New Testament and for some of the scholarly presuppositions with which it is regularly studied would, as I said, be considerable.

8

How Small was the Seed of the Church?[1]

One of the contributions to New Testament study for which I am personally most grateful to Professor Bo Reicke has been his unabashed attention to the significance of names of persons and places for the locating and dating of early Christian writings. His use of the personalia in the Captivity and Pastoral epistles has been particularly illuminating for establishing, in my judgment, the setting in Caesarea not only of Colossians, Philemon and Ephesians (I myself would add Philippians) but also of II Timothy during the two years of Paul's imprisonment there. Indeed it played a decisive role for me in making sense of the whole Pauline chronology in my investigation *Redating the New Testament*.[2] His detective work in tracing connections which it is hard to believe could have been fabricated reveals the clues which names can supply if we are prepared to take them seriously, but not uncritically. It also raises the wider question of the interest that the early church had in such details of personalia and topography.

It has been too readily *assumed* in recent scholarship that the only motive for taking them seriously must be a conservative and harmonizing one. This is because it has also been assumed that the early church had no historical or geographical interest in them for their own sakes and that their occurrence in the narratives – especially of the gospels – can only be attributed to some kind of *Tendenz*. Proper names have been heavily suspect as indicators of lateness and elaboration – despite the fact that Mark, which has normally been accepted as the earliest of the synoptic gospels, is also richest in these and similar details. The form critics have tended to take over the presupposition of Old Testament scholars, with their far longer time-span, that place-names are to be explained in terms of aetiological legend. Again, they have read back into the apostolic writings the hagiographical interests of subsequent apocrypha in

[1]First published in William C. Weinrich, ed., *The New Testament Age: Essays in Honor of Bo Reicke*, Macon, Georgia, 1984, Vol. II, pp. 413–30.
[2]Op. cit., pp. 57–80.

satisfying the curiosity of a more distant age for personal details. Yet E. P. Sanders has demonstrated how unreliable, subjective, and themselves tendentious, have been the criteria employed.[3] Even if latter-day piety thirsted to know the names of the Magi or the Queen of Sheba, of Jesus' sisters or Pilate's wife, of the centurion at the cross or the two thieves,[4] it is arbitrary to assume that the names in our first-century documents[5] are there for the same reason, or if so that they are fictitious. It is entirely possible that the Markan community should have had a special interest in the sons of Simon of Cyrene (Mark 15.21), perhaps because the same Rufus and his mother were members of the Roman church (Rom. 16.13), or the Matthaean community in the mother of the sons of Zebedee (Matt. 20.20; 27.56), or the Johannine in the name of the high priest's servant (John 18.10); and yet each of these details could be as factual as the Kidron ravine, which John alone of the New Testament writers happens to mention (18.1) – just because it was there.

Community interest is in itself no criterion of historicity – nor is the symbolic or theological significance that an evangelist may see in a place-name. John detects depths of meaning in the name Siloam ('sent' or conduit) (9.7), but it does not follow that he invented it or Jesus' association with it[6] – nor *per contra* that the far larger number of locations he mentions with no apparent symbolic significance or theological axe to grind are *for that reason* historical. Similarly, Matthew sees prophetic fulfilment in Jesus' residence in Capernaum because it lay in the district of Zebulun and Naphtali (4.13–16); yet that of itself says nothing as to whether at this point he is interpreting or inventing. Evidently also, especially in ch. 2, he attaches theological significance to Bethlehem and Nazareth,[7] but the tradition of Jesus's association with both of these places, attested independently by Luke and probably by John (cf. the deliberate irony (?) of John 7.41f.), is not for that reason created by the theology. The same applies to Luke's 'doctrinal' interest in 'locality' detected by R. H. Lightfoot[8] and H. Conzelmann.[9] All one can ask is that a genuinely

---

[3] *Tendencies of the Synoptic Tradition*, ch. 3, esp. pp. 183–9.

[4] Ibid., pp. 131f.

[5] For the evidence cf. Sanders, op. cit., pp. 170f. He shows that Mark is proportionately more detailed than both Matthew (14 to 4) and Luke (10 to 4) and Matthew more detailed than Luke (9 to 5). His treatment does not, regrettably, take into account the Fourth Gospel.

[6] C. H. Dodd, *Historical Tradition in the Fourth Gospel*, p. 184, shows how implausible this would be.

[7] Cf. K. Stendahl, 'Quis et Unde?' in W. Eltester, ed., *Judentum – Urchristentum – Kirche*, 1960, pp. 94–105.

[8] *Locality and Doctrine in the Gospels*, London and New York 1938.

[9] *The Theology of St Luke*: ET, London 1960, New York 1961.

open-ended attitude be retained: the evidence of names should not be either discarded or accepted uncritically.

The same must be said of the piecing together of evidence from diverse sources. Obviously one can do this in a conflationary and harmonistic manner, ironing out genuine divergences and failing to respect differences of context and intention. But, as Professor Reicke has shown, it is also possible that connections may be the more credible precisely because there is no interdependence or collusion. There is a true synthesis as well as a false; and the fitting together of clues and the hypothesizing of missing ones is as an important a part of the professor's trade as of the policeman's. It is perfectly legitimate to begin by presuming the validity of details and interrelationships until proved otherwise and then to assess them by the coherence and convincingness of the picture they provide and by the data which this picture then enables us to explain. Naturally the results can never yield more than a greater or lesser degree of probability, but the procedure must be judged by the light which it throws on the total pattern of Christian origins and by the further questions to which it leads.

The particular aspect of Christian origins to which I should here like to address myself is the very beginning – the seed from which the tree of the church grew to branch out over all the earth. For this we must go behind the day of Pentecost, which we are told 'added' about three thousand souls (Acts 2.41), and behind the immediate post-resurrection community, which the author of Acts informs us numbered about one hundred and twenty (1.15). But we must also go behind the 'heavy crop' (Matt. 9.37 = Luke 10.2) from the Galilean sowing (Mark 4.3–8 and pars.); behind too the earlier Judaean ministry, of which it is already said in John 4.35–38 that the fields are white for reaping and that the followers of Jesus have come in for the harvest of 'other men's labours', meaning, as I believe, the mission of John the Baptist and his disciples.[10] For 'the Christian thing', what Peter calls τὸ γενόμενον ῥῆμα, is traced back not merely to the baptism of Jesus but to 'the baptism proclaimed by John' (Acts 10.37), which the traditions agree, *preceded* Jesus's arrival in the Jordan valley (Matt. 3.13; Mark 1.9; Luke 3.21; John 1.29–31).

For further light on this period we are completely dependent on the witness of the Fourth Gospel, which claims to embody testimony reaching back into pre-Christian days. For we read of two disciples of the Baptist who make the crucial transition from his following to

[10]For substantiation of this, cf. my article 'The "Others" of John 4.38', *Twelve New Testament Studies*, pp. 61–6.

form the nucleus of the Christian church (John 1.35–39). We are given the name of one of them only, Andrew (1.40). He finds his brother Simon, and the next day they are joined by Philip, all of whom are linked by coming from Bethsaida (1.41–44). The other disciple remains anonymous and the question naturally arises whether he is the same as that other nameless disciple of this gospel, the one whom Jesus loved, who it is in my judgment very difficult to believe is not intended to be John son of Zebedee,[11] whether or not one goes on to say that he is the source of the tradition or even the author of the gospel. Certainty is impossible. One can simply make the points: (*a*) as is regularly the case with 'the beloved disciple', and indeed with the anonymous disciple of 18.15f., he is closely associated with Peter; (*b*) the call of Simon and Andrew is also connected in the Markan and Matthaean accounts with that of James and John (Mark 1.16–20; Matt. 4.18–22); and (*c*) in the independent Lukan tradition the four brothers are in business partnership (Luke 5.10). If in John 1.41 we read πρῶτος, the inference could be drawn that after Andrew found his own brother (τὸν ἀδελφὸν τὸν ἴδιον) the other disciple found his, and that he was also therefore one of a pair (viz., James or John). But πρῶτον is probably to be preferred and the inference is in any case indemonstrable. Nevertheless some such connection between the two sets of brothers in the Johannine tradition as in the synoptic is entirely likely, if not probable.

In fact, if we are prepared to make this hypothesis, then I believe that a good deal is accounted for which is otherwise inexplicable. In particular the Markan story of the call of the two pairs, who have previously no apparent connection with Jesus or with each other, is made much more credible. Both the unexplained summons and the instant response cry out for some earlier association. If we trust the inference from the Fourth Gospel we shall be led rather to a group of friends and relations whom Jesus did not come to know then for the

[11]The absence of any reference otherwise in the body of the gospel to so central a figure as John (or his brother James), and the unique designation of the Baptist simply as 'John' without fear of confusion, both seem to point in this direction, quite apart from other internal arguments. I am not persuaded by R. Schnackenburg's abandonment of this position in 'Der Jünger, den Jesus liebte' in *EKK*, Vorarbeiten Heft 2, Zurich, 1970, pp. 97–117, or R. E. Brown's in his *Community of the Beloved Disciple*, New York and London, 1979, pp. 33f., or by O. Cullmann's very similar conclusion in *The Johannine Circle*, ET London and Philadelphia 1976, pp. 71–85. To posit a Jerusalem disciple with intimate (and profound) knowledge of Jesus, who was yet entirely forgotten and not one of the Twelve, seems to me to raise more problems than it solves. The presence of such a man among a group of Galilaean fishermen (John 21.7) is explained away as 'redactional'. But *why*?

first time but who came to know and follow him in a new way. This is the thesis that I should like to take up and trace further back. For if their meeting in Galilee was not fortuitous, what about their meeting in Judaea? Is it not still more strange that they should be together there, so far from home? Have we done more than push the problem back and indeed make it more difficult? I believe that further illumination is to be found by following the trails first of relationship and then of friendship.

Why was Jesus and why were these other Galilaeans down in the Jordan valley with John the Baptist at all? Of course we can say that they were attracted there by his spiritual appeal, though the impression we receive is that the great majority of those who 'went out' to him at Bethany beyond Jordan (John 1.28; 10.40), in all probability near the north-east corner of the Dead Sea, would, naturally, have come from Jerusalem and Judaea (Mark 1.5 and pars.; John 1.19, 24; 4.1–3; 5.33–35; Matt. 21.32).[12] But there may also have been other more personal factors at work. According to Luke, Jesus was related to John on his mother's side, for Elizabeth was a relative (συγγενίς) of Mary (1.36). Jesus and John could have been second cousins, probably at one remove since Elizabeth was 'well on in years' (1.7) and indeed 'in her old age' (1.36), while Mary was a παρθένος or young girl (1.27). Or Elizabeth and Mary's mother could have been sisters and Elizabeth therefore Mary's aunt: in this case Jesus and John would have been first cousins once removed. At any rate the families were sufficiently close for Mary to set off eagerly for the uplands of Judaea to keep Elizabeth company for the last three months of her pregnancy (1.39, 56). That Jesus should have been drawn to the Jordan valley by the reputation of his cousin is therefore a factor we may not discount. Born within half a year of each other, they were very likely by now complete strangers, if indeed John was brought up in the desert (1.80), perhaps at Qumran, on the death of his aging parents.[13] According to John 1.31–34 the Baptist did not know Jesus – or at any rate had no notion that this was the coming one of whom he had been speaking. Their subsequent association and parallel ministries in Judaea and Samaria (3.22–4.2) evidently rested on spiritual affinity, and nothing is made later of their blood-relationship. The very fact that there seems to

[12] Herod's precoccupation with him would be explained not because of any links with Galilee but by the fact, which John alone records, that the Baptist began his ministry in Peraea, where he would come under Herod's jurisdiction and where later he was imprisoned and beheaded by him (Josephus, *Ant.* 18.5.2, § 119).

[13] Cf. my article 'The Baptism of John and the Qumran Community', *Twelve New Testament Studies*, pp. 11–27, esp. 11f.

have been no theological interest in it or capital made out of it, or of Elizabeth's priestly descent (Luke 1.5), suggests that connection between the families is not simply a pious fiction of the church and may have had a historical basis.

Yet, while this relationship could help to account for Jesus' presence in the Jordan valley, it would not explain the earlier and apparently independent arrival of those who were subsequently to become his first disciples. Here however there may have been a further family connection at work. For according to John 19.25 Mary the mother of Jesus had a sister. She is unnamed, like the mother of Jesus herself in the Fourth Gospel – which in this tradition may be as much a sign of intimacy as of ignorance. For there is at least the possibility, if not the probability, that she was the mother of John the son of Zebedee himself. If we seek to correlate the figures at the cross of Jesus in the various gospels (Matt. 27.55f.; Mark 15. 40f.; John 19.25; Luke mentions no names at this point, though cf. 24.10), we find that Mary Magdalene appears in all of them, Mary the mother of Jesus in John alone. In the synoptic accounts two others are named. One is Mary the mother of James and Joses (or Joseph) (cf. also Mark 15.47; 16.1; Luke 24.10), whom Matthew subsequently calls simply 'the other Mary' (27.61; 28.1). The second is, according to Mark, Salome (cf. also 16.1), in whose place Matthew has 'the mother of the sons of Zebedee' (cf. also 20.20), evidently intending the same person. In John, as we have seen, there is Jesus' mother's sister, (and?) Mary (the wife?) of Clopas. The first question is whether these two figures stand in apposition (there is no conjunction in the Greek) or whether they are separate persons. The strong probability must be that they are separate persons, otherwise we should have two sisters in the same family called Mary.[14] If they are separate, then it is reasonable to equate 'Mary of Clopas' with 'the other Mary', the mother of James and Joses. This leaves us with the sister of Jesus' mother and Salome, the mother of the sons of Zebedee. Are they to be equated? There is nothing to compel it, for it is made clear that there were other women besides those named (Mark 15.40f.; Luke 23.49; cf. 8.3; 24.10). Yet since all the others singled out from the crowd appear to correspond it is natural to

[14]Jerome identified the two and equated her sons (James and Joses) with those of the same name who are described as Jesus' 'brothers' in Mark 6.3 and with James the son of Alphaeus in Mark 3.18. Others went on to include in the family Jude (the brother??) of James mentioned in Luke 6.16 and Acts 1.13 and even Simon the Zealot. For decisive arguments against this entire position, which is a good example of quite uncritical harmonization, cf. J. B. Lightfoot, 'The Brethren of the Lord' in *The Epistle to the Galatians*, London ⁴1874, pp. 247–81, esp. 255–8.

presume that not only Matthew and Mark but John are referring to the same person under different designations.[15] If so, then Mary the mother of Jesus and Salome were sisters, and John the son of Zebedee was a first cousin of Jesus and a remoter cousin of John the Baptist. This cannot be more than a hypothesis, and the fact that the realtionship is not taken up anywhere else speaks neither for nor against it. For it was certainly not exploited by the apostolic church and may therefore be presumed not to have been created by it. All we can do is to test the hypothesis by what it might help to explain.

The first thing it would explain is the commission to the beloved disciple, whom I am presuming to be John, to care for her who on this hypothesis would be his aunt (John 19.26f.). It might perhaps have been expected that this task would have fallen on one of Jesus' brothers, whether or not they were Mary's own sons,[16] since they are always elsewhere associated with her. But Jesus' earlier response to family claims, 'Who is my mother? Who are my brothers?' (Mark 3.31–35 and pars.; cf. 10.29f. and pars.; Matt. 10.37; Luke 14.26), suggests that for him spiritual affinity overrode natural ties with unbelievers, as his brothers then were (John 7.5). The handing over of his mother to her closest nephew would thus be entirely explicable. Less explicable is the designation of Mary as John's 'mother' in the presence of his own natural mother. But this, like 'son', obviously here implies a spiritual relationship (as in Rom. 16.13), which again takes priority over the natural. The relationship of 'favourite son' would also help to account for the designation 'the beloved disciple' and for the presumption of the sons of Zebedee, or their mother, of entitlement to privileged seats in the kingdom (Mark 10.35–45; Matt. 20.20–28). It would be natural too that Jesus's two cousins, James and John, should constitute with Peter, the designated leader, the nucleus of the inner circle of the Twelve. The fact that on his mother's side John would have had priestly connections (cf. Luke 1.5) could explain why the unnamed disciple of John 18.15f., if

[15]Cf. the judicious note by Brown, *John*, p. 906. The equation was strongly urged by T. Zahn, 'Brüder und Vettern Jesu', *Forschungen zur Geschichte des NT Kanons 6*, Leipzig 1900, pp. 338–41.

[16]Lightfoot, *Galatians*, pp. 264f., regarded this as a 'fatal objection' to the 'Helvidian' theory that the brothers were Mary's own children, preferring the 'Epiphanian' view that they were children of Joseph by a former marriage. But even on this latter theory 'the sacred ties of natural affection' would surely have suggested that it should be they who took responsibility for their step-mother rather than one who on Lightfoot's reckoning was no relation at all (for he questions the equation of Mary's sister with the mother of the sons of Zebedee, merely on the ground that there is 'no hint' of it elsewhere). The same applies to J. Blinzler, *Die Brüder und Schwestern Jesu*, Stuttgart 1967, pp. 113f.

again he is to be identified with the beloved disciple (as I believe from his association with Peter to be likely),[17] was a γνωστός of the high priest, which probably implies a relationship of some familiarity,[18] at any rate with names (18.10) and affinities (18.26) in the servants' quarters, and perhaps a base in Jerusalem (cf. 19.27; 20.10). It *could* also throw some light on the curious statement of Polycrates[19] that 'John was a priest, wearing the sacerdotal plate (πέταλον)'.

If then this John is also, as we have argued, the unnamed disciple of John 1.35, family connections would account not only for Jesus' presence in the Jordan valley but for John's earlier and independent association with his cousin the Baptist. This could have started at the purely natural level, but, as a result of the Baptist's recognition and disclosure of Jesus as the coming one, both Johns were to relate to him in an entirely new way, no longer κατὰ σάρκα but κατὰ πνεῦμα.

So much for the trail of relationship. Let us next pursue that of friendship.

We have already seen that John the son of Zebedee, if this is who he is, is at Bethany beyond Jordan with his friends Andrew and Simon. These are the sons of yet another John (John 1.42; 21.15–17) or Jona (Matt. 16.17), where the difference of nomenclature shows that there has been no assimilation between the gospels, except in the subsequent manuscript tradition.[20] Their connection with the next character on the scene, Philip, is supplied, as we have seen, by their coming from the same town, Bethsaida (John 1.43f.). Now this explains, and is borne out by, the otherwise unaccountable order of the disciples in the list of Mark 3.16–19, where Andrew is paired with Philip, whereas we should expect him to be bracketed (like the sons of Zebedee in every list) with his brother Peter, as in Matthew (10.2) and Luke (6.14).[21] Andrew's special association with Philip, which recurs in John 6.1–13; 12.20–22 and is again explained by their same (Greek-speaking) birth-place (12.21), could not credibly

[17]Cullmann, *Johannine Circle*, pp. 71f., also argues for the identity of the unnamed disciples both in 18.15f., and in 1.35 with the disciple whom Jesus loved – but of none of them with John!

[18]So Dodd, *Historical Tradition*, pp. 86f., who does not however make the other identifications. Cf. Luke 2.44, where γνωστοί are grouped with relatives, and 23.49 where they are certainly not mere acquaintances.

[19]*Apud* Eusebius, *HE* III. 31.3; V. 24.3.

[20]Cf. Dodd, *Historical Tradition*, 308: 'The conclusion may be drawn, with the greatest degree of probability that such matters admit, that Matthew and John represent divergent and independent traditions regarding the name of Peter.'

[21]The same order in Acts 1.13 could be attributed to the displacement resulting from the bringing up of John to second place in importance after Peter; but this does not happen in Mark.

have been concocted by dependence of John on Mark or *vice versa*. It is therefore to be taken seriously.

From Philip we move to his friend Nathanael (John 1.45–51), who we are subsequently told (in an entirely incidental and appended note) came from Cana in Galilee (21.2). This would account for the sequence between John 1 and 2, where we are introduced without explanation to a wedding at Cana (2.1–11), with which the family of Jesus evidently has some close connection. Mary's independent presence ('the mother of Jesus was there, and Jesus and his disciples were guests also'), her sense of responsibility for the proceedings, and her association with the bridegroom's party suggest he was a relative or close family friend.[22]

Immediately after this there follows a historical note (2.12) which has defied theological interpretation: 'After this he [Jesus] went down to Capernaum in company with his mother, his brothers, and his disciples, but they [i.e., evidently, Jesus and his disciples; cf. 2.13–22] did not stay there long.'[23] It is hard to see what to make of this except a piece of biographical reminiscence emanating from the inner circle. The natural interpretation is that Jesus went back home for a few days with his new disciples to pay a visit on the family. If so this would be important corroboration of Matthew's statement (4.13) that Capernaum, not Nazareth, was now his home-town. This is never made explicit in Mark, but there are numerous small connections pointing in this direction which it is difficult to believe are either fortuitous or fictional.

We may start with Mark 2.1, which I believe is rightly rendered by the NEB (and the RSV): 'When after some days he returned to Capernaum, the news went round that he was *at home* (ἐν οἴκῳ).' In his parallel Matthew has 'he came to his own town', εἰς τὴν ἰδίαν πόλιν (9.1), in contrast with εἰς τὴν πατρίδα αὐτοῦ (13.54), his place of origin, or 'where he had been brought up' (Luke 4.16), though neither Mark nor Matthew specifically names this as Nazareth. But in their story Jesus leaves the lake-side in order to get there (Mark 6.1 = Matt. 13.53; cf. Mark 5.21 and Matt. 13.1f.), and in Luke he goes

---

[22]Apocryphal tradition later makes Mary the aunt of the bridegroom, whom a third-century Latin preface identifies as John son of Zebedee! (cf. Brown, *John*, p. 98) – an entirely baseless presupposition, especially if John arrived at the wedding with the other disciples from the Jordan valley. But it nevertheless shows a feel for the connection.

[23]Cf. Dodd, *Historical Tradition*, p. 235: 'This passage is completely out of relation to any other topographical data supplied, and does not in any way contribute to the development either of the narrative or of the thought of the gospel. . . . Clearly therefore the itinerary datum that Jesus κατέβη εἰς Καφαρναουμ is not the product of any particular interest of the evangelist.'

from there to Capernaum (4.31), *to* which later on he and his disciples also return from their secret journey through Galilee (Mark 9.30–33; Matt. 17.22–24). Mark records too that after Jesus left the lake-side for the hills to call the Twelve (3.7–19) he 'went home' (3.20), as the RSV again renders it; and it is here (rather than in Nazareth, as we might expect) that his 'family' (οἱ παρ' αὐτοῦ 3.21, NEB), his mother and his brothers (3.31), seek to rescue him from the crowds and from himself. Matthew once more points up the location by adding to the Markan material following this incident: '*That same day* Jesus went *out of the house* and sat beside the sea' (Matt. 13.1; contrast Mark 4.1, and cf. Matt. 13.36). Mark subsequently goes on (4.35): 'That day, in the evening, he said to them, "Let us cross over to the other side of the lake".' Matthew's parallel to this is placed elsewhere (8.18), but it is significant that it follows the healing of the centurion's servant, which his Q source had fixed in Capernaum (Matt. 8.5 = Luke 7.1), and Jesus' visit to Peter's home (8.14f.), which Mark had also located in Capernaum (1.21, 29). In Mark Jesus first enters the house of Simon and Andrew with James and John, whom, we are told (1.19), he had just found 'a little further on' from where the other two were at work. If, as Luke confirms in a non-Markan passage (5.1–11), these pairs of brothers were in partnership, then Zebedee and his family lived in Capernaum as well.

At this point I would return to the Fourth Gospel. Apart from the statement from which we began in John 2.12, this tradition reflects even greater emphasis than the synoptic upon Capernaum. In fact apart from Cana (2.1–11; 4.46) it is the only Galilean town that Jesus is specifically recorded in John as visiting, though he goes about Galilee generally (4.45; 6.1f.; 7.1) as in the synoptists. Yet his information is clearly not derived from theirs. His story of the healing of the court-official's son, like the parallel but very different Q version, is also connected with (though not set in) Capernaum (4.46–54). After the feeding of the five thousand the disciples start rowing back to Capernaum (6.17), as if this were home, though in Mark Jesus sent them to Bethsaida (6.45) while they actually came to land at Gennesaret (6.53). The following day in John the crowds also set out for Capernaum, evidently expecting to find Jesus there (6.24), which eventually they do, for the dialogue that follows takes place in the synagogue at Capernaum (6.59). Indeed this synagogue, which Mark mentions as the place of Jesus' first public teaching (1.21) and which is probably also that referred to in 3.1 and 5.21f., and which Luke alludes to quite independently (7.5), could be said to be the equivalent of Jesus' parish church.

The Johannine tradition about Capernaum, which fits at so many detailed yet independent points with the synoptic and has therefore strong claim to be authentic, is the more significant if, as John does not tell us but Mark does, this town was the home not only of Jesus and of Peter but of John himself. In fact this may provide the clue to why they were all there. The Zebedees had their trade in the town, and unlike the others, had, as far as we know, always lived there.[24] Peter and Andrew, with Peter's (widowed?) mother-in-law (Mark 1.30 and pars.), had joined them and they had set up together in business. Now if Zebedee's wife Salome was Mary's sister, what more natural than that after the presumed death of Joseph (absent from the scene since Luke 2.41–52, when Jesus was twelve) Mary with her sons would also have moved there to be near her sister's family? We may surmise that the daughters had already got married to local lads and stayed behind, for in Mark 6.3 a distinction is drawn by the townsfolk of Nazareth: 'Is not this the carpenter, the son of Mary and brother of James and Joses and Judas and Simon, *and are not his sisters here with us?*' Their name and number (Matt. 13.56 has 'all his sisters') seem to have been forgotten and they evidently dropped out of the company of Jesus.[25] On the basis of the singular in Matt. 4.13 ('leaving Nazareth he went and settled at Capernaum on the sea of Galilee'), the move could well have been undertaken on the initiative of the eldest son, now the head of the family. It is also perhaps no accident that Matthew should combine this information about the move with his special interest in the mother of the sons of Zebedee (20.20; 27.56). Thus bonds of blood and friendship would explain not only why Andrew and Peter and later Jesus should have been down in the Jordan valley but why they were together in Capernaum. And a key link in each case would have been John son of Zebedee. Whoever eventually wrote the Fourth Gospel – I actually believe John did[26] – he is, many would now again agree, the source and guarantor of vital parts of its tradition – though the significance of the information it supplies often only emerges if it is held together with other quite independent tradition which both supplements and confirms it. The clues and interconnections are

[24]On one of the rare occasions on which Lightfoot nodded he said that John too came from Bethsaida (*Biblical Essays*, London 1893, p. 128). But there is no evidence for this.

[25]Later legends agree (against Matthew) only on their number – two. Epiphanius (*Haer.* 78.8 and *Ancor.* 60) calls them Mary and Salome. Elsewhere other names appear. Cf. *NTApoc*, I, p. 418.

[26]Cf. my *Redating the NT*, esp. pp. 298–311.

scarcely such as are likely to have been invented or planted. But together they reinforce what separately may sometimes seem tenuous links.

The picture constructed so far of an initial group of close friends and relations is further supported by the evidence of the lists of the Twelve in the synoptists and Acts (Matt. 10.2–4; Mark 3.16–19; Luke 6.14–16; Acts 1.13). The order of the names appears to indicate two things. The first is order of importance. In every list Simon Peter stands first, which is explained by his designation as the foundation-stone of the church (Matt. 16.18) and his later position of leadership (Mark 16.7; Luke 22.31f.; John 21.15–17; Acts 1.15; 2.14; etc). The nickname Πέτρος, which all the evangelists record, is given him in the Fourth Gospel in the pre-Galilean period and, uniquely, in the original Aramaic Κηφᾶς (1.42), a usage confirmed by the early and independent witness of Paul (I Cor. 15.5; etc.). John comes second in the list of Acts 1.13, which evidently reflects the pre-eminence that he and Peter quickly assumed in the early church (Acts 3.1–4.31; 8.14–25), which is again confirmed by Paul (Gal. 2.9). In the other lists, including that of Luke's Gospel, John follows his (presumably elder) brother James, though elsewhere in the Lukan tradition (Luke 8.51; 9.28 – but the manuscript evidence is divided) the later pre-eminence of John over James is reflected back. What began as 'John the brother of James' (Mark 3.17) ends as 'James the brother of John' (Acts 12.2).

But the second thing which the synoptic lists appear to reveal is the order of adhesion. There are certain disciples who are always in the first half – and they are the same ones already mentioned in, or deduced from, the Johannine evidence: Peter, Andrew, James, John and Philip. Moreover, not only, as John alone explains, is Andrew closely associated with Philip, but so is Bartholomew, who comes immediately after Philip in all the gospel lists and in Acts is separated from him only by Thomas. Bartholomew is, of course, a patronymic, like (Simon) Barjona in Matt. 16.17 or (Joseph) Barsabbas in Acts 1.23, and he must have had a given name as well. If, as later tradition has maintained, this was Nathanael, then his proximity to Philip woud again be explained by the acquaintance between them that John alone describes (1.45–51). But this cannot be more than speculative.[27] Next to Bartholomew in Matthew and

---

[27]Cf. the discussion of the matter by U. Holtzmeister, 'Nathanael fuitne idem ac S. Bartholemaeus Apostolus?', *Bibl* 21, 1940, pp. 28–39.

Acts (though Mark and Luke interpose Matthew) is Thomas, again a name of relationship, which John translates for us as $\Delta i\delta\upsilon\mu\sigma\varsigma$ 'the twin' (11.16; 20.24; 21.2). His given name was probably Judas, as in the heading to the Gospel of Thomas (Didymus Judas Thomas) and in the Syriac tradition,[28] the nickname perhaps being explained by the need to avoid confusion not only with Judas Iscariot but with the other Judas, whom the Lukan lists alone mention but whom John again confirms (14.22). When and where Thomas came on the scene we do not know, but he is associated with others of the inner group not only in the synoptic lists but in John 14.5 and 21.2.[29]

That there was within the Twelve such an inner circle, however variously demarcated, is evident from all the traditions. Sometimes it consists of two (Peter and John) (Luke 22.8; John 20.2–10; Acts 3 and 4; 8.14–25; and, with James the Lord's brother, Gal. 2.9); sometimes of three (Peter, James and John) (Mark 5.37; 9.2; 14.33 and pars.), sometimes of four (Peter James, John and Andrew) (Mark 13.3); sometimes of five (John [?], Andrew, Peter, Philip and Nathanael) (John 1.35–51); sometimes of seven (Peter, Thomas, Nathanael, James, John and two others) (John 21.2). The same names tend to recur in the post-apostolic tradition: Andrew, Peter, Philip, Thomas, James, John and Matthew in Papias (*apud* Eusebius, *HE*. III 39.4); John and Andrew in the Muratorian Canon (9–14); Thomas, Andrew and John in Eusebius, *HE*. III. 1.1. There is also the Talmudic tradition (*b. Sanh* 44) that Jesus had five disciples (of quite different names).[30]

The outsiders to this inner group begin with the call of Levi = (?) Matthew (Mark 2.13f. and pars.), whose adhesion definitely belongs to the period of Galilean ministry. Thereafter the circle is enlarged only by a few names before the ranks are closed. All of these second-liners have explanatory additions in some of the lists: Matthew, the tax-gatherer (Matt.: cf. Mark 2.14, Levi, the son of Alphaeus); James, the son of Alphaeus (Matt., Mark, Luke and Acts); Simon the Cananaean (Matt. and Mark) or Zealot (Luke and Acts); Judas, the son of James (Luke and Acts; Mark has instead Thaddaeus[31] and

[28]*Ev.Thom.* 1; *Act. Thom.* 1, *et passim*; Eusebius, *HE* I. 13.11; John 14.22 (syr[c]); cf. *NTApoc* I, pp. 285–7.

[29]In the *Acts of Thomas* 39 (*et passim*) he is the twin of Jesus himself and therefore privy to his most secret sayings!

[30]On this cf E. Bammel, 'What is thy Name?' *NovTest* 12, 1970, pp. 223–8, who argues that while the names are secondary the number five represents good tradition.

[31]J. Jeremias, *New Testament Theology* I, pp. 232f., suggests that Thaddaeus (= Theodotos) could well be a nickname (cf. e.g. Barnabas in Acts 4.36) by which after the betrayal the surviving Judas preferred naturally to be called. But Nathanael also translates as *Theodotus*. The confusion and lack of agreement seems to show how peripheral some even of the Twelve were.

Matthew either Thaddaeus or Lebbaeus); and finally Judas Iscariot (Matt., Mark and Luke), the son of Simon (John 6.71; 13.2, 26).

Immediately following the names of the Eleven in Acts we have the other components of the earliest Christian in-group: 'The women, Mary the mother of Jesus, and his brothers' (1.14). The last we have so far ignored. Notices of them in the gospels are trustworthy to the extent that they are so uncomplimentary, both in the synoptic and in the Johannine traditions (Mark 3.21, 31–5 and pars.; 6.3 and par.; John 7.1–13). The change of emphasis so shortly after the Resurrection seems to have been presaged by the instruction found in two unconnected traditions (Matt. 28.10; John 20.17), 'go to my brothers', which if it refers, as seems probable (and Dodd agreed), to Jesus' kith and kin, could indicate that their attitude had already softened. The change was sealed, no doubt, by the appearance to James (I Cor. 15.7) which conferred on him 'apostolic' standing. The rapid rise of James to leadership of the Jerusalem church, attested by both Paul and Acts (Gal. 1.19; 2.9, 12; Acts 12.17; 15.13; 21.18) bears out the pattern of family links which we argued earlier. More significantly this pattern continues after James' death. Eusebius, relying on Hegesippus, describes the scene:

> After the martyrdom of James and the taking of Jerusalem which immediately ensued, it is recorded that those apostles and disciples of the Lord who were still surviving met together from all quarters and, together with our Lord's relatives after the flesh (for the more part of them were still alive), took counsel, all in common, as to whom they should judge worthy to be the successor of James; and, what is more, that they all with one consent approved Symeon the son of Clopas, of whom also the book of the Gospels makes mention, as worthy of the throne of the community in that place. He was a cousin – at any rate so it is said – of the Saviour; for indeed Hegesippus relates that Clopas was Joseph's brother.[32]

Now if, as Eusebius asserts, this Clopas was the one mentioned in John 19.25 as the (husband) of Mary, this would mean that she too was related to Jesus by marriage on his father's side. The story may be credited, not only because of the inherent probability of the family nexus being perpetuated, but because Symeon the son elected, unlike

---

[32]*HE* III.11; cf. III.32.1–6; IV.22.4. In III.32.4 Eusebius says 'one might . . . reasonably conclude that Symeon was an eyewitness and actual hearer of the Lord.' Indeed on his (evidently legendary) figures he would have been about ten years his senior.

his brothers James and Joses, is never mentioned in Scripture. One would have expected a concocted story to have drawn upon the biblical tradition. If, again, this Clopas was the same man to whom Luke (24.18) gives the parallel Greek name Cleopas (on the analogy of Symeon/Simon), we have a further possible connection. For certainly with his companion he was a member of the intimate circle (cf. 24.24, τῶν σὺν ἡμῖν. Indeed, according to Origen and the margin of Codex S, this companion was called Simon; and Zahn,[33] followed by A. Mayer and W. Bauer,[34] regarded it as entirely likely that these should be father and son, the uncle and cousin of Jesus. This last is of course speculation (on which nothing hangs), but in view of the previous pattern it would not be improbable.

Perhaps we could sum up by setting down in parallel columns those of whom we have individual mention as belonging to the immediate in-group, which Luke (23.49) describes as Jesus's γνωστοί and John (13.1) as his ἴδιοι:

Relations	*Friends*
Mary (mother)	Simon Peter
James (brother)	Andrew
Joses (brother)	Philip
Jude (brother)	Nathanael (= Bartholomew?)
Simon (brother)	Thomas
Salome (aunt)	Matthew (Levi?)
James (cousin)	James son of Alphaeus
John (cousin)	Simon the Zealot
Clopas (uncle)	Judas son of James (= Thaddaeus?)
Mary (aunt by marriage)	Judas Iscariot
James (cousin)	Mary Magdalene
Joses (cousin)	Joanna
Symeon (cousin)	Susanna[35]

This does not of course mean that there were not 'many others' especially among the women who accompanied him from Galilee (cf. Luke 8.3). But these are distinguished from the γνωστοί (Luke 23.49)

[33]*Forschungen* 6, pp. 352, 363.

[34]'The Relatives of Jesus', *NTApoc* I, p. 426.

[35]The last is mentioned only in Luke 8.3, but Joanna, the wife of Chuza, a steward of Herod's, is present also in Luke 24.10. It is at least possible that she could be part of the household of the βασιλικός or 'officer in the royal service' at Capernaum converted by the healing of her son in John 4.46–53. There is subsequently too Mary, the mother of John Mark (Acts 12.12), but whether she was also, as tradition asserts, the host at the Last Supper is pure speculation.

And for the inner circle the above list of some two dozen is likely to be a generous estimate, since several, even of the Twelve, seem to have been fairly marginal.

If then we ask, 'How small was the seed of the church?', the answer apears to be 'like the mustard-seed, which is smaller than any seed in the ground at its sowing' (Mark 4.31). Indeed what may have occasioned the simile was the incredible contrast, humanly speaking, between the all-too-rapid burgeoning of the movement in Galilee and the tiny group of friends and relations from which it all began. The picture we have sought to reconstruct reinforces this. Admittedly it depends on some signs smaller than a man's hand and connections which look thin-spun. Yet the very fact that the web rests on many separate supports, and that no obvious theological or religious interests are visible in the spinning (at any rate until very much later), gives confidence rather than the opposite. Above all it reveals the rich complementarity of the evidence from John and the synoptists. Either taken alone, especially the latter, leaves us with a great many unanswered questions about Christian origins. Perhaps we should give up trying to answer them. Yet it seems foolish gratuitously to discard the clues supplied by proper names or to ignore bits of evidence which, if pieced together, can disclose an overall picture that is both coherent and, I believe, credible. Moreover, if it is credible, it can restore our trust in the details of the gospel traditions, not least those of the Fourth Gospel, and make it seem less ridiculous than it has to many recent critics that the men of the first century were interested in and cared for the history as much as the theology of the Word made flesh.

Though he uses very different categories and appears to have a diametrically opposed estimate of the historicity of the Fourth Gospel, John Knox tells me that he was trying to make much the same point when he spoke of the 'memory' of the church telling us a good deal more about the inner life of Jesus than do 'the gospels'. But he confesses that by the latter he did not make it clear that he meant 'the synoptic gospels'.

> These are, generally speaking, strangely silent about Jesus' own inner attitudes, states of mind and heart. They tell us where he went, what he did or said, what happened to him, but rarely give us any hint of what he was feeling. One may infer from his teaching about God how he himself felt toward God, but we are not explicitly told. One may draw conclusions from his ethical

teaching, not only how he *thought* about one's duty towards others, but also as to what his actual feelings toward others were; but these are never described and are seldom referred to. Sometimes in his most passionate (and most characteristic) teachings, his inner feelings break through what may appear to be the determined objectivity of the Gospel record, and one seems for a moment to hear his very voice.[36] But these occasions are rare indeed; and I wonder just what impression of the inner personal life of Jesus we should have if we needed to depend on the Gospels alone, or whether we should be able to hear his voice in his recorded words if we were not also hearing it in the common life of the Church. . . . Undoubtedly one reason why the Church has always cherished the Fourth Gospel and has been unable to believe that it does not contain authentic historical truth about Jesus is that one can read there, and there only, such words as 'Having loved his own . . . he loved them to the end' and 'This is my commandment, that you love one another as I have loved you' (John 13.1; 15.12) – words which express a love of Jesus for his own which has a deep, sure place in the memory of the Church.[37]

But I question whether he has not set up a false division between 'the Gospels' and his elusive and much debated category 'the memory of the Church' because he confines the former to the synoptists and does not treat John (whom he firmly classes with 'the Epistles') as just as authentic a source of knowledge about Jesus, if not a more penetrating one, than the other three.

[36] Cf. Jeremias' *ipsissima vox*; see *The Prayers of Jesus*, pp. 108–15.
[37] *The Church and the Reality of Christ*, New York 1962, London 1963, p. 55f.

9

'His Witness is True': A Test of the Johannine Claim[1]

In any study of the Jesus of history the place of the Fourth Gospel and the use to be made of its evidence is problematic. And nowhere is this issue more acute than in the events leading up to his conviction and death. For John has an extensive and detailed narrative of these events which differs at a number of vital points – not least in its chronology – and yet where the degree of overlap with the other accounts is greater than anywhere else. C. H. Dodd has observed how extensive and detailed this parallelism is[2] – so much so that one of two conclusions is inevitable. Either John's account evinces literary dependence on that of the synoptists or it embodies an independent tradition with serious claims to take us back to the facts and interpretation that created and controlled the common Christian preaching. With now the growing weight of contemporary scholarship, I cannot find the former a credible explanation, and Dodd's own examination of the passion narrative, from which he begins his massive exposition,[3] is a sufficient statement of the case.[4]

[1]First published in E. Bammel and C. F. D. Moule, eds., *Jesus and the Politics of his Day*, Cambridge and New York 1984, pp. 453–76.

[2]*Historical Tradition in the Fourth Gospel*, pp. 29f.

[3]Ibid, p. 21–136.

[4]Cf. the conclusion of R. E. Brown, *The Gospel according to John*, p. 791: 'The Johannine Passion Narrative is based on an independent tradition that has similarities to the Synoptic sources. Where the various pre-Gospel sources agree, we are in the presence of a tradition that had wide acceptance at a very early stage in the history of the Christian Church and, therefore, a tradition that is very important in questions of historicity.' He goes on: 'The acceptance of the thesis of an independent, early tradition underlying John should make us cautious about assuming too quickly that the doctrine, apologetics, and drama *created* the raw material basic to the scenes involved. In our opinion, John's genius here as elsewhere consisted in re-interpreting rather than in inventing.' F. Hahn, 'Der Prozess Jesu nach dem Johannesevangelium – Eine redaktionsgeschichtliche Untersuchung', *EKK* 2, Zürich 1970, p. 23–96, and A. Dauer, *Die Passionsgeschichte im Johannesevangelium*, Munich 1972, both support the fundamental independence of the Johannine tradition but give more weight to redactional motifs. I do not myself share the presupposition, common to Dodd and the form-and redaction-critics, that this

But if John's is an independent voice, how are we to assess how he stands to the truth of the matter? For the claim of the Johannine community is that 'his witness is true' (John 21.24), which in turn is based on the personal testimony of 19.35: 'This is vouched for by an eyewitness, whose evidence is to be trusted. He knows that he speaks the truth, so that you too may believe.' While it is the truth of faith that he is primarily concerned with, this is not to be dissociated from the truth of fact. For to him the faith is the truth *of* the history, what *really* happened, from the inside.

How may we test his claim? It can only be *a posteriori*, by asking whether, in the light of all the evidence, his account yields a credible picture of the total situation, explaining not only what *he* gives us but what others independently tell us. This does not involve saying that John states the whole truth or nothing but the truth. But he does claim that in the essential relation of the Word to the flesh he is giving us the truth. The purpose of this chapter is to test that claim with specific reference to the relationship of the spiritual to the political in the life, teaching and death of Jesus.

We may begin by noting two tributes in recent writing on this subject to the testimony of John. In the course of his balanced discussion of the political question in *Jesus and the Revolutionaries*, Oscar Cullmann writes:

> According to John 18.36 Jesus replies to the political question of Pilate (the only one which interested him), 'Are you the King of the Jews?' with the decisive answer, *which I could have used as the motto for this presentation*: 'My kingdom is not of this world.'[5]

In other words, Cullmann believes that John has got it right – that his interpretation provides the correct clue to the essential understanding of the matter.

Equally, Alan Richardson punctuates his treatment of the gospel evidence in his book *The Political Christ* with reluctant tributes to the testimony of John. For he is one of those who start with a very low expectation at this point. Indeed, in his own earlier commentary[6] he committed himself to the position that John is not only

---

evangelist stood in an external relationship to his tradition and that one can separate out pre-Johannine material; cf. my *Redating the New Testament*, ch. 9. But that does not affect the value of their contributions, as Dodd himself, *Historical Tradition*, p. 17, recognized that it would not undermine his case if the opposite presupposition were made.

[5]ET New York, 1973, p. 42. Italics mine.
[6]*The Gospel according to St John*, London and Naperville 1959.

historically worthless as an independent source but that he had no
concern for historical or chronological accuracy. Yet time and again
in Richardson's later book we have such concessions as:

> Here again John (19.13) brings out the truth of history, even if he
> composed the trial speeches himself.[7]
> Does John in 6.15 in his characteristically allusive way hint that
> this [viz., being taken for the leader of a nationalist movement]
> was a serious danger to Jesus during his ministry?[8]
> John with his usual penetrating eye for the real issue brings out the
> truth of the matter when he makes the Jews (the Jews!) protest to
> Pilate, 'Everyone who makes himself a king is an enemy of Caesar'
> (19.12).[9]
> John repeatedly shows that he is very well informed about Jewish
> affairs in the period before the Jewish War.[10]

At this stage we merely note these as impressions that, whether for
reasons of theological insight or historical information (or both), the
Johannine picture is not as far removed from reality as it has been
customary to assume. But we can only convert impressions into
something more substantial by working through the evidence in
greater detail. This we may do by fastening upon the incidents, in the
order John records them, that bring into focus the relationship
between the spiritual and the political, between the kingship of
Christ and the kingdoms of this world.

The first, that of the cleansing of the temple as recorded in John
2.13–22, is chiefly significant for what it does not say. It constitutes
the first and most dramatic challenge to the synoptic picture. Not
only in its placing, at the very beginning rather than at the very end of
Jesus' ministry, but in its significance, it stands in striking contrast to
the Markan tradition. Few have thought that John is nearer to the
truth in this regard. Dodd himself believed that the synoptists were
here to be preferred.[11]

In John the cleansing of the temple has nothing to do with the
challenge that culminated in the arrest of Jesus. According to Mark
(11.18) it served as the trigger for the final determination of the chief
priests and scribes to do away with Jesus. It is interesting that there is
no sign of this link in Matthew, and in Luke (19.47) it is the *teaching*
of Jesus in the temple that decides them to act. Indeed, in all four

---

[7]*The Political Christ*, London and Philadelphia 1973, p. 28.
[8]Ibid, p. 37.
[9]Ibid, p. 38.
[10]Ibid, p. 41.
[11]*Historical Tradition*, pp. 162, 211.

gospels it is his teaching that is given as the real ground of their fear and
opposition (Mark 11.18; 12.12 and pars.; 14.64 and pars.; Luke
19.47; 20.1; John 18.19–21; 19.7). It looks as though we have here a
purely Markan piece of editorial interpretation. For if the cleansing of
the temple had really provided the occasion of the arrest, it is
remarkable that it should receive no mention at all in the subsequent
proceedings. It was the threat to *destroy* the temple that was brought
up against Jesus (Mark 14.57f. *et passim* = Matt. 26.60f.; cf. Mark
15.29 = Matt. 27.39f.; Luke refers to it only, indirectly, in Acts 6.14),
and this in the synoptists is not associated with the cleansing of the
temple. If the cleansing had occurred in the highly-charged context in
which the synoptists place it, it could not but have assumed, whatever
its motivation, a political significance. Indeed the dilemma is, Why
was Jesus not apprehended on the spot? S. G. F. Brandon, who sees it
as a political coup not merely in consequence but in intention, is
acutely aware of this, and he can explain it only by the totally
unsupported hypothesis that Jesus *must* have been accompanied by an
armed force powerful enough to have prevented his arrest.[12] It is at
least worth asking whether the Johannine version may not be correct
in saying that it was political neither in intention nor in consequence,
and was not followed by arrest or prosecution because it occurred in a
totally different context.

For John the cleansing of the temple has nothing to do with the
political scene. It is an act of religious zeal for the purity of the holy
place, a prophetic protest by Jesus against turning his Father's house
into a market (cf. Zech. 14.21; I Macc. 2.24–26; II Macc. 10.1–8;
Mark 11.16), that is, against trying to serve God and money (cf. Matt.
6.24 = Luke 16.13). It is explained by a different scripture (Ps. 69.9)
from those adduced in the synoptists (Isa. 56.7; Jer. 7.11), and this
scripture is introduced not as Jesus' motive at the time (as in Mark
11.17 and pars.) but as the disciples' subsequent reflection that such
zeal for God would be the death of him (John 2.17; cf. 12.16). To the
evangelist himself the incident would appear to be a sign of the
spiritual truth that in order to give life the temple of Jesus' own body
must be consumed (χαταφάγεται) and die (cf. 2.17, 21; 6.51–58;
12.24; and 2.18–21 with 6.30–35). Despite assertions to the
contrary, it is not presented as an act of *force majeure*. The 'whip of
cords' (2.15) was, it seems, 'something like (ὡς – supported now by

---

[12]*The Fall of Jerusalem and the Christian Church*, London 1951, ²1957, pp.
103f.; *Jesus and the Zealots*, Manchester 1967, New York 1970, pp. 332–4; *The Trial
of Jesus of Nazareth*, London 1971, pp. 83f.

p^{66} ^{and} ^{75}) a whip' made up on the spot (ποιήσας) from the rushes
(σχοινίων) used for the animals' bedding[13] and (if the phrase τά τε
πρόβατα καὶ τοὺς βόας is taken in apposition to πάντας[14]) confined in
its application to the sheep and oxen. But, whatever precisely
happened, the act is presented as one of religious enthusiasm, not to
say spiritual fanaticism, with no perceptible political overtones. In
this it differs from the purging of the temple described in Josephus
(*Ant.* 17.6.1–3, §§ 149–63) by two men with good Maccabaean
names, Judas and Matthias, of the image of the golden eagle set
over the great gate by Herod, which was clearly political in
motivation and immediately provoked military reprisals.

Jesus' words in John, 'Destroy this temple and in three days I will
raise it again' are not, as in the 'false witness' reported by the
synoptists, a threat that *he* would destroy the temple (those who
will do this are the Romans, 11.48), but a statement that *if* this
temple is demolished,[15] Jesus will raise up another, 'in a trice'. The
nearest parallel is the saying connected with the cursing of the fig-
tree, which is closely associated in the synoptists with the cleansing
of the temple: 'If you say to this mountain, "Be removed and
thrown into the sea", it will happen' (Matt. 21.21), where 'this
mountain' (cf. 'this temple' in John 2.19) probably has the overtones of the holy mount of Zion, as in Isa. 25.6f., etc. In other
words, the debate in John 2.13–22, as in 4.20f. (where 'this
mountain' for the Samaritan woman means Gerizim), concerns the
offering of worship in spirit and in truth in contrast with its
materialistic corruption. The saying 2.19 is not throwing down a
political gauntlet but challenging to purity of faith (cf. again Mark
11.22f.). There follows (John 2.20) the same crude misunderstanding between Jesus and 'the Jews' as there is later between Jesus and
Nicodemus. For Jesus is not talking of rebuilding Herod's temple,
any more than spiritual rebirth has to do with entering the womb a
second time (3.4): 'the temple he was speaking of was his body'
(2.21). The political dimension is at this point far removed. Later it
will be very relevant, but not now.

---

[13]So Brown, *John*, p. 115.
[14]So RV; E. Hoskyns and F. N. Davey, *The Fourth Gospel* I, 203; and Dodd,
Historical Tradition, p. 157, who compares Matt. 22.10 and defends the use of the
masculine πάντας where nouns of different genders are comprehended under a
collective term.
[15]For the imperative for the conditional, cf. Dodd, *The Interpretation of the
Fourth Gospel*, Cambridge and New York 1953, p. 302, who argues that the
Johannine form of the saying is more primitive than the Markan.

R. E. Brown, while siding with the majority of commentators in preferring the synoptic dating of the cleansing,[16] agrees that the saying about the temple's destruction could scarcely have left such a dim and divisive memory at the trial (cf. Mark 14.59) had it only been uttered shortly beforehand. He therefore allows that this points to an earlier context for the saying. But I have long been convinced[17] that John's setting of the entire complex makes much better sense – quite apart from removing the very real difficulty to which Brandon's hypothesis of a *force majeure* represents such a desperate solution.

It has often been observed that the synoptists' placing of the cleansing was forced upon them. It is one of the few incidents outside the passion narrative which they had no option but to locate in Jerusalem, and their outline included only one visit to Jerusalem. John, on the other hand, could have put it at the beginning, middle or end of the ministry. That he puts it at the beginning is, I believe, due to the fact that it belongs, as J. Armitage Robinson observed a long time ago in his book, *The Historical Character of St John's Gospel*,[18] to that period in Jesus' ministry when the understanding of his role was dominated by the figure of 'the coming one' designated for him by John the Baptist. As M. Goguel put it,[19] 'When Jesus preached and baptized in Peraea, it was as a disciple of John the Baptist that he did it.' When therefore he first went up to Jerusalem it was deliberately to set in motion the opening act of the programme of Malachi that had inspired John's preaching, the promise of the messenger of the Lord coming suddenly to his temple like a refiner's fire to 'purify the sons of Levi and refine them like gold and silver, till they present right offerings to the Lord' (Mal. 3.1–3, 8f.)[20]

Then there was a connection between this action of Jesus

---

[16] One of the exceptions, ironically, is V. Taylor, *The Gospel according to St Mark*, London and New York 1952, [2]1966, pp. 461f., who prefers John to Mark. Similarly J. Blinzler, *Johannes und die Synoptiker*, Stuttgart 1965, p. 84f.

[17] Cf. my 'Elijah, John and Jesus', in *Twelve New Testament Studies*, especially pp. 40f. I reproduce some sentences from that article here.

[18] London, 1908, [2]1929, pp. 27–31.

[19] *Jean-Baptiste*, Paris 1928, pp. 250f.

[20] For the connection between the cleansing of the temple and the religious ideal of zeal for the purity of Israel that inspired both the Baptist and Qumran, cf. E. Stauffer, 'Historische Elemente im vierten Evangelium', in E. H. Amberg and U. Kühn, eds., *Bekenntnis zur Kirche: Festgabe für E. Sommerlath*, Berlin 1960, pp. 31–51 (especially p. 48). He accepts the Johannine placing of the story in the 'Baptist' period of Jesus' ministry (pp. 38, 41, 49f.).

and the mission of John is borne out by the association of the two in the synoptic account. Jesus, challenged for the authority by which he purges the temple, refers his questioners to the baptism of John (Mark 11.27–33 and pars.). In the position which it occupies in the synoptists it appears to be a trick question parried by a clever riposte. The Baptist has been off the stage for a long time and the source of his activity seems to have nothing to do with the case. As H. E. Edwards put it, 'Is it likely that if John the Baptist had disappeared from public view *two years before* this incident it would still have been dangerous for any member of the Jerusalem aristocracy to disavow belief in him?'[21] But if the Johannine placing is correct, the connection is at once apparent. Jesus' right to act can be accepted only if the source of the Baptist's mission is acknowledged. For the authority behind the one is the authority behind the other: if John's activity was 'from God', then so was Jesus'. It was a complete answer. Were the Markan question in John or the Johannine placing in Mark, I suggest that no one would doubt that the cleansing of the temple occurred during the period when the people were still 'all wondering about John, whether perhaps he was the Messiah' (Luke 3.15).

Moreover the dating of the incident in the Fourth Gospel fits with the external evidence in so far as we can reconstruct it. In John 2.20 the Jews say, 'It has taken forty-six years to build this temple.' Now Josephus tells us in *Ant.* 15.11.1, § 380, that the reconstruction of the temple by Herod began in the eighteenth year of his reign – that is, in the year 20–19 BC.[22] The forty–sixth year would then be AD 27–28 on inclusive counting. It is impossible to arrive at certainty for the absolute dating of Jesus' ministry, but on balance it seems most probable that Jesus was baptized towards the end of 27 and crucified in 30.[23] The Passover referred to in John 2 would then be that of 28, with the final Passover, at which the synoptists place the cleansing, in 30. The forty-six years would therefore fit the earlier occasion with remarkable precision, but not the latter. Now, according to the Mishnah (*Shek.* 1.3), the tables of the money-changers for converting into the temple currency the annual half-

[21] *The Disciple who Wrote these Things*, London 1953, p. 191.
[22] Cf. J. Finegan, *Handbook of Biblical Chronology*, Princeton 1964, pp. 276–80. Josephus has another statement in *BJ* 1.21.1, § 401, putting it in Herod's fifteenth year, but it is generally agreed that this is less reliable. In any case this would make the date earlier still and even less compatible with the synoptic placing of the cleansing.
[23] Cf. the judicious article by G. B. Caird, 'The Chronology of the NT', *Interpreter's Dictionary of the Bible* I, New York 1962, pp. 601–3.

shekel tax enjoined by Exod. 30.13 were set up in the temple from the 25th day of Adar, that is, three weeks before Passover.[24] This comports with the statement in John 2.13 that Passover was 'near' when Jesus went up to Jerusalem, which is then followed in 2.23, after the cleansing, by the time-reference 'at the Passover, during the feast'. R. Schnackenburg, who rejects the Johannine placing, nevertheless concedes that this looks like 'a precise detail which seems to support the date given by the evangelist for the cleansing of the temple, the beginning of the public ministry of Jesus'.[25] The only way to set aside the otherwise irrelevant and apparently motiveless reference to forty-six years (a number for which no convincing symbolic reason has been found)[26] is to insist, with C. K. Barrett,[27] that the aorist must mean that John was mistaken, supposing that the construction of the temple had by then stopped, whereas we know that it went on till 63 (Josephus, *Ant.* 20.9.7, § 219). But Brown[28] cites what he calls the 'perfect parallel' from Ezra 5.16 (LXX): 'From that time until now [the temple] has been in building ($\dot{\omega}\varkappa o\delta o\mu\dot{\eta}\theta\eta$) and is not yet finished'. It is surely easier to believe that the evangelist knew what he was talking about and got the date right.

Though it is peripheral to our purpose here, I would venture the suggestion that other material associated with the Jerusalem minis-

---

[24]That the cleansing of the temple occurred at Passover-time is the one common factor in the divergent datings, and the burden of proof must lie heavily on those who would wish to put it at any other season. F. C. Burkitt, 'W and Θ: Studies in the Western Text of Mark', *JTS* 17, 1916, pp. 139–50, argued for the feast of the Dedication, and T. W. Manson, 'The Cleansing of the Temple', *BJRL* 33, 1951, pp. 276–80, for Tabernacles. But the specific provision for the money-changers' tables to be set up prior to Passover makes this very arbitrary. Manson's attempt to get round this by saying 'there would probably always be some tables in the Temple precincts' is unconvincing. And unless, with him, we gratuitously excise Mark 11.13b ('for it was not the season of figs') in the interests of a naturalistic easing of the offence of the story, the closely-attached cursing of the fig-tree precisely fits the Passover season – one of leaves without fruit – in a way that Tabernacles (autumn) or the Dedication (winter) does not.

[25]*The Gospel according to St John* I, ET London 1968, p. 352.

[26]Augustine, for instance, *In Joh.* 10, noting that in Greek letters 'Adam' had the numerical value of 46, applied it to Jesus' own age (cf. John 8.57, 'not yet fifty years old'). But this bears no relation to the quite explicit statements of the text.

[27]*The Gospel according to St John*, London and New York 1955, p. 167.

[28]*John*, p. 116. It had already been cited by J. H. Bernard, *St John*, ad loc.; C. H. Turner, 'Chronology of the New Testament', in *Hastings' Dictionary of the Bible* I, Edinburgh and New York 1898, p. 405; and earlier by J. B. Lightfoot, whom little escaped, in an unpublished section of his lectures at Cambridge in 1873 (see the reference in my *Redating the NT*, p. 277). John 2.20, he said, 'speaks volumes for the authenticity of the gospel'. Cf. also his *Biblical Essays*, pp. 30f.

try and placed, unavoidably, by the synoptists in the final visit, may also properly belong to the period when Jesus is still acting out the Baptist's programme. We have seen how the cursing of the fig-tree, symbolizing the doom of Israel (cf. Hos. 9.10, 16f.), which is intertwined by Mark with the cleansing of the temple, supplies the closest parallel to the saying in John, 'Destroy this temple. . . . ' The cursing might almost be designed as an act of prophetic symbolism to spell out the Baptist's warning: 'Bring forth fruit worthy of repentance. . . . Every tree that fails to produce good fruit is cut down and thrown on the fire' (Matt. 3.8–10 = Luke 3.8f.). The *parable* of the fig-tree in Luke 13.6–9, instead of being, as is often supposed, a variant tradition of the same incident, could then be Jesus' reflection upon his own action two years previously (counting inclusively in the Jewish manner) and thus bear out its early dating.

> A man had a fig-tree growing in his vineyard; and he came looking for fruit on it, but found none. So he said to the vine-dresser, 'Look here! For the last three years (or, this is now the third year) I have come looking for fruit on this fig-tree without finding any. Cut it down. Why should it go on using up the soil?' But he replied, 'Leave it, sir, this one year while I dig round it and manure it. And if it bears next season, well and good; if not, you shall have it down.'

If then the cursing, like the cleansing, belongs to Jesus' early Judaean ministry, this could explain why the withering attack on the Jewish leaders which follows in Matthew contains two further echoes of the Baptist – the accusation of not believing him when even tax-gatherers and prostitutes did (21.32) and the adoption by Jesus of his description of them as a 'viper's brood' (23.33; cf. 3.7). Perhaps therefore what seems to us so harsh was a deliberate part of that ministry of the mightier one to winnow and to burn (Matt. 3.11f. = Luke 3.16f.) which at that time Jesus was content to accept from John.[29]

After John's arrest (Mark 1.14) Jesus is presented as coming into Galilee with an understanding of his mission very different from that of this Elijah figure drawn from Mal. 3 and 4. Luke (4.16–19) makes Jesus introduce it in terms of Isa. 61, and according to the Q tradition Jesus justifies his activity to John's emissaries by referring them to Isa. 35 and 61 (Matt. 11.2–6 = Luke 7.18–23). The role is no longer that of the mighty one sent to purge and to judge but of the gracious

---

[29]For further such connections, lying behind John 3.5 and Luke 9.52–56, cf. again my *Twelve New Testament Studies*, pp. 41f.

one anointed to seek and to save and to heal. Between the Jordan and Galilee the synoptists set the story of a spiritual crisis which is depicted in Q as three successive temptations that Jesus faces and rejects. Doubtless this is a schematized account of temptations born of real-life situations over a longer period (cf. Luke 22.28), though the news of John's arrest (Matt. 4.12) could well have forced reappraisal of the role that his preaching had sanctioned. For was the confrontation and violence to which it led really the way of the kingdom? The path of precipitate action in the temple (Matt. 4.5–7; Luke 4.9–12) began to look less compelling. Rejection of it could perhaps have stemmed from the incident described in John 2.13–22.[30] For on reflection the evangelist sees it as suicidal, the action of a religious enthusiast whose zeal is self-consuming. In itself it was a spiritual rather than a political act, motivated by purity of passion for his Father's house rather than the quest for popular support or temporal power. But the Q narrative sees it as linked with two other highly political temptations, whose origin in life could well be associated with the next incident in John to be considered. It is interesting that Matthew relates the incident to the news, this time, of the Baptist's *death* and to another withdrawal to the wilderness (ἔρημον τόπον) which that provoked (14.13).

If it is John who enables us to understand the religious *rather than* the political significance of the temple cleansing (and there is in fact nothing in the synoptic accounts themselves as opposed to their context to suggest otherwise), it is John in 6.1–15 who enables us to appreciate the political *as well as* the religious meaning of the desert feeding.[31] This meaning could not be deduced from the Markan

[30]R. E. Brown, 'Incidents that are Units in the Synoptic Gospels but dispersed in St John', *CBQ* 23, 1961, pp. 152–5, while agreeing with what I go on to say below about the other two temptations, parallels this one with the urging of Jesus' brothers in 7.1– 4 to him to go up to Jerusalem and show himself to the world. This cannot be excluded, but the correspondences are not great. In an earlier attempt at the same exercise (which Brown does not mention) H. Preisker, 'Zum Charakter des Johannesevangeliums', in F. W. Schmidt, R. Winkler and W. Meyer, eds., *Luther, Kant, Schleiermacher in ihrer Bedeutung für den Protestantismus: Festschrift für G. Wobbermin*, Berlin 1939, pp. 379–93, parallels Luke 4.2–4 (improbably) with John 4.31–34; Luke 4.5–8 with John 6.14f.; and Luke 4.9–12 with John 7.4–6. He argues that the temptations are lifted out of the 'mythical settings' given to them by the synoptists and later suplied with historical ones by John. But again, if the 'mythical' settings had occurred in John and the 'historical' in the synoptists, no one would have dreamt of making such a judgment of priority.

[31]On this, cf. Dodd, *Historical Tradition*, pp. 212–17, and *The Founder of Christianity*, New York 1970, London 1971, p. 131–9; T. W. Manson, *The Servant Messiah*, Cambridge 1953, pp. 69–71; H. W. Montefiore, 'Revolt in the Desert?', *NTS* 8, 1962, pp. 135–41; and earlier, as so often, Lightfoot, *Biblical Essays*, pp. 151–3.

narrative, yet when introduced makes startling sense of it. The clue lies in the Johannine conclusion, 'Perceiving that they were about to come and take him by force to make him king, Jesus withdrew again to the hills by himself' (6.15). There is indeed good manuscript support here for the reading 'fled' (φεύγει)[32] – which is scarcely likely to have been invented. Jesus' hand is forced and he finds himself compelled to rapid evasive action. Suddenly the political and paramilitary overtones of this messianic meal become evident. From Mark we could, if we were looking for it, sense the manic excitement of the crowds and their lost and dangerous condition of lacking and looking for a leader (Mark 6.33f.; for the political background of 'sheep without a shepherd', cf. Num. 27.17; I Kings 22.17; Ezek. 34.5). Then there is the significance, again if we were looking for it, of the fact that they were all men (ἄνδρες). John (6.10) agrees with Mark (6.44) and Luke (9.14) in so describing the five thousand. Matthew appears to miss the point in order to heighten the miraculous by adding 'besides women and children' (14.21; and also in 15.38).[33] For the context of this desert assembly is evidently the same as that described in Acts 21.38: 'Then you are not the Egyptian who started a revolt some time ago and led a force of four thousand terrorists (ἄνδρας τῶν σικαρίων) out into the wilds?' The wilderness was the natural place from which false prophets and messianic pretenders might be expected (Matt. 24.24–6) and Josephus testifies later (*Ant.* 20.5.1; 20.8.6, 10, §§ 97–9, 167–72, 188) to several such abortive risings by individuals promising signs and giving themselves out to be prophets (John 6.14; cf. Mark 13.6; Acts 5.36f.).[34] Of the same Egyptian that Acts mentions Josephus writes:

> A charlatan, who had gained for himself the reputation of a prophet, this man appeared in the country, collected a following of about thirty thousand dupes, and led them by a circuitous route from the desert to the mount called the mount of Olives. From there he proposed to force an entrance into Jerusalem and, after overpowering the Roman garrison, to set himself up as

---

[32]Including ℵ*, the old Latin, Tertullian and Augustine. It is adopted by brown.

[33]Unless χωρίς could here mean 'without any admixture of women and children', as Dodd suggested to Montefiore (*NTS* 8, 1962, p. 137). But he did not repeat this in his own discussion of the passage.

[34]Cf. P. W. Barnett, 'The Jewish Sign Prophets – AD 40–70 – Their Intentions and Origin', *NTS* 27, 1981, pp. 679–97.

tyrant of the people, employing those who poured in with him as his bodyguard.[35]

Such, no doubt, was the kind of programme that many of the crowd were expecting from Jesus in the wilderness. If, as John says, they proposed to make him 'king', it could for them have meant no more than when Josephus uses the same word to describe how, 'as the several companies of the seditious lighted upon anyone to head them, he was immediately created a king (βασιλύς)' (*Ant.* 17.10.8, § 285).[36] Yet a bid for national power was a serious possibility, for with 'the country . . . a prey to disorder . . . the opportunity induced numbers of persons to aspire to sovereignty (βασιλείαν)' (*BJ* 2.4.1, § 55). Indeed of John 6.15 William Sanday wrote: 'There is no stronger proof both of the genuineness and of the authenticity of the Fourth Gospel than the way in which it reflects the current Messianic idea.'[37]

This clue explains also the sudden and otherwise unaccountable ending to the story in Mark (6.45): 'As soon as it was over he made (ἠνάγκασεν, forced) his disciples embark and cross to Bethsaida ahead of him, while he himself sent the people away.' Evidently Jesus could not trust his associates not to share the surge of the crowd and constitute themselves his bodyguard. Then, we read, 'after taking leave of them (ἀποταξάμενος αὐτοῖς), he went away εἰς τὸ ὄρος to pray' (6.146). Here perhaps we may have the setting in life for the temptations to a populist programme which the synoptists represent him as rejecting in principle from the beginning (Matt. 4.1–4, 8–10; Luke 4.1–18) but which could well have taken their particular form from the loaves and the mountain (cf. Matt. 4.8, εἰς ὄρος) of this desert crisis. If so, they will belong not so much to the first transition in Jesus' self-understanding, from the prophet of doom to the charismatic liberator, but to the second critical turning in his ministry – though, as we have said, if Matthew is right, this too may have been triggered off by reflection upon the fate of John (with Matt. 14.13 cf. also 11.12–14 and 17.9–13). This time it was the shift arising from the dangerous misunderstanding to which the title

---

[35] *BJ* 2.13.5, §§ 261f. Tr. H. St J. Thackeray (Loeb Classical Library), London and New York 1927.

[36] I have followed here the translation of A. N. Sherwin-White, *Roman Society and Roman Law in the New Testament*, Oxford and New York 1963, p. 25. R. Marcus in the Loeb edition takes προϊστάμενος to mean 'made himself king', which seems less likely in the context.

[37] *The Authorship and Historical Character of the Fourth Gospel*, London 1872, p. 124.

of Messiah, or anointed one, lay exposed. For it was open to be interpreted not only in religious but in political terms, as the equivalence of 'Christ' and 'king' in popular usage makes clear (Mark 15.32; Luke 23.2, 35, 37; cf. Acts 17.7, 'They . . . assert there is a rival king, Jesus'). When therefore, as John 6.15 records, this equation became explicit, Jesus was compelled to a corrective, beginning with the Twelve. For the reply elicited from Peter in Mark 8.29, 'You are the Christ', is followed not, as in Matthew's addition (16.17–19), by acclamation, but by rebuke, the verb ἐπιτιμάω recurring three times in 8.30, 32, 33. Thenceforward Jesus must insist with uncompromising abruptness on spelling out his mission in terms rather of a Son of Man vindicated only out of suffering and death, for which the models were this time to be found in Dan. 7 and Isa. 53. (For the same contrast between Christ on the lips of others and the Son of Man on Jesus' own, cf. Matt. 26.63f.; Luke 22.67–69.) This testing of the terms on which he could count on the disciples' loyalty is presented by the synoptists without occasion or motive as the climax of the Galilean ministry (Mark 8.27–30 and pars.). But in John it is explained by the desert crisis. It is this last which was the real turning point, of which the testing of the disciples' faith (6.66–69) and the need for withdrawal (7.1) were the consequences. Thereafter care to avoid a premature dénouement, which this crisis so nearly provoked, becomes decisive (7.2–9).

Yet John makes it clear that the real truth of what it is to be the Messiah or king of Israel (both of which titles he uses more than any of the synoptists) is not to be denied or repudiated of Jesus. Indeed they are introduced in the opening chapter (1.41, 49) as essential ingredients of what it means to confess him as the Son of God (1.49). But after ch. 6 the debate about how, and in what sense, Jesus can be the Messiah becomes more subtle and more ironic (7.25–52). Then in ch. 10 the argument focuses upon the category of the shepherd, which, as Walter Grundmann has rightly stressed,[38] is intimately associated with that of divine kingship. In Ezek. 34, a chapter which underlies the whole of John 10 (and cf. again Ezek. 34.5 with Mark 6.34 – the sheep without a shepherd), the shepherd is linked with the hope of a Davidic Messiah: 'Therefore I will save my flock, and they shall be ravaged no more . . . I will set over them one shepherd to take care of them, my servant David; he shall care for them and become their shepherd. I, the Lord, will become their God, and my servant David shall be a prince among them' (34.22–24). It is

[38] *Jesus and the Politics of his Day*, pp. 295–318.

understandable therefore that the claim by Jesus to be the true shepherd of Israel provokes the question, 'How long must you keep us in suspense? If you are the Messiah say so plainly' (10.24). It is the same question that in Luke (22.67) is later thrown at Jesus by the Sanhedrin. And the answer, though superficially different, is in fact the same: 'If I tell you', he says in Luke, 'you will not believe.' 'I have told you', he says in John, 'but you do not believe' (10.25; cf. 8.25, 'Who are you?'. . . . 'What I have told you all along' (NEB margin)). For in John the messianic secret is not that Jesus says nothing, but that he says everything openly to the world (18.20) – yet only his own sheep can hear and believe (10.26f.).

Throughout this tenth chapter Jesus is at pains to distinguish himself as the good from the worthless shepherds of Israel,[39] echoing in 10.12 the words of the prophet Zechariah: 'Alas for the worthless shepherd who abandons the sheep' (Zech. 11.17). In particular he dissociates himself from the pretenders claiming to enter and control the sheep-fold of Israel. The contrast is not with those who have gone before him, as the $\pi\rho\grave{o}$ $\grave{\epsilon}\mu o\widehat{u}$ of 10.8 has inevitably suggested. But this is very doubtfully part of the true text.[40] The contrast is with those who come without authorization and 'climb in some other way' (10.1). Jesus does not come 'of his own accord', but with the authority of him who sent him (7.28f.; 8.42f.): they come in their own name, saying $\grave{\epsilon}\gamma\acute{\omega}$ $\epsilon\acute{\iota}\mu\iota$, and claiming to be the Christ (Mark 13.6 and pars.; 13.21–23 and pars.; Luke 17.23). The purposes for which the two come are diametrically opposed: for Jesus it is to give life, for them it is to take life (10.10). And whereas he voluntarily and of his own accord lays down his life for the sheep (10.11, 15, 17f.), they by their resort to violence have their lives taken from them (10.18). So far from being the nationalists they claim, true Israelites (cf. 1.47), they are $\grave{a}\lambda\lambda\acute{o}\tau\rho\iota o\iota$ (10.5), foreigners to God's people (cf. Matt. 17.25f.). They are burglars and bandits (10.1, 8), $\lambda\eta\sigma\tau a\acute{\iota}$, the word that is to be used subsequently for the political insurrectionary Barabbas, who is contrasted with the true 'king of the Jews', Jesus (18.40). It is the term too that Josephus uses for the Zealots, and he gives vivid examples of these terrorists and their methods (*Ant.* 17.10.4–8, §§ 269–85; 20.8.5f., §§ 160–72; *BJ* 2.4.1–3, §§ 55–65; 2.13.6, §§ 264f.; 2.17.8, §§ 433–40; 4.9.3f., §§ 503–13). One in

[39]For the setting in life of this parable in the concluding challenge to the Jewish leadership, see further 'The Parable of the Shepherd' (John 10.1–5) in my *Twelve New Testament Studies*, pp. 67–55.
[40]It is omitted *inter alia* by p[45 vid, 75], ℵ*, R, *al*, lat, sy[s, P], sa – a powerful combination. It is bracketed in the United Bible Society's text.

particular (*Ant.* 17.10.6–8, §§ 277–84; *BJ* 2.4.3, §§ 60–65) offers an ironic commentary on John 10. After speaking of 'the great madness that settled upon the nation because they had no king of their own to restrain the populace by his moral example (ἀρετῇ), Josephus goes on to tell of an unknown shepherd Athronges, who 'had the temerity to aspire to the kingship, thinking that if he obtained it he would enjoy freedom to act more outrageously; as for meeting death, he did not attach much importance to the loss of his life' (very different from voluntarily laying it down). He 'donned the diadem' and took the title of 'king', and with his marauding bands slaughtered Romans and compatriots alike, killing, as Josephus puts it, 'sometimes in hope of gain and at other times from the habit of killing'. The contrast with the 'good' shepherd, especially as it is drawn out in John 10.10, could scarcely be more striking.

It is the determination to present Jesus as the true Messiah or king of Israel and yet to make clear that he repudiated the overtones of political violence with which it was *bound* to be associated that dominates the tragic irony of the Johannine passion story. Before moving to this, however, we should note the build-up to the arrest and trial of Jesus which John is careful to record. In Mark there is an early reference to a plot of Jewish factions to make away with Jesus (3.6), but then no plans or procedures are mentioned until the very end (11.18; 12.12; 14.1f.), when things are rushed through in hugger-mugger fashion (14.55–64; 15.1–15). In John there are a series of abortive attempts at arrest or violence to Jesus's person (7.30, 32, 44; 8.20, 59; 10.31, 39), leading to a formal meeting and resolution of the Sanhedrin when a warrant is issued for his arrest and he is publicly declared a wanted man (11.46–57). Bammel[41] has subjected this passage to close analysis and concluded that its parallels with Jewish usage and tradition afford good confidence that it represents reliable historical material. He summarizes its main points as follows:

(*a*) a picture of the prosecution of Jesus which makes the legal proceedings begin a considerable time before the crucifixion;
(*b*) the fact that the legal processes are started and carried out solely by the Jews;
(*c*) the part played by Caiaphas and the arguments presented by him;
(*d*) the withdrawal of Jesus.

---

[41]'*Ex illa itaque die consilium fecerunt*' in E. Bammel, ed., *The Trial of Jesus*, London and Naperville 1970, especially pp. 29–35. Cf. Brown, *John* pp. 441f., 799; Dodd, *Historical Tradition*, pp. 27f.

He goes on: 'Each of these elements looks strange, but together they give a picture which is thoroughly consistent, and is paralleled in more than one detail by traditions which do not merely reproduce the Fourth Gospel.'[42] Indeed the meeting and resolution of the Sanhedrin and the part played by Caiaphas seem to be reflected independently in Matt. 26.3f. There however this tradition is combined with Markan material which sets it a bare two days before Passover and with a dating of the crucifixion which contradicts the clear determination that 'it must not be during the festival . . . or there may be rioting among the people' (Matt. 26.2, 5). The Johannine chronology is altogether more intelligible.[43]

In John, Jesus goes into hiding after the warrant for his arrest until six days before Passover (11.54; 12.1). Then 'the next day the great body of pilgrims who had come to the festival, hearing that Jesus was on the way to Jerusalem, took palm branches and went out to meet him' (12.12f.). In all the records of the triumphal entry[44] there is the same tense mixture of the spiritual and the political. The distinctive emphasis of John is to present Jesus' action as the conscious *corrective* of a planned political ovation. In the synoptists it is Jesus himself who stage-manages his entry on a donkey (Mark 11.1–7 and pars.) and the crowd which spontaneously cuts brushwood from the fields (Mark 11.8) or branches from the trees (Matt. 21.8). In John it is the crowd which takes the initiative, coming out from Jerusalem to greet him with a reception calculated to evoke the spirit of Maccabaean nationalism (12.13).[45] It is Jesus who counters this by an apparently spontaneous action: 'But (δέ) Jesus found a donkey and mounted it' (12.14). The 'but' is omitted in the NEB. J. N. Sanders[46] however is

[42] *Trial*, p. 35.

[43] It would take us wide of our purpose to enter in detail into the whole question of the dating of the crucifixion, but it is one where (in contrast with the cleansing of the temple) there is substantial critical support for the Johannine chronology.

[44] Cf. E. D. Freed, 'The Entry into Jerusalem in the Gospel of John', *JBL* 80, 1961, pp. 329–38 (for dependence upon the synoptics), and D. M. Smith, Jr, 'John 12.12ff. and the Question of John's Use of the Synoptics', *JBL* 82, 1963, pp. 58–64 (against dependence).

[45] Cf. W. R. Farmer, 'The Palm Branches in John 12.13', *JTS* n.s. 3, 1952, pp. 62–3; and R. H. Lightfoot, *St John's Gospel*, Oxford and New York 1956, p. 238. Cf. in particular I Macc. 13.51 (the only other occurrence of βαΐα in the biblical writings) and II Mac. 10.7 (φοίνικας). The fact, if it were a fact (which it is not), that palms did not grow in Jerusalem (e.g. R. Bultmann, *The Gospel of John*, p. 418); to the contrary, H. St J. Hart, 'The Crown of Thorns in John 19.2–5', *JTS* n.s. 3, 1952, p. 72), would not necessarily indicate that John did not know his topography but that they had been brought in earlier (for liturgical purposes; cf. Neh. 8.15) and were used with premeditated purpose; cf. Brown, *John*, 456f.

[46] J. N. Sanders and B. A. Mastin, *The Gospel according to St John*, London and New York 1968, p. 288.

surely right in interpreting it as 'a prompt repudiation of the crowd's acclamations'. The purpose of the act of prophetic symbolism is clear. It is to say 'King of Israel' (12.13), yes: but not that sort of king (12.15).[47] There is no suggestion in John, as in Luke (19.37), that the disciples had any part in the demonstration, or even in finding and preparing the donkey (Mark 11.1–7 and pars.). They are merely recorded as not understanding. For, as the evangelist stresses, the true significance of what happened could only be understood later in the light of the distinctive and paradoxical manner in which Jesus was in fact to enter upon his glory (12.16). Like all the history in the Fourth Gospel it is written 'from the end' and its telling has been moulded by that 'calling to mind' which must wait upon the gift of the Spirit (14.26). Yet what is 'remembered' is not only 'that this had been written about him' but 'that this had happened to him': not merely interpretation but event. J. N. Sanders' comment at this point is again apposite:

> So far from being 'hardly possible as history' (Barrett, p. 347 [²416]), his [John's] account may well reveal a better understanding than the other evangelists' of Jesus' dilemma, as 'Son of David' by right, and conscious of a mission to save Israel, yet refusing to adopt the only policy that the majority of his people would understand or accept.[48]

For John the entry into Jerusalem, with its tragic-comic 'God bless the king of Israel!', presents the reader in advance with the clue by which the trial of Jesus is to be interpreted: its proceedings turn more insistently than in any other gospel upon the question, 'Are you the king of the Jews?' (18.33).[49]

Indeed the whole of the latter part of John's Gospel is presented as a kind of cosmic political trial, of which it is the function of the last discourses to supply the heavenly dimension or spiritual interpretation. This was brought out in a most original but neglected article by Théo Preiss, 'Justification in Johannine Thought', originally submitted to the *Festschrift* for Barth's sixtieth birthday in 1946 and translated in the posthumous collection of his essays, *Life in Christ*.[50]

[47]The point of the quotations from Zech. 9.9 and (as he argues) Zeph. 3.16 is well brought out by Brown, *John*, pp. 462f.

[48]*John*, pp. 288f.

[49]In John's passion narrative there are 12 occurrences of βασιλεύς (plus 3 of βασιλεία), compared with 4 in Matthew, 6 in Mark and 4 in Luke. This is the more notable in view of only 2 occurrences in John of ἡ βασιλεία τοῦ θεοῦ.

[50]ET London and Chicago 1954, pp. 9–31.

As far as I know, it has received no mention in any subsequent commentary on John.[51] Preiss drew attention to the markedly juridical emphasis in John's Gospel (and Epistles), in such categories as legal agent, witness, judge, judgment, accuse, convict, advocate.[52] The whole action is viewed as a 'gigantic juridical contest' between Jesus as the authorized *persona* of God and 'the Prince of this world', culminating in a great reversal of judgment, when it will be seen that it is the latter who is condemned and Jesus who has won the case by his exaltation to the Father. This will become apparent only in the light of the work of the Paraclete; for he, as both defending and prosecuting counsel, will call the victorious lives of Christians to witness in the court of heaven to clinch the demonstration of how matters really lie.

Meanwhile in the earthly events, for those who have the eyes to see it, 'the judgment of this world' (12.31) is about to be played out with all its ambiguities and double meanings. It is the world that supposes it is doing the judging. Pilate, as the unwitting representative of the higher power, not merely of Caesar but of God, exercises the royal ἐξουσία granted to him (19.11). He takes his seat on the tribunal as judge (19.13). Yet the ἐκάθισεν could be deliberately ironical, carrying the overtones also of the transitive sense of 'setting' upon the judgment-throne the Man to whom the right to pass judgment has been committed (cf. 5.27). The transitive sense cannot be the primary one,[53] though echoes of this way of thinking in the early church are to be found in the Gospel of Peter 3.7, 'They put upon him a purple robe and set him on the judgment-seat and said "Judge righteously, O King of Israel!"', and in Justin, *Apol.* I. 35.6, 'They tormented him, and set him on the judgment-seat, and said, "Judge us".' In both these cases it is the Jews who do this; but in John it would be part of the irony of Pilate's action. For, in contrast with the

[51]It is one of the merits of Hahn's article, 'Der Prozess Jesu nach dem Johannesevangelium', *EKK* 2, p. 95, that he commends it albeit briefly. Surprisingly, it does not even receive mention in A. E. Harvey's *Jesus on Trial. A Study in the Fourth Gospel*, London 1976, which came out too late to be taken fully into account here, but which expands the same thesis in a most suggestive manner.

[52]Key passages for these terms are John 5.22–47; 7.45–52; 8.13–18, 28, 45f.; 12.31–33, 44–50; 14.30f.; 15.22–27; 16.7–11, 33; 18.29–19.16.

[53]Despite Harnack, Loisy, Macgregor, and most recently I. de la Potterie, 'Jésus, roi et juge d'après Jn. 19.13: ἐκάθισεν ἐπὶ βήματος', *Bibl* 41, 1960, pp. 217–47. for a full survey, cf. Dauer, *Passionsgeschichte*, pp. 269–74, who comes down against. As Bultmann observes, *John*, p. 664, 'an αὐτόν would be indispensable'. Dodd, *Historical Tradition*, p. 119, and Hahn, *EKK* 2, pp. 48–50, are also decisive for the intransitive. (For striking parallels for the procurator taking his seat on the βῆμα cf. Josephus, *BJ* 2.9.3, §, 172; 2.14.8, § 301.) Yet other commentators are surprisingly open to a secondary meaning: e.g. Barrett, R. H. Lightfoot, Brown, and Lindars, ad loc.

synoptists, John has Pilate himself bring out the prisoner in his purple cloak and mock radiate crown[54] and publicly present him to the Jews as their king (19.14). And the political implications of the scene are drawn out to the full: 'If you let this man go, you are no friend to Caesar;[55] any man who claims to be a king is defying Caesar' (19.12); '"Crucify your king?" said Pilate. "We have no king but Caesar", the Jews replied' (19.15).

Of course the story is written up to bring out the theological dimensions of the drama that is being enacted. But once again John appears to be giving the truth, as he sees if, *of* the history, rather than creating *ex nihilo*. As Brown says,[56]

> The Synoptic Gospels never adequately explain why Pilate yielded to the importunings of the crowd and the priests. . . . John's picture of Pilate worried about what might be said at Rome has a very good chance of being historical. According to Philo, *Ad Gaium* xxxviii. 301f., Pilate was naturally inflexible and stubbornly resisted when the Jews clamored against him until they mentioned that the Emperor Tiberius would not approve his violating their customs. 'It was this final point that particularly struck home, for he feared that if they actually sent an embassy, they would also expose the rest of his conduct as governor'. . . . A shrewd ecclesiastical politican like Caiaphas would have been quite aware of the prefect's vulnerability and prompt to probe it.[57]

Yet in all this the non-political and non-violent nature of Jesus' kingship is made explicit in John 18.36f.:

> 'My kingdom does not belong to this world. If it did, my followers would be fighting to save me from arrest by the Jews. My kingly authority comes from elsewhere.' 'You are a king, then?' said Pilate. Jesus answered, '"King" is your word. My task is to bear witness to the truth. For this was I born; for this I came into the world, and all who are not deaf to truth listen to my voice.'[58]

---

[54] Cf. Hart, *JTS* n.s. 3, 1952, pp. 66–75. Even if this theory is not substantiated the irony remains. The Turin Shroud, if authenticated, would count against it, since it points to real thorns and not to a circlet of acanthus leaves.

[55] For 'Caesar's friend' as a title of honour, cf. E. Bammel, Φίλος τοῦ καίσαρος', *TLZ* 77, 1952, pp. 205–10; E. Stauffer, *Jesus and his Story*, ET London 1960, pp. 109f.; Sherwin-White, *Roman Society*, p. 47.

[56] *John*, pp. 890f.

[57] It was precisely this sort of denunciation to Rome by his subjects that led to Pilate eventually losing his post in 36–37 (Josephus, *Ant.* 18.4.2, §§88f.

[58] Cf. the echo in the last words of the test of messiahship in 10.27: 'My own sheep listen to my voice.'

Taking up, as the passage does, the previous injunctions at the arrest, 'Let these others go' (18.8) and 'Sheathe your sword' (18.11), there could not be a clearer disavowal of power-politics. Yet, equally, the manner in which the religious charge against Jesus, which for the Jews is the real gravamen in all the gospels (Mark 14.63f. and pars.; John 19.7), was capable of being twisted into the political is nowhere more fatefully evident than in John.

He stresses that the two aspects were inseparable. In this gospel the arrest of Jesus is already the work of Roman soldiers, as well as of the constables of the Jewish court (18.3, 12).[59] This Roman involvement has been much questioned, and even denied.[60] But if one's first reaction is to find it strange and historically improbable, it may on reflection again bear out, and indeed explain, the synoptic account. All the synoptists concur – and it is the only point in the story at which Luke agrees verbatim with Matthew and Mark – that Jesus asked the question of his captors, 'Do you take me for a bandit, that you have come out with swords and cudgels to arrest me?' (Mark 14.48 and pars.) Now if we stop to ask who would arrest a λῃστής, and how, the answer is obvious. It was certainly not the Jews who apprehended Barabbas (John 18.40) or the two λῃσταί crucified with Jesus (Matt. 27.38; Mark 15.27). It was the Romans; and they would take the proper military precaution of doing it in force. What

---

[59]The ὑπηρέται, a word which John always uses in its technical sense, were not 'temple police' (NEB) but constables of the court of the Sanhedrin acting in its judicial capacity. Cf. Matt. 5.25; Mark 14.65; John 18.22; Acts 5.21f.; and note the irony of John 18.36: 'my ὑπηρέται'.

[60]E.g. by J. Blinzler, The Trial of Jesus, Westminster, Maryland, 1959, pp. 63–70, and Bammel, Jesus and the Politics of his Day, p. 439. It seems to me most improbable that John did not intend to use σπεῖρα and χιλίαρχος, like the rest of the New Testament writers, as the equivalents of the Roman cohors and tribunus. (So in E. Schürer, History of the Jewish People in the Age of Jesus Christ, revised ET, I, Edinburgh and Naperville 1973, p. 372 n. 86.) Of course the LXX does not do so because it is not talking about the Romans; but its parallels certainly do not bear out the desired meaning of σπεῖρα as a small detachment (e.g. II Macc. 12.20!). Such resort becomes plausible only if Roman participation is utterly improbable – but see below. M. Goguel, The Life of Jesus, ET London and New York 1933, pp. 468f., and P. Winter, On the Trial of Jesus, Berlin 1961, pp. 44–9, make the point that Roman participation in the arrest goes against John's tendency (as they see it) to place responsibility for the death of Jesus on the Jews while exonerating Pilate, and cannot therefore be regarded as his invention. H.-W. Bartsch, 'Wer verurteilte Jesus zum Tode?', NovTest 7, 1964/65, pp. 210–16, does not think Winter establishes this. But I would regard Roman participation as in any case entirely natural under the circumstances, and in no way 'astonishing' (C. K. Barrett, The Gospel of John and Judaism, London and Philadelphia, 1975, p. 71; though he is wrong in saying that in John 'the Romans rather than the Jews arrest Jesus' (italics mine)).

is distinctive about the arrest of Jesus is that the Jewish authorities took the initiative and *collaborated*. They did so because the informer was in their pay and was answering the call of the Sanhedrin, which John alone reports, 'that anyone who knew where he was should give information, so that they might arrest him' (11.57). The words of Jesus to Pilate in 18.36 ('my followers would be fighting to save me from arrest by *the Jews*')[61] presuppose again that it was the Jews, not the Romans, who were out to seize him (cf. 19.11). Their reasons for wanting him were religious (11.47f.), though doubtless the Jewish establishment was able easily enough to obtain Roman assistance by representing him, then as later, as a danger to the peace. But in the first instance he was a wanted man on the Jewish list, for whom a summons was out from a properly convened Jewish court. So it is to this court that he was handed over – by the Romans.

So far from this being irregular or improbable there are close parallels in the story of Acts 21–23.[62] There too 'the officer' ($\chi\iota\lambda\acute{\iota}\alpha\rho\chi o\varsigma$) commanding 'the cohort' ($\tau\tilde{\eta}\varsigma$ $\sigma\pi\epsilon\acute{\iota}\rho\eta\varsigma$)[63] took a force of soldiers to keep the peace (21.31f.), and he too suposes he has gone out against a $\lambda\eta\sigma\tau\acute{\eta}\varsigma$: 'Then you are not the Egyptian that started a revolt some time ago and led a force of four thousand terrorists out into the wilds?' (21.38). We are not told how many troops he took – obviously not the whole cohort of six hundred men (later he detached two hundred to convoy Paul to Caesarea (23.23)). As Bernard comments on John 18.3:[64]

> It is not . . . to be supposed that John means that the whole strength of the regiment (cf. Mark 15.16) was turned out to aid in the arrest of Jesus; the words $\lambda\alpha\beta\grave{\omega}\nu$ $\tau\grave{\eta}\nu$ $\sigma\pi\epsilon\tilde{\iota}\rho\alpha\nu$ indicate no more than that Judas had got the help of 'the cohort', i.e. a detachment, with whom the commanding officer of the garrison came (v. 12), in view of possible developments.

Moreover, there is no difficulty about the fact that the Romans deliver the prisoner bound to the Jewish authorities. For in Acts, even though

---

[61] I owe this point to Hahn, *EKK* 2, 40.

[62] On the legal aspects of this, cf. Sherwin-White, *Roman Society*, pp. 48–70.

[63] As has often been observed (e.g., Lightfoot, *Biblical Essays*, pp. 160f.), John's similar use of '*the* cohort' in 18.3, 12 may reflect knowledge of the fact (cf. Josephus, *BJ* 2.12.1, § 224; 5.5.8, §. 244) that prior to the Jewish war a Roman cohort was regularly quartered in the Turris Antonia and always mounted guard to prevent disorders at the feasts. After 70 a radical change took place in the garrisoning of Palestine; cf. Schürer, *History*, I, pp. 366f.

[64] *John*, p. 584.

Paul is a declared Roman citizen (22.25–29) and is in Roman
protective custody, he is on a charge before the Jewish high court
(22.30; 23.28f.), and it remains within the power of the Sanhedrin
to apply to the commandant to bring him before them (23.15).
Subsequently Lysias reports: 'I found that the accusation had to do
with the controversial matters in their own law, but there was no
charge against him meriting death or imprisonment' (23.29).[65] That
would have been the end of it as far as the Romans were concerned,
were it not that, thanks to information received ($\mu\eta\nu\upsilon\theta\epsilon\iota\sigma\eta\varsigma$, the
same technical term as in John 11.57), a plot against Paul's life had
been uncovered (23.30).

With Jesus too, since the threat of civil violence turned out to be
equally unfounded, that would have been the end of it for the
Romans – *had not the Jews been able to represent their religious
charge of blasphemy as at the same time the political one of high
treason*. And this is really the nub of the whole affair. The strength
of the Johannine account is that it gives, I believe a better
explanation of the relationship of the two than any other.

All the gospels agree that Jesus went to his death on a political
charge and yet that the participants in the drama, the Jewish
leaders, Pilate, and Jesus himself, all knew in their hearts that this
was a false charge. The real accusation lay elsewhere, yet it was the
political one that could, and must, be made to stick. As Dodd
succinctly sums up the situation,

> The priests had a double aim in view: Jesus must be removed by
> death; he must also be discredited. The death sentence therefore
> must be legally and formally pronounced by the governor. The
> surest way to secure such a sentence would be to cite the
> Defendant on a charge of political disaffection. But such a
> charge would by no means discredit him in the eyes of the Jewish
> public; quite the contrary. It was for the Sanhedrin to show that

---

[65]This had not prevented the commandant, like the magistrates at Philippi
(16.22), ordering a preliminary flogging (22.24f.), and it is interesting that it comes at
the same stage and is described by the same term ($\mu\alpha\sigma\tau\iota\zeta\epsilon\iota\nu$) as in John's account of
the trial of Jesus (19.1). Yet it is regularly asserted (e.g. by B. A. Mastin in Sanders and
Mastin, *John*, pp. 399f.; and B. Lindars, *The Gospel of John*, London 1972, pp. 363f.)
that John has deliberately or ignorantly turned upside down the Markan-Matthaean
order, where, quite properly, the (severer) *flagellatio* occurs after the sentence (Matt.
27.26; Mark 15.15) as a regular part of the preliminaries to crucifixion (cf. Josephus,
BJ 2.14.9, §§ 306–8; 5.11.1, § 449; Livy xxxiii. 36; Sherwin-White, *Roman Law*, pp.
27f.). Luke (23.16, 22) also mentions the threat of a preliminary beating in the same
place as John, but we are not told whether it was carried out.

he was guilty of an offence against religion.[66]

The one charge that met both requirements was that of claiming to be the Christ, which could be interpreted from the religious point of view as the blasphemous one of making himself Son of God (John 10.33–36;[67] cf. 5.18; 19.7) and from the political point of view as the seditious one of pretending to the throne. And the gospels agree on the fatal way in which these three terms, Christ, Son of God and King, could slide, or be made to slide, into one another (Matt. 26.63; 27.42f.; Mark 14.61; 15.32; Luke 22.67–70; 23.2, 35, 37; John 1.41, 49; 18.33; 19.7).

The first requirement of any satisfactory account of the trial is that it should be able to show how the political charge, though recognized to be disingenuous, could still have seemed plausible. The strength of an interpretation like Brandon's is that Jesus' position must have been *patient* of the construction put upon it in Luke 23.2, 'We found this man subverting our nation, opposing the payment of taxes to Caesar and claiming to be Messiah, a king.' The weakness of such an interpretation is that it does not do justice to the knowledge that this construction was fundamentally a lie. This is nowhere made clearer than in John. Not only is the reader appraised unequivocally of the inner truth, but the disingenuousness of the Jewish leadership over their real charge against Jesus is subtly conveyed. They begin their dealings with Pilate by trying to get away without being specific at all: 'Pilate went out to them and asked, "What charge do you bring against this man?" "If he were not a criminal", they replied, "we should not have brought him before you"' (18.29f.). When that fails, as it must, they go for the capital charge of treason (18.33–19.6). When Pilate finds no case on that one, they fall back on the real offence (for the Jews) of his blasphemous claim to be Son of God (19.7) – though taking the trouble to dress up their charge in the pagan terms of being a son of God (υἱὸν θεοῦ)[68] or a θεῖος ἄνθρωπος and thus play on the Roman prefect's fear of the supernatural (19.8f., cf. Matt. 27.19).[69] Finally,

[66] *Founder*, p. 156. For the interrelation of the religious and political charges, cf. also Brown, *John*, p. 798–802.

[67] Cf. the βλασφημία here with that in Mark 14.64 = Matt. 26.65. It appears to attach to the theological implications of 'Son of God' rather than of 'Christ' (cf. Luke 22.66–71).

[68] Dodd, *Historical Tradition*, pp. 113f., rightly draws attention to the absence of articles here – though I would hold that they should be omitted with strong manuscript support, in 10.36, where, for different (and this time Jewish) reasons, the logic of the argument equally requires it (cf. my *Human Face of God*, p. 189). The absence of articles in 1.14 and 5.27 shows that John's usage in this regard is far from accidental (cf. also Mark 15.39 = Matt. 27.54).

[69] Cf. Dodd, *Historical Tradition*, p. 114: 'The whole episode therefore is entrely in character, and to all appearances it owes nothing to theological motives. Thus in the one place where the course of the narrative directly invites theological exploitation, it remains on a strictly matter-of-fact level. This is surely a very remarkable feature in a work so dominated by theological interests.'

with that getting them nowhere, they return to the political tack and outmanoeuvre Pilate with the utterly cynical claim of being more loyal to Caesar than he (19.12–16).

Of the three charges in the Lukan indictment – that Jesus was a disturber of the peace, a rebel against Rome, and a claimant to the throne of Israel – it is the last which stands out, and upon which alone Pilate seizes (Luke 23.3; though cf. 23.14). The trial turns on his supposed claim to kingship (Mark 15.2 and pars.; John 18.33): it is not simply that he is one more insurrectionary like Barabbas (Mark 15.7; Luke 23.19; John 18.40) or the two others crucified with him (Matt. 27.38; Mark 15.27). The gospels are unanimous that he was condemned to execution as a messianic pretender to the throne of Israel, 'the king of the Jews' (Mark 15.26 and pars.; John 19.19). They all agree too that he did not express it in this way himself, but threw the question back when it was put to him with 'The words are yours' (Mark 15.2 and pars.; John 18.37). Pilate's refusal therefore, according to John (19.21f.), to alter the *titulus* at the request of the Jews to 'He said, I am king of the Jews' was entirely correct. It was not he who said it but they – as Mark also makes Pilate insist: 'the man *you call* the king of the Jews' (15.12). Yet, for John, in the deepest and truest sense he *was* 'the king of the Jews'. So Pilate is made to testify to it. As Dodd put it earlier,[70] with a true sense of the juridical context in which the whole drama is being played, 'He is thus, as it were, subpoenaed as an unwilling witness to Christ's authority, as Son of Man, to judge the world (as Caiaphas was subpoenaed to testify that He died to gather the scattered children of God [11.50–2]).'

No one is arguing that the Johannine account of the trial or of anything else is to be assessed primarily by the canons of factual accuracy. That indeed is to judge things 'as the eyes see' (7.24), 'by worldly standards' (8.15), rather than with true discernment, and inevitably to misunderstand and misrepresent. John is concerned primarily with theological verity rather than with historical verisimilitude.[71] Yet, once again, it is the truth of the history that he claims to present, not of a fictitious tale. So we may end with Dodd's concluding assessment of the Johannine trial scene:

> Here we have for the first time an account which, though it leaves some gaps, is coherent and consistent, with a high degree of

---

[70] *Interpretation*, p. 436.
[71] For the elaboration of this, cf. my 'The Use of the Fourth Gospel for Christology Today' in B. Lindars and S. S. Smalley, eds., *Christ and Spirit in the New Testament: Studies in Honour of C. F. D. Moule*, Cambridge 1973, pp. 61–78; re-printed as ch. 10 below.

verisimilitude.... It is pervaded with a lively sense for the situation as it was in the last half-century before the extinction of Jewish local autonomy. It is aware of the delicate relations between the native and the imperial authorities. It reflects a time when the dream of an independent Judaea under its own king had not yet sunk to the level of a chimera, and when the messianic ideal was not a theologumenon but impinged on practical politics, and the bare mention of a 'king of the Jews' stirred violent emotions; a time, moreover, when the constant preoccupation of the priestly holders of power under Rome was to damp down any first symptoms of such emotions. These conditions were present in Judaea before AD 70, and not later, and not elsewhere. This, I submit, is the true *Sitz im Leben* of the essential elements in the Johannine trial narrative.[72]

The case we have been arguing does not depend on claiming that John alone gives us the truth, or that his account is distinctively different. Indeed the argument has at most points been that it is he who enables us to make full sense of the synoptists, even when he diverges from them. Yet it is not primarily in additional information, however valuable and illuminating, that his contribution lies, but in the interpretation that he allows us to see in, rather than imposes upon, the common story. In particular he draws out the fascinating and fateful ambiguities, religious and political, inherent in the categories in which the person and work of Christ were compassed. I believe therefore that Cullmann was correct in saying that his reconstruction in *Jesus and the Revolutionaries*, based as it is on material supplied by the synoptists, receives its most succinct and profound expression in John. Whether John has got it right (if he has)

---

[72] *Historical Tradition*, p. 120. Cf. C. H. Turner, *Studies in Early Church History*, Oxford and New York 1912, p. 191: 'I should feel minded to urge every student who wants to understand the meaning of the Roman empire in history to master two brief passages in the Bible, the story of the opening of relations by Judas Maccabaeus with Rome in I Macc. 8, and the fourth evangelist's account of the trial before Pilate.' Sherwin-White, *Roman Society*, p. 47, concludes: 'After the survey of the legal and administrative background it is apparent that there is no historical improbability in the Johannine variations of this sort from the synoptic version.' He strongly defends (p. 32–43) the historicity of John 18.31, 'we are not allowed to put any man to death', which is crucial also to the credibility of the synoptic accounts. So too Dauer, *Passionsgeschichte*, pp. 143–5.

Since completing this study I have seen an unpublished paper. 'The Trial of Jesus', by Fergus G. B. Millar, editor of the *Journal of Roman Studies*, from which he kindly allows me to quote. In it he says, 'I wish to suggest that the most convincing account we have of the events leading up to the Crucifixion is that of John. ... It is John who allows us to see what really happened.'

from theological insight or from inside historical knowledge, or both, depends upon judgments about his tradition that involve far wider considerations. But that 'his witness is true' on the fundamental issue of the relationship of the spiritual to the political is a claim which must be judged to have stood the test.

IO

The Use of the Fourth Gospel
for Christology Today[1]

Nothing colours the presuppositions lying beyind the christology of an age or an author more than the position given to the evidence of the Fourth Gospel. In the patristic age it was taken for granted that texts from this gospel were to be regarded as primary data of the problem which had to be solved.[2] No christology which did not do justice, for instance, to both the sayings 'I and the Father are one' and 'my Father is greater than I' or which failed to posit in Jesus both genuine human limitations and a consciousness of pre-existent glory could satisfy the 'facts'. It was material from John which more than any other compelled, and tested, the doctrine of the Two Natures in its various forms. (Most of the illustrations, for instance, in the *Tome* of Leo of what it meant for Jesus to do some things as God and some things as man are drawn from this gospel.) Still a century ago so liberal a theologian as Schleiermacher regarded the Fourth Gospel as having priority in date and authority,[3] and his picture of the absolute, changeless, sinless perfection of one who did not have his origin in this world clearly reflects this – though ironically the Fourth Gospel really gives remarkably little basis for the sinlessness of

[1]First published in B. Lindars and S. S. Smalley, eds., *Christ and Spirit in the New Testament: Studies in Honour of C. F. D. Moule*, Cambridge 1973, pp. 61–78. As the title implies, this question raised itself for me in the course of preparing my Hulsean Lectures on a christology for today. I have therefore myself used certain sections of it in the published version of these lectures, *The Human Face of God*.

[2]Cf. M. F. Wiles, *The Spiritual Gospel*, Cambridge and New York 1960; T. E. Pollard, *Johannine Christology and the Early Church*, Cambridge 1970.

[3]Cf. A. Schweitzer, *The Quest of the Historical Jesus*, ET London [3]1954, pp. 66f.: 'It is, according to him, only in this Gospel that the consciousness of Jesus is truly reflected', since it alone has behind it the authority of an eyewitness. 'The contradictions could not be explained if all our Gospels stood equally close to Jesus. But if John stands closer than the others. . . .'

Christ.[4] Even up to the First World War it was possible for a person like Bishop Frank Weston to write his great book *The One Christ* as though the data for the problem of the self-consciousness of Christ were still basically set, largely by the Fourth Gospel, in the way that they had been for Cyril of Alexandria. What Weston claimed to do, with some success, was to produce a more adequate hypothesis to account for the same evidence: he did not question, let alone set aside, the evidence of John. 'The most important evidence', he wrote, 'to the divine nature of the Christ is that which is based upon the revelation of His self-consciousness, His knowledge of His pre-existence, and His memory of the state of eternal glory.'[5]

The swing away from this position, which of course had set in in liberal circles long before Weston,[6] has been almost total. It hardly needs illustration to show that the prevailing assumption in recent christological writing is that the only secure foundation (if indeed there is *any* secure foundation) for the kind of way Jesus thought, spoke or acted is the synoptic material. Among dozens of judgments that might be quoted I cite two from theologians who are far from extreme. The first is W. R. Matthews in *The Problem of Christ in the Twentieth Century*:

> There are still eminent authorities who hold that the Gospel of John is a primary historical source for the life and words of Jesus. And yet I must express my clear view that they are advocating a lost cause. . . . No: the supreme value of the Fourth Gospel lies else-where. . . . It is the primary document for all Christian mysticism and it is the noblest landmark in the course of the development of Christian doctrine.[7]

The second is Hugh Montefiore writing in *Soundings*:

[4]The key text, John 8.46, classically translated 'Which of you convicteth me of sin?', is much more likely in the context to have the limited reference given it in the NEB: 'Which of you can prove me in the wrong?' In fact, nowhere more than in this gospel is the opinion canvassed that Jesus is bad (7.12; 9.16, 24; 10.21, 33) quite apart from the more frequent suggestions that he is mad or unbalanced (2.17; 6.42; 7.20; 8.48, 52; 10.20).

[5]Op. cit., London ²1914, p. 38.

[6]Cf. P. W. Schmiedel, *The Johannine Writings*, ET London and New York 1908, whose conclusion is that the gospel 'is 'dominated by complete indifference as to the faithfulness of a record; that importance is attached only to giving as impressive a representation as possible of certain ideas; and that the whole is sustained by a reverence for Jesus which has lost every standard for measuring what can really happen' (p. 139).

[7]Op. cit., London 1950, New York 1951, pp. 7f.

The testimony of Jesus himself is far more important than the interpretation that the early Church put on his person and status, for, if his claims about himself are true, he alone would have been in a position to know his relationship to his Father. Here the challenge of higher criticism must be accepted, and an attempt must be made to distinguish the words of Jesus from the logia of the Gospels; and, although the case cannot be argued in this essay, the synoptic gospels must be set apart from the Fourth Gospel: only the former may confidently be used for this purpose.[8]

On the Continent the swing away has, of course, been still more pronounced, but even so relatively conservative a scholar as Günther Bornkamm says at the beginning of his *Jesus of Nazareth*:

The gospel according to John has so different a character in comparison with the other three, and is to such a degree the product of a developed theological reflection, that we can only treat it as a secondary source.[9]

And it has so far largely been ignored in the 'new quest' of the historical Jesus.[10]

There is another, equally powerful school which would take the line that since *all* the gospels contain practically no history worth mentioning John and the synoptists can for doctrinal purposes be used more or less indifferently. Of this Paul Tillich is representative:

It was the desire of so-called *liberal theology* to go behind the biblical records of Jesus as the Christ. In such an attempt the first three Gospels emerge as by far the most important part of the New Testament, and this is what they became in the estimation of many modern theologians. But the moment when one realises that the Christian faith cannot be built on such a foundation, the Fourth Gospel and the Epistles become equally important with the Synoptics.[11]

---

[8]'Towards a Christology for Today', *Soundings*, ed. A. R. Vidler, Cambridge and New York 1962, pp. 157–8.

[9]Op. cit., ET London 1960, New York 1961, p. 14.

[10]It is characteristic that R. S. Barbour's excellent little survey and critique should be called *Traditio-Historical Criticism of the Gospels*, London 1972, and then confine itself, without explanation, entirely to the synoptic gospels. Of the one book mentioned by Norman Perrin in his *What is Redaction Criticism?*, Philadelphia and London 1970, as applying this method, so far, to the Gospel of John, J. Louis Martyn's *History and Theology in the Fourth Gospel*, New York 1968, he writes, almost in commendation (!), that 'both the history and the theology mentioned in the title are those of the evangelist and his church, not of Jesus' (p. 84).

[11]*Systematic Theology* II, Chicago and London 1957, p. 135.

As is well known, a considerable critical reaction has more recently set in in New Testament circles against writing off the historical value of the Johannine tradition – a reaction with which I have long been in sympathy.[12] It is conveniently summarized in A. M. Hunter's *According to John*[13] and documented in a masterly way in C. H. Dodd's *Historical Tradition in the Fourth Gospel,* which is the more impressive because he came to his conclusions from a very different position. At all sorts of points, from the broadest outline of the ministry to the minutest topographical detail, the Fourth Gospel is coming to be seen as preserving tradition not only in regard to the events of Jesus' life but also in regard to his teaching which has claim to go back at least as far as and sometimes further than anything in the synoptic gospels. Nevertheless, when it comes to the central issue of all, the picture which John gives us of Jesus and the use that we can make of it for doctrine, the criteria have not, I think, been adequately reassessed. Clearly the clock cannot be put back to the pre-critical position, but do the recent emphases make no difference? What is the proper, as opposed to the improper, use of the Johannine material today? This seems to me to depend upon clarifying what the author's own concerns really were and what they were not.

We may fairly take as representative his key christological text from the climax of the prologue: 'The word became flesh: he came to dwell among us, and we saw his glory, such glory as befits the Father's only Son, full of grace and truth.'[14] Though it is only in the prologue, which I believe the author to have added later,[15] that the λόγος terminology is used, the theme of the whole gospel is the interrelation of the two levels of reality – λόγος, spirit, the eternal glory of the divine, on the one hand, and flesh, this world of space and time, on the other. The great affirmation of this writer is that they coincide in Christ: the Word becomes flesh and the glory of the invisible God is seen and heard and handled. Both the spirit and the flesh are of equal importance and must be taken with equal seriousness. Flesh without spirit is of no significance (3.6; 6.63), but the flesh is utterly indispensable as the

[12]See my lecture 'The New Look on the Fourth Gospel' given to the international conference on 'The Four Gospels' at Oxford in 1957, reprinted in my *Twelve New Testament Studies,* pp. 94–106, and my essay 'The Place of the Fourth Gospel' in *The Roads Converge,* ed. P. Gardner-Smith, London and Toronto 1963.

[13]London and Philadelphia 1968; cf. A. J. B. Higgins, *The Historicity of the Fourth Gospel,* London 1960, and R. E. Brown, 'The Problem of Historicity in John', *New Testament Essays,* Milwaukee 1965, London 1966, pp. 143–67.

[14]1.14 (NEB). On the proper translation of this see below.

[15]'The Relation of the Prologue to the Gospel of St John', *NTS* 9, 1962–3, pp. 120–9; reprinted as ch. 5 above.

locus of the revelation. The overriding purpose of the gospel is to show these coinciding and coinhering in Jesus as the Christ, the Son of God (20.31).

Beside the truth of this nothing else matters. John is content to hold them together, to allow one to shine through the other, to let the flesh be 'diaphanous' of the spirit (to use Teilhard de Chardin's word), so that the glory is visible in and through it. About the verity of this he cares intensely. That in the process verisimilitude suffers he cares little. For flesh that is diaphanous does not look like flesh: the shining through of the divine gives a docetic appearance. Hence the sense that many have felt, like John Knox[16] and still more Ernst Käsemann,[17] that John does not give us a genuinely human Christ at all. And this indeed was clearly the earliest reaction. John was adopted by the Gnostics as 'their' gospel and the stress in the Johannine epistles on Jesus come in the flesh (I John 1.1; 4.2; II John 7) must be seen as reaction to the docetic impression his teaching evidently provoked. But the very fact that the reaction was so vehement suggests that this is genuinely a *misinterpretation* of his intention: indeed for him it is very 'antichrist'.[18]

Perhaps the balance can best be held by saying that John is insistent, with equal emphasis, on the Word and the flesh, but is ready by comparison to sit light to the mediating connections involved in the 'becoming'. He is prepared to treat freely all the questions of 'how', the processes of coming into being and coming to know, the lines of temporal and psychological development. In this gospel there is little interest if any in the progression by which men reach the truth

[16] *The Humanity and the Divinity of Christ*, Cambridge and New York 1967, p. 62: 'One may affirm the humanity as a formal fact and then proceed so to define or portray it as to deny its reality in any ordinarily accepted sense.' Cf. E. L. Titus, 'The Fourth Gospel and the Historical Jesus', in *Jesus and the Historian: Written in Honor of Ernest Cadman Colwell*, ed. F. T. Trotter, Philadelphia 1968, pp. 98–113.

[17] *The Testament of Jesus*, ET London and Philadelphia 1968. He sees in this gospel an unashamedly 'naive docetism' (p. 26), 'the consistent presentation of Jesus as God walking on the face of the earth' (p. 73). 'The Church committed an error when it declared the Gospel to be orthodox' (p. 76): 'neither apostolic authorship nor apostolic content can be affirmed for it' (p. 74). See the reply by G. Bornkamm, 'Zur Interpretation des Johannes-Evangeliums', *Geschichte und Glaube*, erster Teil, *Gesammelte Aufsätze*, Band III, Munich 1968, pp. 104–21; cf. S. S. Smalley, 'Diversity and Development in John', *NTS* 17, 1970–1, pp. 278–81.

[18] This reaction in the Johannine epistles is, as Bornkamm points out, completely ignored by Käsemann, who regards them as composed by a different writer as a corrective. But the epistles read as a *recall* to teaching given, not as an attack upon it.

about Jesus. He is acknowledged as Christ from the beginning, (John 1.29, 34, 41, 45, 49) and is prepared to declare himself such (John 4.25f.; 9.36f.). There is no 'messianic secret' in the Markan sense. As Jesus says to the high priest at the end, 'I have spoken openly to all the world . . , I have said nothing in secret' (John 18.20). The fact nevertheless that the truth about him has been veiled and, in contrast with Mark,[19] must remain so even to the disciples till the Spirit brings to clarity what has hitherto come in riddles (John 16.12–15, 25–32), does not mean that all along the light has not been shining in its fullness of grace and truth. Nor is there any sign of growth in Jesus' own awareness. There is no suggestion that he 'learned' from the things he suffered (Heb. 5.8)[20] – merely a waiting for his 'hour' to come and his 'time' to ripen (John 2.4; 7.6, 8, 30; 8.20; 12.23; 13.1; 17.1). Whereas in Hebrews it is he who is subject to $\tau\varepsilon\lambda\varepsilon\acute{\iota}\omega\sigma\iota\varsigma$ or maturation (Heb. 2.10; 5.9; 7.28), there is no hint of this in the $\tau\varepsilon\tau\acute{\varepsilon}\lambda\varepsilon\sigma\tau\alpha\iota$ of John (John 19.30): he never develops. All that we moderns are naturally interested in from the scientific and historical point of view, and in particular from the psychological point of view, is fundamentally uninteresting to this evangelist. He is consumed with the one need to present the truth of Jesus as he has come to know it. And this truth Jesus himself cannot help but express in every word he speaks and every deed he does. They are all 'signs', sacramental of the reality which shines through him. By comparison *how* he thought or spoke is entirely subordinate. He speaks 'Johannine' language –in the same way as the Italian painter paints him as an Italian.[21] John is interested in verity not verisimilitude, in the real not the realistic, in history not historicism. And he is not worried by anachronisms. Indeed the whole gospel is deliberately anachronistic: it is an attempt see Jesus *from* the end, from the age of the Spirit who alone clarifies, declares and brings to remembrance[22] what was the truth all along. And if it was the truth all along, then that is what it is important to present, even if no one recognized it at the time.

It is no wonder therefore that by the standards of verisimilitude the gospel *looks* docetic, static and unhistorical. Indeed, taken literally, as a biography, it *is* docetic, and it is not in the least surprising that this has been the charge it has invited from the beginning. Yet we should do

---

[19]Mark 4.11. I take $\grave{\varepsilon}\nu$ $\pi\alpha\rho\alpha\beta o\lambda\alpha\tilde{\iota}\varsigma$ here to mean originally the same as $\grave{\varepsilon}\nu$ $\pi\alpha\rho o\iota\mu\acute{\iota}\alpha\iota\varsigma$ still means in John 16.25, as 'dark sayings'.

[20]For a justification of this, cf. ch. 11 below, pp. .

[21]It is notoriously difficult to know in ch. 3, for instance, where the speech of Jesus ends and the comment of the evangelist begins. See the footnotes in the RSV at John 3.15 and 30.

[22]John 14.25–6; 15.26; 16.12–15, 23–30; cf. 2.22; 20.9.

the author the justice of accepting that such a judgment is in his eyes a fearful misunderstanding. For this point of view is not the point of view from which it should be assessed. For that is to judge things 'superficially' (John 7.24), 'by worldly standards' (John 8.15), rather than with true discernment.

Yet, with all this said, this does not mean that John is unconcerned with historicity. Nor is to 'remember', however creatively, to invent. Rather, it is, in the power and truth and freedom of the Spirit, to take the things of Jesus and hold them up to the light, so that the light can transfigure them and show them in their true glory. It is *not* to make up things about Jesus in order to illustrate timeless truths. For John has a profound reverence for history, for happenedness. As the locus of incarnation it cannot be treated lightly or wantonly: it is holy ground. I am not persuaded that he is simply prepared to play ducks and drakes with the history, as many commentators suppose, in the interests of theology.[23] Indeed, so many of the details, especially of location and topography, which have been verified in recent study, have apparently no conceivable theological point or motivation. He has occasion to mention them simply because they were 'there'. At points where he differs from the synoptists (of whom I believe, with an increasing weight of scholarship, his tradition is fundamentally independent) his evidence is to be taken very seriously – e.g. on the early Judaean ministry, the duration of the ministry as a whole, the political significance of the desert feeding, the timing of the cleansing of the temple, the date of the crucifixion, and even, I believe, with Jeremias,[24] the empty tomb tradition. This does not, of course, mean that John is always to be preferred, let alone that every historical statement he makes is correct. But I am convinced he has every claim to be heard as history and not simply as theology.

How then does this comport with his admitted disinterest in empirical realism or historical reconstruction? The lines of demarcation may in practice be thin and difficult to draw and the kind of judgment involved is not the sort that makes easily for objective consensus. But what we can say, straight away, is that John is not evidence, and does not set out to be evidence, of how things looked to Jesus or the disciples or for that matter to anyone else before the resurrection. Nor does John supply material for the reconstruction of Jesus' self-consciousness.[25] The fact that Jesus speaks in this

[23]As a test of his method, see my article 'The "Others" of John 4.38', *Twelve New Testament Studies*, pp. 61–6.

[24]*New Testament Theology*, I, pp. 304f.

[25]Again I would now wish to qualify this remark by distinguishing between 'self-consciousness' and 'self-knowledge'. See ch. 11 below.

gospel of his eternal existence or his pre-incarnate glory or of his heavenly origin and destination, and indeed the whole impression he gives of spiritual aloofness and superiority, not to say of arrogance and megalomania – all this is to be judged not as data for psychological analysis but as declaring the truth that, while unquestionably *a man* in the fullest sense of both words (and no other gospel uses ἄνθρωπος anything like as much of Jesus),[26] he was veridical also of another entire world of being. Like almost every incident and indeed phrase in the Fourth Gospel, Jesus' whole life speaks at two levels of meaning. But the 'how' of the signs and the lines of connection or causation between the flesh and the spirit, the history and the theology, are of utterly subordinate interest. They can therefore be written up (in every sense of the word) freely and are not to be estimated by the canons of historicism. But equally the events described are not just fiction nor is the Fourth Evangelist writing a novel, not even a historical novel.

Where in particular the line is to be drawn is bound, as I said, to differ from one assessment to another. But I am sure there is all the difference between saying that a line *is* there, however difficult to determine, and saying that there is no line at all. And, greatly daring, I should like to try to indicate where I would come down, not on subordinate incidents, but on the total impression given by the Johannine portrait of Jesus.

Reading the gospel through at a sitting, one is left with the overwhelming impression of a man whose life was lived in *absolutely intimate dependence*[27] (stressing all three words) upon God as his Father. Everything Jesus was and said and did has its source in this utter closeness of spiritual relationship which he describes as sonship or 'sent-ness'.[28] Now clearly, as I have said, the *way* this is described is governed not by psychological realism but by theological reality – though this is *not* the same as saying that it is to be interpreted (as we tend instinctively to do with this vocabulary of 'the Father' and 'the Son') in terms of Nicene ontology. Indeed, even in regard to language we are coming to recognize that John is nearer to source than we should recently have dared to think, and that he is drawing out the remembered tradition rather than simply imposing upon Jesus categories of his own. Particularly is this proving to be so where the

[26]The figures are: Matt. 3; Mark 2; Luke 6 (the Matthaean and Markan parallels, plus 4 times on the lips of Pilate, with ἀνήρ once); John 15 (and ἀνήρ once).

[27]For the stress on the dependence of Christ in this gospel, cf. J. E. Davey, *The Jesus of St John*, London 1958.

[28]John 3.17, 34; 4.34; 5.23f., 30, 36–38; 6.29, 38, 44, 57; 7.16, 18, 28f., 33; 8.16, 18, 26, 29, 42; 9.4; 10.36; 11.42; 12.44f., 49; 13.20; 14.24; 15.21; 16.5; 17.3, 8, 18, 21, 23, 25; 20.21.

vocabulary is most theological, and on the face of it most 'Johan-nine'.

Nothing is more characteristic of John's style than such sayings as:

> The Father loves the Son and has entrusted him with all authority (3.35);
>
> I know him because I come from him and he it is who sent me (7.29);
>
> The Father knows me and I know the Father (10.15);
>
> Jesus, well aware that the Father had entrusted everything to him (13.3);
>
> O righteous Father, although the world does not know thee, I know thee, and these men know that thou didst send me (17.25).

Yet these are all variations and meditations upon the theme represented in the Q saying of Matt. 11.27 (Luke 10.22):

> Everything is entrusted to me by my Father;
> and no one knows the Son but the Father,
> and no one knows the Father but the Son
> and those to whom the Son may choose to reveal him.

Now Jeremias has convincingly shown[29] that, so far from this being a metaphysical 'bolt from the Johannine sky',[30] that has dropped unaccountably into the synoptic tradition, it is in origin parabolic language, the 'the' before father and son being not ontological but generic – as in 'the sower went forth to sow' (Mark 4.3) or 'the grain of wheat remains solitary' (John 12.24), where English idiom requires an 'a'. The Q saying is a parable of the intimate knowledge that only a father and a son have of each other (this was before the generation gap!), which Jesus is using to describe the *abba*-relation-ship to God that he is claiming for himself, and ideally for every child of man. Of course this parabolic language is interpreted or allego-rized – and correctly so – by the evangelists to designate Jesus in his unique relationship to God – just as, in the parable of the Wicked Husbandmen (Mark 12.1–9), the son who is heir to the estate in contrast with the servants clearly stands for Jesus. Indeed, I believe it is inconceivable that Jesus did not intend it to be taken thus – the story having no point unless in some sense it is a picture of God's

[29] *The Central Message of the New Testament*, ET London and New York 1965, pp. 23–6.
[30] K. von Hase, *Die Geschichte Jesu*, Leipzig ²1876, p. 422.

dealings with Israel through the prophets and now through himself.[31] 'The Father' and 'the Son' thus come to stand in Mark 13.42 and Q (Matt. 11.27 = Luke 10.22) as in John simply as proper names for God and Christ. But it is in John that the original parabolic foundation of this language is still most clearly visible beneath the theological surface.

In fact where he first introduces it, at the climax of the prologue, it is specifically in the form of a simile from human relationships: 'glory *as* of a father's only son' (δόξαν ὡς μονογενοῦς παρὰ πατρός).[32] There are no articles in the Greek, and yet they are constantly supplied by translators and interpreters (Moffatt's 'glory such as an only son enjoys from his father' being a rare exception). The simile was already a familiar one in describing Israel in relation to God: 'Thy chastisement is upon us as upon a first-born, only son.'[33] I have not been able yet to find a precise parallel for an only son being called his father's glory.[34] But δόξα and εἰκών were used as equivalents in contemporary Judaism to mean 'reflection',[35] as in I Cor. 11.7: 'Man is the image and glory of God; but the woman is the glory of man.'[36]

[31]Cf. Dodd, *The Parables of the Kingdom*, pp. 124–32. This is not, of course, to say that there is no pointing up or elaboration in the transmission. Indeed, Dodd's reconstruction of the original form of the story as telling of two servants followed by a son (Mark 12.5 being later expansion to fit the history of Israel) has been strikingly vindicated by the version in the *Gospel of Thomas* 66. See ch. 2 above.

[32]John 1.14; cf. the ὡς υἱός of Heb. 3.6.

[33]Ps. Sol. 18.4; cf. 13.8. For the metaphor applied to Israel, cf. II Esdras 6.58, 'We thy people whom thou hast called thy first-born, the only-begotten, thy beloved', and, earlier, Exod. 4.22; Ps. 89.27; Jer. 31.9.

[34]Prov. 17.6 has 'the glory of sons is their father', but here 'glory' means 'pride', as in Sir Walter Scott's 'his mother's pride, his father's glory'. The nearest parallel I know to what I believe to be the *sense* is Ecclus. 30.4, where it is said of a son, 'When the father dies it is as if he were still alive, for he has left a copy of himself (ὅμοιον γὰρ αὐτῷ) behind him'.

[35]See J. Jervell, *Imago Dei*, Göttingen 1960, especially pp. 174f., 180, 299f., 325f. He takes this to be the meaning in John 1.14, but does not notice it as a simile from human relationships. I am grateful to Professor Moule for putting me on to this reference, and indeed for supplying, and gently correcting, so much else. See also L. H. Brockington, 'The Septuagintal Background to the New Testament Use of δόξα', *Studies in the Gospels: Essays in Memory of R. H. Lightfoot*, ed. D. E. Nineham, Oxford 1955, pp. 7f., and the extensive literature cited by R. P. Martin, *Carmen Christi: Philippians 2.5–11 in Recent Interpretation and in the Setting of Early Christian Worship*, Cambridge and New York 1967, pp. 102–19.

[36]Cf. II Cor. 3.18, 'We all reflect as in a mirror the glory of the Lord; thus we are transfigured into his image, from glory to glory', and 8.23 (as rendered in NEB margin), 'They are delegates of our congregations: they reflect Christ (δόξα Χριστοῦ)'. For the association of εἰκών and δόξα: Rom. 1.23; I Cor. 11.7; 15.43, 49; II Cor. 3.18; 4.4; of εἰκών and πρωτότοκος: Col. 1.15; of δόξα and υἱός: John 14.13; 17.1; Rom. 8.14–23; 9.4; Eph. 1.5–6; Heb. 2.10; and of all four words: Rom. 8.29–30 and Heb. 1.2–6 (where χαρακτήρ replaces εἰκών).

The idea behind John 1.14 is therefore almost certainly that the incarnate Christ is the exact counterpart or reflection of God, his spit and image, as we should say, like an only son of his father. Indeed, words used by Montefiore in exegesis of Heb. 1.3[37] get precisely what I believe John is here saying: 'As a son may be said to reflect his father's character, so the Son is the refulgence of his Father's glory, and so the exact representation of God's being.' But what is introduced as a simile in v. 14 is already fully allegorized by v. 18, especially if the astonishing μονογενὴς θεός, 'the only one who is himself God', is indeed the right reading.

At other points too in the gospel the parabolic basis of this father–son language still shows through. Dodd has argued this of John 5.19–20,[38] where, again transposing from the definite to the English indefinite article, we have what he calls the parable of the Apprentice:

A son can do nothing on his own;
he does only what he sees his father doing:
what father does, son does;
For a father loves his son and shows him all his trade.[39]

There is also what must be recognized[40] as the parable of the Servant and the Son in 8.35:

A servant has no permanent standing in the household,[41]
but a son belongs to it always.[42]

Moreover, nowhere in the New Testament are we closer than in the Fourth Gospel to the fundamental Hebraic use of sonship to designate not an absolute status or title but a functional relationship

[37]*The Epistle to the Hebrews* (Black's New Testament Commentaries), London and New York 1964, ad loc.

[38]'Une parabole cachée dans le quatrième Évangile', *RHPR*, 1962, nos. 2–3, pp. 107–15; *Historical Tradition*, p. 386.

[39]Cf. Phil. 2.22, 'He has been at my side . . . like a son working under his father'.

[40]Dodd, *Historical Tradition*, pp. 380–2.

[41]Cf. 15.15, 'A servant does not know what his master is about', which is clearly parabolic.

[42]The same contrasts occur in the synoptic parables of the Prodigal Son (Luke 15.19, 'I am no longer fit to be called your son; treat me as one of your paid servants'; 15.31, 'My boy, you are always with me, and everything I have is yours') and the Wicked Husbandmen (Mark 12.1–9, where the son is the heir while the servants are thrown out.). The Johannine point of the freedom enjoyed by the son of the house (8.36) is reflected in the parable of Jesus' other great figure for God, the king, in Matt. 17.25f.: '"What do you think, Simon? From whom do kings of the earth take toll or tribute? From their sons or from others?" And when he said, "From others", Jesus said to him: "Then the sons are free".'

marked by character. This comes out very plainly in the dialogue that follows in 8.37–47. To be a son is to show the character, to reproduce the thought and action, of another, whether it be Abraham, or the Devil, or God. To claim therefore to be a son of God is not blasphemy, as the Jews suppose. Their Bible should have taught them better. This is made explicit in Jesus' reply in 10.34–38:

> Is it not written in your Law, 'I said: You are gods'? Those are called gods to whom the word of God was delivered – and Scripture cannot be set aside.[43] Then why do you charge me with blasphemy because I, consecrated and sent into the world by the Father, said 'I am a son of God'?[44] If I am not acting as my Father would, do not believe me. But if I am, accept the evidence of my deeds, even if you do not believe me, so that you may recognize and know that the Father is in me, and I in the Father.

This argument which places Jesus on exactly the same metaphysical level as every other son of God yet attests him functionally unique, because he alone 'always does what is acceptable to him' (John 8.29), could not have been invented later,[45] nor even, I believe, in a Greek-thinking milieu.[46] It carries us back as near to source as we are likely to get – to very early Jewish-Christian

[43]This is not such an artificial argument as it sounds to us. Those who are called 'gods' in Ps. 82.6, which Jesus quotes, are judges. (The interpretation of them as angels by J. A. Emerton, *JTS*, n.s. 11, 1960, pp. 329–32, and 17, 1966, pp. 399–401, even if made in Judaism, fits the context neither of the Psalm (cf. vv. 2–4) nor of John (cf. 10.33, 'a mere man').) And the judges are called 'God' (cf. Exod. 21.6; 22.8f., 28) because they 'represent' him, just as Jesus is claiming to do. Indeed H. Odeberg, *The Fourth Gospel*, Chicago 1928, Uppsala 1929, p. 292, argues that in using the phrase 'your law' (10.34; cf. 8.17; 15.25) Jesus is not saying something un-Jewish (as is often supposed) but is claiming to stand in the same relation to the *Torah* as his Father (cf. 7.16–22). While the Jews say 'our law' (7.51; cf. 18.31; 19.7), God says 'my law' or 'your law'.

[44]Again no articles, except in MS readings that are evidently secondary. Their absence would not in itself be decisive for the sense, for 'definite predicate nouns which precede the verb usually lack the article' (C. F. D. Moule, *An Idiom Book of New Testament Greek*, Cambridge and New York 1953, p. 115, citing E. C., Colwell's rule). But the logic of the passage would be destroyed if Jesus were here claiming to be *the* son of God in a sense that could not be true of the men of the Old Testament.

[45]So too Hunter, op. cit. p. 94.

[46]Cf. J. H. Bernard, *St John*, ad loc: 'The argument is one which would never have occurred to a Greek Christian, and its presence here reveals behind the narrative a genuine reminiscence of one who remembered how Jesus argued with the Rabbis on their own principles.'

controversy in Palestine, if not to Jesus himself. Historically we cannot say more, nor, I think, less.[47]

This does not mean, of course, that in theological reflection John does not see Christ as *also* being unique – a distinction he recognizes by reserving the word 'son' for Jesus and 'children of God' for Christians.[48] But, unlike later dogmaticians, he shows no awareness of a contradiction or even of a tension at this point. Indeed it is of the essence of his insight into the incarnation that moral affinity and metaphysical union should not be seen as the alternatives they so

---

[47]Cf. Dodd on the relation between John 10.15, 'The Father knows me and I know the Father', and Matt. 11.27 = Luke 10.22: 'The saying we are now considering belongs to the earliest strain of tradition to which we can hope to penetrate, since it can be traced to the period before the formation of the common source (whether oral or written) of Matthew and Luke (Q), and the evidence suggests that before any written record of it appeared it had developed variant forms, three of which appear independently in Matthew, Luke and John, while others appear in ancient versions and patristic citations', *Historical Tradition*, p. 361. It would be tempting to pursue the implications of this for the origins of the Johannine linguistic tradition. Jeremias makes the comment: 'Matt. 11.27 is not a Johannine verse amidst the synoptic material, but rather one of those sayings from which Johannine theology developed. Without such points of departure within the synoptic tradition it would be an eternal puzzle how Johannine theology could have originated at all' (*Central Message*, p. 25). But if this is so, what comes through John's style cannot merely reflect the coloration of his glass: there must have been something of it in the light itself. The Johannine sayings with close verbal parallels in the other traditions, analysed by Dodd (op. cit. pp. 335–65) as going back at least as far as their synoptic counterparts, raise the question whether their 'Johannine' tinting is any further from the original style of Jesus than, say, the increasingly apocalyptic tone given to it, as I believe, by Mark and Matthew (cf. my *Jesus and His Coming*, p. 94–102). I discussed this, all too briefly, in my essay, 'The Place of the Fourth Gospel', *The Roads Converge*, p. 63–7. To the evidence I assembled there I would add the question raised by W. H. Brownlee, 'Jesus and Qumran', in *Jesus and the Historian*, ed. F. T. Trotter, p. 76: 'The really serious question posed by the Scrolls is whether the two types of vocabulary belonged authentically to Jesus, with a polarization of the two elements taking place in different Gospel traditions: the Synoptics preserving and emphasizing Jesus' ethical teaching in an apocalyptic context and the Fourth Gospel preserving and elaborating his mystical teaching in a dualistic context. Palestinian Judaism contained both elements, not simply in different communities but also in the same community. More than this, apocalypticism and light-darkness dualism were blended together in the same passages.' Of course, in John we are still not reading the *ipsissima verba*, but may we not, in Jeremias' useful distinction, be hearing the *ipsissima vox*? At the end of his discussion of this distinction in his *New Testament Theology* I, p. 37, he formulates the following 'principle of method': 'In the synoptic tradition it is the inauthenticity and not the authenticity of the sayings of Jesus that must be demonstrated.' With every proper regard for the differences of aim I mentioned before, I would ask why this methodological principle needs to be prefaced with the words 'in the synoptic tradition'. *As authenticity is understood in John* (which is certainly not literalistically), I believe it may be just as applicable to his material.

[48]John 1.12; 11.52; I John 3.1–2, 8–10; 5.2.

disastrously were in the subsequent disputes between Antioch and Alexandria. Jesus can say in the same discourse that 'the Father is in me, and I in the Father' (10.38) and 'my Father and I are one' (10.30) *because* he is acting as his Father would (10.37) and his deeds are done in his name (10.25). Again he says in a later discourse (14.9– 10), 'Anyone who has seen me has seen the Father' because 'I am *not* myself the source of the words I speak to you: it is the Father who dwells in me doing his own work'. He is 'God's only son', the very 'exegesis' of the Father (1.18), indeed himself θεός, 'what God is' (1.1), because as a mere man (10.33) he is utterly transparent to *another*, who is greater than himself (14.28) and indeed than all (10.29). The paradox is staggering, and it is no wonder that this christology later fell apart at the seams. But for John there is no antithesis, any more than there is for the author to the Hebrews, between the humanity and the divinity, the historical and the theological.

Yet the question remains, Is this impression which John leaves us of Jesus fundamentally one that is invented or one that is 'remembered' in the pregnant sense in which the evangelist uses that word, of *history really entered into?* I suggest that there is every reason to believe, from his whole theology of history, that the latter is what he intended, and that we should take his intention seriously. In other words, he is elucidating ('What first were guessed as points, I now knew stars')[49] the inexpungeable impression of man whose entire life was lived 'from God',[50] and whose words and actions bespoke a relationship in which he was in the deepest sense 'at home' and where as a truly normal (and *for that reason* unique) human being he 'belonged'.

It is this sense of belonging elsewhere, this sense that the source and ground of his being and acting and speaking is not 'of himself' (5.19, 30; 7.16–18, 28; 12.49), nor 'of this world' (8.23; 17.14, 16; 18.36), but 'from above' (3.31; 8.23), that the evangelist seeks to express, spatially and temporally, in the Hellenistic-Jewish myth of pre-existence. His being is 'with God' (1.1) 'in the bosom of the Father' (1.18); his home is 'in heaven',[51] from which he 'comes down' (John 3.13, 31; 6.33–58) and to which he will return in ascent

---

[49] R. Browning, 'A Death in the Desert', which from his early essay in *Foundations*, ed. B. H. Streeter, London 1913, p. 216, to his *Readings in St John's Gospel* London and New York 1939, p. 17, William Temple called 'the most penetrating interpretation of St John that exists in the English language'.

[50] παρὰ τοῦ θεοῦ: John 6.46; 7.29; 8.26, 40; 9.33; 10.18; 15.15, 26; 16.27; 17.7–8; ἐκ τοῦ θεοῦ: 8.42, 47; 10.32; 16.28; ἀπὸ τοῦ θεοῦ: 3.2; 13.3; 16.30.

[51] John 3.13. But the words ὁ ὢν ἐν τῷ οὐρανῷ, which might be taken to imply that the Son of Man is (really) still in heaven even during the Incarnation, are almost certainly not part of the original text (despite the NEB – against the RSV).

(John 3.13; 6.62; 13.1, 3; 20.17). Equally his ἀρχή or origin is not just the moment of his historical birth, but is before Abraham (John 8.58), before the world (John 17.5, 24), and indeed at the beginning of all things (John 1.1f.).

Take this language literally, whether as history or psychology, let alone the consciousness of it, and you have shattered the conditions of genuine humanity. As John A. Baker has said,[52]

> It is simply not possible at one and the same time to share the common lot of humanity, and to be aware of oneself as one who has existed from everlasting with God and will continue to do so. . . . You cannot have both the Jesus of John 8.58 as a piece of accurate reporting and the doctrine of the Incarnation.

But the crux of the matter is what is meant by 'accurate reporting'. If this refers to the language of 'the flesh', to psychological description, to what can be seen and judged as the eyes see, then of course the conclusion follows. But it is precisely not accuracy of this kind, I submit, that the evangelist is seeking to report. ἀκρίβεια (and its cognates) is characteristically the virtue extolled by Luke–Acts:[53] John's consuming interest is rather in ἀλήθεια and its cognates.[54] Yet as testimony to the impact Jesus made at the deepest spiritual level his report may be properly and profoundly accurate. In this sense we could concur with his own claim that 'his witness is true' (19.35). But, as the context of this claim makes clear, truth at this level is not independent of history nor indifferent to it: for the claim proceeds from the statement, 'This is vouched for by an eyewitness'. It is the truth *of* the flesh.

Perhaps the 'feel' of such a man as John is seeking to depict, who is utterly human and yet whose entire life is lived from God as its centre and source, can be captured from a picture drawn from human experience, and with no reference to the Fourth Gospel, which has been given by Greville Norburn of the mysterious quality of the 'charismatic' man.[55]

Such a person, says Norburn, speaks with an authenticity and

---

[52]*The Foolishness of God*, London 1970, p. 144.

[53]Especially Luke 1.3; cf. Acts 18.25f.; 22.3; 23.15, 20; 24.22; 26.5. Elsewhere in the New Testament it occurs only of Herod's anxious interrogations of the wise men (Matt. 2.7f., 16) and in Eph. 5.15 and I Thess. 5.2.

[54]The Gospel and Epistles of John contain almost as many instances as the rest of the New Testament put together.

[55]With permission and gratitude I paraphrase and then quote from an article, 'Kant's Philosophy of Religion: A Preface to Christology?', *SJT* 26, 1973, pp. 431–48.

personal authority. He tells of what he has seen and known. He has been there. He lives, sometimes fitfully, in other cases more permanently, on intimate, confident and even confidential terms with the object of his vision. That with which he claims to be in touch is a mystery that lies too deep for words, of which he can only say 'Not this', 'Not that', and yet which he frequently speaks of in terms of 'I' and 'Thou'. There is about him a certain distance and remoteness from the rest of us – a quality of holiness which brings us up with a sense of uneasiness in his presence.[56] He is rejected, inevitably, by the majority, yet attracts the few who know they must learn of him. But he is fascinating to friend and foe alike. For he has achieved, or been given, emancipation from the anxiety of finitude which is the lot of ordinary mortals: he is whole, undivided, reconciled. He bears a quality of saintliness which transcends goodness as the expert transcends the amateur. He seems to be given to us unaccountably, even arbitrarily.

Such men, goes on Norburn, 'summon their contemporaries, by the fact of their numinous existence, to make the crucial choice as to whether they are right or whether they are wrong'. They serve as midwives of faith for the rest of us:

> They do surrogate-duty in the sphere of religion for the empirical control which in its own sphere science requires for the confirmation of its hypotheses. They *certify* as true what we can only *think*. They authorize us to make the venture of faith for ourselves. For by the wholeness of their character, by the hidden source of their confidence and power, by their distance from the rest of us, by the self-authenticating hallmark of truth which they exemplify, they produce the indefeasible impression that they are just the sort of persons we should expect to occur, if a reality corresponding to our own inchoate idea of God really exists.

Of course, the fourth evangelist is saying *more* than this of Jesus. He is giving a theological interpretation of the impression Norburn is describing in purely human categories. But I suggest that at least something remarkably like that impression lies behind the picture John presents to us, and that it is not invented. Indeed, I am persuaded that it is as authentic historically of the impact left by

---

[56]Cf. the effect of the 'righteous man' in Wisd. 2.12–20, a passage which seems to have been strangely neglected by early Christian apologetic, except *possibly* in Luke 23.47, where 'righteous (or innocent) man' replaces 'God's son' of Mark 15.39. The two are equated in Wisd. 2.18: 'If the righteous man is God's son, God will stretch out a hand and save him.'

Jesus as any we get in the New Testament (which include not only those in Mark, Luke and Matthew but, I increasingly think, the Epistle to the Hebrews).[57] And John's picture is the more whole. As long as we do not misuse the portrait by treating it as a photograph (either here or indeed in any of the other sources), then I believe it has a quite indispensable contribution to make to the total 'synoptic' material out of which an adequate christology has to be fashioned today.[58]

[57]The picture of Jesus perfected out of temptation and suffering (especially in Heb. 5.7–9) rests, I am convinced, on oral tradition independent of, and indeed perhaps earlier than, that of the gospels. Cf. H. Montefiore, *The Epistle to the Hebrews*.

[58]Since writing this I have re-read the essay by Dodd, 'The Portrait of Jesus in John and in the Synoptics', in *Christian History and Interpretation: Studies Presented to John Knox*, ed. W. R. Farmer, C. F. D. Moule and R. R. Niebuhr, Cambridge and Toronto 1967, pp. 183–98. Concentrating on an aspect on which I have not touched (Christ as judge), he comes nevertheless to a very similar conclusion: 'John's rendering of the portrait of Jesus will be neither his own invention nor the re-colouring of another artist's sketch. He will have had, through memories or traditions available to him, access to the sitter, and the similarities we have noted will go far to assure us that behind the two renderings of the portrait [viz. of John and the synoptics] there stands a real historical person' (p. 195).

In a comment on the draft of this essay Dodd has kindly written to me with regard to John 1.14: 'I think we should now agree that the true rendering is "a father's only son", the statement being, as in other similar passages, essentially a parable.'

11

The Last Tabu? The Self-Consciousness
of Jesus[1]

Each generation of students inherits from its predecessor certain 'no go' areas that have been thoroughly worked over and had warning notices erected. There is little point in going over *that* ground again: it has been exhausted and declared barren. Certain negative results are implicitly communicated to the undergraduate beginning on his search. There are issues, it is suggested, which may be set aside as a waste of time to reopen; and slogans are passed on which it would not be intelligent or respectable to question. Some of those with which my generation was brought up, beginning its theology more or less with the Second World War, were:

The parables are not allegories;
The gospels are not biographies;
It is impossible to write a life of Jesus;
We can never get behind the Christ of the church's faith;

and above all

Of the self-consciousness of Jesus we may say nothing.

The previous generation had been through all that and had its fingers burnt. So there was no need to read it up or to work it through for oneself. All of us, I suppose, are worst read in any field in the period immediately prior to our own, which our own is struggling to leave behind. And this came as a special relief to my generation, since so much of it was in German and still untranslated. Indeed, until the spate of Continental theology made available by the post-war SCM Press under Ronald Gregor Smith we were unbelievably insular. Jülicher on the parables (which had given the quietus to allegory) is

[1]Given as the Presidential Address to the Cambridge Theological Society, 12 May 1983.

untranslated (and as far as I am concerned unread) to this day. Wrede, whom my supervision pupils still serve up to me as 'Reade' (this always seems to me the best argument for getting them to read their essays, quite apart from what one is saved in hand-writing and spelling) – Wrede on the Messianic Secret, published in 1901, was translated only in 1971. Bultmann's *History of the Synoptic Tradition* remained in 'the decent obscurity of a learned language' for forty-two years and Martin Kähler's most influential book of all, *The So-Called Jesus of History and the Historic Biblical Christ*,[2] for nearly seventy. If we had read Schweitzer's *Quest of the Historical Jesus*, it was only the last chapter. That area could safely be relegated to the background of one's studies and a censor posted at the threshold, secure in the reassurance, to quote the verdict of Kähler's translator, that 'the Life of Jesus movement' had proved itself 'historically impossible, theologically illegitimate and apologetically irrelevant'. So who in his senses would wish to revive that corpse?[3]

Above all was this true of the self-consciousness of Jesus – and instinctively it rose to the mind as *Selbstbewusstsein*, though there was a perfectly good English equivalent, as there was for *Sitz im Leben* (though not for the elusive, and often one suspects deliberately obfuscating, distinction between *Historie* and *Geschichte*). But somehow to give the monster a German name put it in its place and made it easier to tame. 'We can, strictly speaking, know nothing of the personality of Jesus', declared Bultmann in his *Jesus and the Word*, by which alone he was known in English until after the war. Therre was no gold there. And still the area was fenced off by Bornkamm in pioneering 'the new quest'. The 'messianic consciousness' of Jesus, he wrote in his *Jesus of Nazareth*, is 'all too psychological' for theological investigation. So the sensible student is advised to this day to give it wide berth if he does not wish to tread on mines still lying around.

Intimately bound up with this issue was the use, or rather the non-use, to be made of the evidence of the Fourth Gospel. This too had been put away into an isolation ward labelled 'Christian mysticism' and severely discounted in any reconstruction of the historical Jesus. Even the so-called 'bolt from the Johannine blue' in the Q logion of Matt. 11.27 and Luke 10.22 was pronounced guilty by association.

---

[2]W. Wrede, *The Messianic Secret*, ET London 1971; R. Bultmann, *The History of the Synoptic Tradition*, ET Oxford and New York 1963; *Der sogennante historische Jesus und der geschichtliche, biblische Christus*, Leipzig 1892; [2]1896, ET Philadelphia 1964.

[3]E. Bratten, Introduction to ET, p. 36.

For the pre-critical use made of the Fourth Gospel in the history of christology had given scholars a bad conscience, which has still not been exorcized. Since the Johannine material was so heavily affected, not to say infected, by this 'history', it could not be approached dispassionately. One must not be caught using *those* texts even with a long spoon! But cut out the Johannine texts, and even Johannine-sounding texts, and could the question of Jesus' inner life ever be asked, let alone answered? For in the classical debates of the Christian church it was taken for granted that texts from this gospel were primary data of the problem to be solved.[4] No christology which did not do justice to both the sayings 'I and the Father are one' (10.30) and 'my Father is greater than I' (14.28), or which failed to posit in Jesus both genuine limitations, like tiredness, tears and thirst (4.6; 11.35; 19.28), as well as a memory of pre-existent glory (8.58; 17.5), could satisfy the 'facts'. It was material from the Gospel of John which more than any other compelled, and tested, the doctrine of the Two Natures in its different presentations, and most of the patristic examples of what it meant for Christ to do some things as God and some things as man were drawn from this Gospel. Still as late as the nineteenth century so liberal a theologian as Schleiermacher used as an argument for the priority of John the authority of its eyewitness to the person of Christ. 'It is, according to him', wrote Schweitzer, 'only in this Gospel that the consciousness of Jesus is truly reflected.' 'The contradictions', Schleiermacher maintained, between this and the others 'could not be explained if all our Gospels stood equally close to Jesus.'[5] But if John stands closer than the others, as he believed, then the problem could be resolved. Even up to the First World War it was possible for Bishop Frank Weston to write his great book *The One Christ* as though the data for the self-consciousness of Jesus were still basically set, largely by the Fourth Gospel, in the way they had been for Cyril of Alexandria. What Weston claimed to do, not without some success, was to produce a more adequate hypothesis to account for the same data: he did not question, let alone set aside, the Johannine material. 'The most important evidence', he wrote, 'to the divine nature of Christ is that which is based upon the revelation of His self-consciousness, His knowledge of His pre-existence, and His memory of the state of eternal glory'.[6]

[4] I have drawn in what follows on some material reprinted in ch. 10 above, pp. 138ff.

[5] *The Quest of the Historical Jesus*, p. 66, quoting Schleiermacher, *Über die Schriften des Lucas*, Berlin 1817.

[6] *The One Christ*, p. 38.

The swing away from this position, which of course had set in in liberal circles long before Weston, has been almost total. Yet nothing has been put in its place. In respect of what Clement of Alexandria called 'the bodily facts', John's evidence has again come back into serious contention. But what lay at the centre of Jesus' life has been left a blank, and indeed been regarded as forbidden territory. We can say what the church said about him, but we cannot say – or apparently be allowed to care – what he thought about himself. He could have meant something entirely different, or been a deluded megalomaniac. But what if he did not understand himself as anything like what the church proclaimed him to be? Is it possible to be content with – let alone to believe – a Christ *malgré lui*? 'Do you think you're what they say you are?', asks the chorus in *Jesus Christ Super-Star*, representing, as choruses are supposed to, the ordinary man. And if he did not, then it is difficult to persuade the ordinary man or 'the simple believer' that it is a matter of complete indifference.

Yet the scholars, particularly those grasping the relief afforded by Kähler's book, which seemed to offer indemnity from what Tillich called 'historical risk' and to secure churchmen from being at the mercy of the latest deliverances of the Herr Professor, have thought it possible to ring off for faith what Kähler called an 'invulnerable area' from 'the papacy of scholarship'. Bultmann's statement of this position in his *Theology of the New Testament* could stand for many:

> The acknowledgment of Jesus as the one in whom God's word decisively encounters man, whatever title be given him – 'Messiah (Christ)', 'Son of Man', 'Lord' – is a pure act of faith independent of the answer to the historical question of whether Jesus considered himself to be the Messiah. Only the historian can answer this question – as far as it can be answered at all – and faith, being personal decision, cannot be dependent on a historian's labour.[7]

One may agree that only the historian can answer this question, and grant too that the historian's labour cannot give faith, but still question whether it may not take it away, by rendering what lay at the heart of the truth about Jesus so uncertain, so vacuous or so culturally conditioned that men and women cease in fact to find it worth believing. I am not persuaded that it is possible to remain indifferent to the findings of the historian on how Jesus understood

[7]ET London and New York 1952–5, I, p. 26.

himself, nor that an ultimate scepticism is either tolerable or necessary. Yet are we in a position to give any answer? Have we the materials? Is it not inaccessible, even if not invulnerable?

At this point a distinction needs to be made. The materials clearly fail for reconstructing Jesus' self-consciousness in psychological terms, for analysing his psyche, its history or its type. The gospels are no more in the business of supplying answers to psychological questions than they are to sociological or economic questions – though this does not mean that it is illegitimate *for us* to ask them. They do not even tell us what he looked like. Nor do they concern themselves with the dawning or development of his self-awareness. They are not bio-graphy, in the sense of writing about his life as βιός, let alone providing fragments of autobiography from the lips of Jesus. But this does not mean that they presuppose there *was* no development in his apprehension of God or himself, or that his was a static perfection. They would surely have agreed with Cullmann that 'the life of Jesus would not be fully human if its course did not manifest a development'.[8] Indeed the writer to the Hebrews is quite clear that he learned obedience through the things that he suffered, that he had to become what he was, to be made perfect, to go through the process of individuation and maturation like every other human being (2.10, 17f.; 4.15; 5.5, 8f.; 6.20; 7.28). Luke certainly recognized its beginning in the boy Jesus (2.52) in words that deliberately echo the growth of the child Samuel (I Sam. 2.26) and which Barth delighted to observe is described by the word προ-κόπτειν, meaning 'to extend by blows, as a smith stretches metal by hammers'.[9] But the gospels are not interested in continuing to trace this process. One only gets glimpses of it, for example, in the story of the Syrophoenician woman, where under pressure Jesus comes through to a position he has apparently no intention of adopting at the outset (Matt. 15.21–28; Mark 7.24–30), or in Gethsemane, where he struggles to align his will with that of his Father (Mark 14.32–42 and pars.; Heb. 5.7). But even here of course the accounts are not written with an interest in tracing the psychological processes involved.

In John, for all the concentration on Jesus' inner life and relationship to the Father, there is even less attention to questions of psychic development or to the human factors that obedience involved. Yet they can be read between the lines of a number of

[8]*The Christology of the New Testament*, ET London and Philadelphia ²1963, p. 97.
[9]*Church Dogmatics*, ET Edinburgh and Grand Rapids, Michigan 1936–69, I. 2, p. 158.

passages, such as 7.1–10 (his prevarication about going up to Jerusalem for Tabernacles: life is easy for those for whom 'any time is right', he must abide his 'hour'; cf. 2.4; 12.23; 13.1); or 11.1–16 (where again in the conflict brought to a head by Lazarus' illness the reluctance to face a return to Judaea comes through); or 12.27–31 (the Johannine equivalent of Gethsemane, with its turmoil of soul and inner dialogue). Indeed the marks of emotional strain and psychic disturbance in Jesus are quite as evident in John as they are in Mark – though this is not the time to set them out in detail.[10] It would, I believe, be quite false to conclude that John supposed there *was* no development in his subject, or that the static effect and the semblance of effortless superiority which his gospel has conveyed *when read from the viewpoint of modern psychology* was his intention.

Nevertheless a distinction needs to be made in the case of Jesus as of every other human being between his ego and his self, his *ego-consciousness* and his *self-knowledge*. Unhappily the Greek ἐγώ like the English 'I' has to stand for both. Who, deep down, was the person who said ἐγώ εἰμί or ἀμην λέγω ὑμῖν? How are we to understand such words, and with what aim are they recorded? There is an important difference to be drawn at this point between psychological verisimilitude and theological verity. None of the gospels is primarily interested in the former; all are deeply concerned with the latter. And particularly of course is this true of John. If the distinction is not grasped, then the misunderstanding in his case will be the greater. If the Jesus of John and his words are taken at the level of psychological verisimilitude, then the impression is indeed left that never did any true man speak as he spoke, or, as those openly say in this gospel who *do* take him at this level, that he was mad (2.17; 6.42; 7.20; 8.48, 52; 10.20) or bad (7.12; 9.16, 24; 10.21, 33; 18.30). And to many since the Johannine Christ has come through as intolerable or repellent.

Yet at the level of theological verity John is simply deepening the question posed by all the gospels, Who is this man? (Mark 4.41 and pars.; cf. 1.27; 2.7). Where is he *from*, that he speaks and acts with such authority, direct 'from source' (ἐξ-ουσία)? '*Quis et unde?*': so Krister Stendahl has brilliantly elucidated the two questions behind the opening chapters of Matthew's Gospel. And these two questions, τίς καὶ πόθεν?, are those round which the whole of John's Gospel may be said to be written. 'Where do you come from?', asks Pilate in desperation and not a little apprehension (19.8f.). At one level

---

[10]Cf. my forthcoming *The Priority of John*.

Jesus' contemporaries claim to know this well enough (7.27f.) – they are perfectly familiar with his parentage and his home (6.42) – and in irony they are represented as saying that if he *were* the Messiah they would *not* know: for 'no one is to know where *he* comes from' (7.27). Yet at a deeper level they do not and cannot know (8.14; 9.29f.). *But he knows* (7.29; 8.14; 13.3). This last is a presupposition of the whole gospel, which is written to draw it out for its readers. In this sense the *self-knowledge* of Jesus is the indispensable heart of the mystery: to regard it as a matter of indifference or as a 'no go' area is to leave a blank at the centre of Christian theology. Rather, John's concern is to take the reader into the very heart of this relationship, to disclose the inside story, what was really going on and who he really was, ἀληθινῶς, at the level of πνεῦμα rather than ψυχή.

In the synoptists the relation of Jesus to God, the distinctive relationship which allows him to speak of 'my Father' and to know himself called in a unique manner to the vocation of sonship, is everywhere presupposed. It is declared by the heavenly voice at his baptism, tested in the wilderness temptations, reiterated at the Transfiguration, and summed up at the close of his public teaching in the distinction between the servants and the son in the parable of the Wicked Husbandmen. The relation to source, the freedom and the authority with which Jesus speaks and acts, the intimacy of his union with God as Father: all these are presupposed and taken for granted. Yet, apart from hints from supernatural powers 'in the know' (Mark 1.24, 34; 3.11; 5.7 and pars.), there is really only one point at which we are permitted a glimpse into the inside of that reality. That is when a door is opened into the relationship between Jesus and his Father which forms the centre and core of his being:

> At that time Jesus spoke these words: I thank thee, Father, Lord of heaven and earth, for hiding these things from the learned and wise, and revealing them to the simple. Yes, Father, such was thy choice. Everything is entrusted to me by my Father; and no one knows the Son but the Father, and no one knows the Father but the Son and those to whom the Son may choose to reveal him (Matt. 11.25–27).

This mutual 'knowledge' is of course that of *connaître*, not *savoir*, even in the Lukan version, 'no one knows who the Son is but the Father, or who the Father is but the Son' (10.21f.). It is the knowledge of personal intimacy, and has been shown to have its closest parallel not in Hellenistic 'gnosis' but in the 'knowledge' of the Dead Sea Scrolls.[11] Indeed the precedence given to the Father knowing the Son, in contrast to what we should instinctively think of or quote, shows that it is grounded in the Hebraic understanding of God's prevenient knowledge and covenant-love (as the presence of the word εὐδοκία, or choice, in the context clearly indicates): 'You only have I known of all the families of the earth' is the presupposition of Yahweh's judgment of Israel (Amos 3.2). Similarly in Isaiah the charge that 'Israel does not know' rests on the divine premise, 'Sons have I reared and brought up' (1.2f.). And within the new covenant the same order still holds: 'I shall know even as also I have been known' (I Cor. 13.12). So in John, the order is 'the Father knows me and I know the Father' (10.15); and the good shepherd knows his sheep before they know him (10.14).

That Jesus is thus known or loved (for the two are practical equivalents) by the Father, that he is 'the son of his love' (Paul's equivalent in Col. 1.13 of υἱὸς ἀγαπητός or ἐκλεκτός), that he finds his entire life and being in responding to this relationship, is, as Jeremias contended, his secret, his revelation, the clue to his whole mission, which, as he tells Peter, flesh and blood cannot reveal, but only his Father in heaven (Matt. 16.17). Without this clue we should miss everything. The synoptic gospels, as we have said, presuppose it, but they do not expose it. And in this , we may judge, they are true to Jesus. It is not, as Bornkamm states,[12] because they are 'extremely indifferent and evasive' to the consciousness of Jesus. It is because they respect the privacy and intimacy of the relationship with the one he called 'my Father'. Like Socrates of his δαιμόνιον, he evidently did not talk of it freely. Yet that Socrates had this inner conviction of a reality that was always with him is deeply embedded in our sources, in Xenophon (*Mem.* 1.1.2; 4.8.1, 5; *Apol.* 4,12f.) as well as Plato (*Apol.* 40A; *Theaet.* 151A; *Euthyd.* 272E; *Euthyphr.* 3B), and has to be regarded as one of the most certainly remembered facts about him. Equally, with Jesus, this inner relationship as the umbilical cord of his life must be accepted as irreducibly necessary to the understanding of who and what he was, and, Riesenfeld has insisted,[13] to the authority of his teaching. Though the passage which brings it to the surface may appear in the synoptic gospels to stick out like a sore thumb and 'gives the impression of a thunderbolt fallen from the Johannine sky',[14] recent critical study has shown that there is less

[11]Cf. W. D. Davies, *Christian Origins and Judaism*, London and Philadelphia 1962, pp. 119–44; especially 141–4.

[12]*Jesus of Nazareth*, p. 169.

[13]*The Gospel Tradition and Its Beginnings*, London 1957, pp. 28f.

[14]K. von Hase, *Die Geschichte Jesu*, Leipzig ²1876, p. 422.

and less ground for doubting its genuineness as a saying of Jesus. This is especially true if, with Jeremias again, we recognize that on Jesus' own lips the 'the' of 'the father' and 'the son' is the generic 'the' constantly to be found in parables, like 'the sower' that went out to sow (Mark 4.3) or 'the grain of wheat' that falls into the ground (John 12.24). In these cases we should use the indefinite article, so Jeremias renders: 'Just as only a father (really) knows his son, so only a son (really) knows his father'. It is still indeed a parable of Jesus' unique relationship to God, like 'the son' in the story of the Wicked Husbandmen. But, as James Dunn has rightly said, it does not by itself commit us to any particular interpretation of 'divinity': 'Schweitzer's claim that Matt. 11.27 "may be spoken from the consciousness of pre-existence" is never more than a possibility, neither finally excluded nor positively indicated by careful exegesis.'[15] To the content of what is or is not here being claimed I shall come back. At this point we are simply concerned with whether such insight into the self-knowledge of Jesus is a legitimate or important quest. And on this Dunn is unequivocal:

> Can the historian hope to penetrate into the self-consciousness (or self-understanding) of a historical individual? The answer must be in the affirmative, otherwise history would be nothing more than a dreary catalogue of dates and documentation.[16]

He goes on to illustrate from Louis XIV and Winston Churchill how particular utterances or revealing comments, especially at crucial moments, may 'provide as it were a key which unlocks the mystery of the historical personality, a clue into his or her character, a window into his or her soul'. He asks whether there are any statements of Jesus which provide similar windows into his inner feelings and consciousness, and he replies: 'In my judgment the answer is almost certainly yes.' He cites those sayings of Jesus which express 'what Bultmann himself called "the immediacy of es-chatological consciousness" (Matt. 11.5f. = Luke 7.22f.; Matt. 13.16f. = Luke 10.23f.; Matt. 12.41f. = Luke 11.31f.; Luke 12.54–56; and he adds Matt. 12.28 = Luke 11.20).[17] But none of these begins to take one inside his relationship to God in the manner of Matt. 11.27 = Luke 10.22. Yet remarkably this saying is never cited anywhere in Bultmann's *Theology of the New Testament*; and it is

[15] *Christology in the Making*, London and Philadelphia 1980, p. 29; so Cullmann, *Christology of the New Testament*, p. 288.

[16] Op. cit., p. 25.

[17] Op. cit., p. 26.

significant that he always speaks of Jesus' 'messianic self-consciousness', asking whether he saw himself as Messiah or Son of Man or
Lord. His relationship to the Father as Son, which Jeremias rightly saw
as central, is not even discussed.

But what is so rare as to be almost unique in the synoptists is
normative in John. And if, as I am convinced, there is no literary
interdependence it is surely very significant that the one synoptic
window should be thoroughly Johannine in colouring. It suggests
strongly that the Johannine picture of Jesus' self-understanding as 'the
unique Son of God who has a unique knowledge of the Father, and a
unique function as Mediator of that knowledge' is not simply of his
creation but a taking up and drawing out of what surfaces so sketchily
elsewhere.

This aspect of 'St John's Contribution to the Picture of the
Historical Jesus' was stressed in an inaugural lecture of that title (the
source of my last quotation), given by T. E. Pollard at Knox
Theological Hall, Dunedin, in 1964. Since it has appeared only in a
privately circulated journal for ministers of the Presbyterian Church
in New Zealand,[18] I should like to give it wider circulation by some
more extended citation than would otherwise be appropriate.

He believes that the paucity of synoptic reference to the self-
consciousness of Jesus represents a faithful reflection of his own
reticence.

> If he avoids using Messianic categories, it is not because he did not
> believe himself to be Messiah; but because, as the sequel to Peter's
> confession of him as the Messiah shows so clearly, there was a vast
> difference between what Peter and the rest understood by the title
> and the meaning it had for Jesus himself. Luke testifies to the failure
> of the disciples to understand the significance of Jesus and his
> words in the disillusionment and perplexity of the two disciples on
> the road to Emmaus. The Synoptics give an accurate picture of this
> failure on the part of the disciples to understand the personality and
> the words and deeds of Jesus. They are recording the consciousness
> and personality of Jesus as they dimly apprehended it in the days of
> his ministry.
>
> On the other hand, John writes in order to bring out the real
> personality of Jesus and the real nature of his ministry, which had
> been there all the time, but which, during Jesus' sojourning with
> them, they had failed to see clearly. . . . It is not that John is reading

[18]*Forum* 16.6, August 1964, pp. 2–9.

back into the earthly life something that was not there; rather, with the penetrating insight born of reflection and faith, he sees the personality of Jesus as it really was, and as the disciples would have seen it had their eyes not been blinded by preconceptions and misunderstanding. As he writes his Gospel John is saying in effect, 'This is what Jesus was really like; we did not realise it then, but now we know it.'

Pollard goes on to use R. G. Collingwood's distinction between the 'outside' and the 'inside' of the same event, between 'everything belonging to it that can be described in terms of bodies and their movements' and 'that in it which can only be described in terms of thought'.[19]

Applying this distinction I would say that the Synoptists are more concerned with the 'outside' of the events they record, even though they record them because they believe that they have a theological or soteriological significance. John, on the other hand, is concerned with the 'inside' of the events; to use Collingwood's words, he 'remembers that the events were actions, and that his main task is to think himself into these actions, to discern the thoughts of the agent'.[20] In other words, the Synoptists see Jesus and his words and actions from the outside through the eyes of the disciples: John 'enters sympathetically into the mind' of Jesus, or 'puts himself into the shoes' of Jesus.

He draws the conclusion that

On Collingwood's definition of the real task of the historian, it could well be argued that John is a better historian than the Synoptists. John portrays Jesus as the one who at every point is conscious of his Messianic function as Son of God, whose every action, thought and word are governed by this consciousness. There is no need to interpret this portrait as an invention by John or a falsification of what Jesus really was. Rather it is an attempt to portray Jesus as he was, in his earthly life, in and for himself. It is not that this Jesus of St John is any less human than the Jesus of the Synoptics; it is rather that John penetrates with deeper insight into the inner springs of the personality of Jesus. Nor was John's portrait a more highly developed theological interpreta-

[19]*The Idea of History*, Oxford and Toronto 1959, p. 174.
[20]Loc. cit.

tion; rather because of his deeper insight he makes explicit what is implicit, and, for the most part, veiled in the synoptics.

And he ends by predicting that, as I am trying to work out at every level in my forthcoming Bampton Lectures,

> As the New Quest progresses, the Gospel of John must come into its own again as a primary source. To quote E. M. Sidebottom, 'The Fourth Gospel is . . . best understood as a complement to the others not in the sense that it interprets them but that it shows us how to interpret them.'

So with this in mind let us look very summarily[21] at the content of the statements about the 'I' of Jesus in the gospels and especially the Fourth.

First it must be stressed again that what we are dealing with in all the gospels (and not only the Fourth) is theological interpretation of his person, not a transcript of his words. This does not mean that we may not catch the *ipsissima vox*, but it certainly does not commit us to claiming the *ipsissima verba*. The Johannine 'I am' sayings above all demand to be understood as interpretative clues of the evangelist to his essential self-understanding, not as materials from a psychologist's note-book for piecing together a reconstruction of his consciousness.

Secondly, I would want to insist again that what John is doing, here as elsewhere, is drawing out and deepening what is already there in the Christian tradition, making explicit what is implicit. For the 'I' of this gospel is already in principle that of the synoptics. It is the 'I' of the numerous 'I have come' sayings that declare the purpose of his mission and which are common to all the gospels; it is the 'I' to whom everything is committed by his Father in whose person and deeds God's rule are made present; who in the name of the divine Wisdom speaks the invitation of God and sends his emissaries; the 'I' of the Sermon on the Mount who goes behind what was said, not merely (as in the AV), *by* them of old time, but to them (by God); who as the Son of Man on earth is lord of the Sabbath, enjoying the same superiority to its rest (as John draws out) as the Creator himself; who pronounces the forgiveness of sins, thereby putting himself in the place of God; who quells the powers of demons and of nature, and exercises before the time the prerogatives of the last judgment; the 'I' who in Luke, as well as in John, will dispense the Father's Spirit and who in Matthew can promise his own abiding presence.

[21] Again for a fuller analysis I must refer to *The Priority of John*.

All of this is in the synoptists; and John is portraying and projecting it in categories, already, it is becoming clear, well understood in Jewish apocalyptic mysticism, of primacy and ultimacy, before and after, above and below. For what is here is a greater than Solomon or Moses, than Jacob or Abraham, and so must be recognized as being before them and above them – and indeed before all and above all. But what is here is a *man*, who has been given an authority, as the authentic son of man, reaching back to the very beginning of God's purpose and extending to its end. Even the most exalted Johannine affirmations of timeless pre-existence and heavenly ascendency, like those of the more prophetically-based categories of foreordination and eschatology common to the synoptists, are made not to question his humanity but to enhance it. In fact when the Baptist reiterates the assertion of Jesus' priority in 1.30 he adds the word ἀνήρ: to say that Jesus is 'before' him is not to lift him out of the ranks of humanity but to assert his unconditional precedence. To take such statements at the level of 'flesh', to imply, as 'the Jews' interpret him, that, at less than fifty, Jesus is claiming to have lived on this earth before Abraham (8.52, 57), is to be as crass as Nicodemus who understands rebirth as an old man entering his mother's womb a second time (3.4). These are not assertions about the ego of the human Jesus, which is no more pre-existent than that of any other human being. Nor are statements about the glory that he enjoyed with the Father before the world was to be taken at the level of psychological reminiscence. As such they would clearly be destructive of any genuine humanness, whereas for the Johannine Jesus the revelation of 'what I saw in my Father's presence' (8.38) is described unequivocally only two verses later as the work of 'a *man* who told you the truth as I heard it from God' (8.40). Again, to confuse theological verity with psychological verisimilitude is to confound everything. Yet at the level of spirit and truth (4.23; 3.6), of ζωή (6.63) rather than βίος, the voice with which Jesus speaks and the authority with which he acts and claims allegiance is that of the Word which transcends time and space.

There are two ways in which Jesus' way of speaking (λαλιά) is misunderstood and his word therefore cannot be 'heard' (8.43) that are reflected in the Fourth Gospel and its subsequent interpretation. The first is to take the 'I' of such utterances at the level of the ego of Western empiricism, and so make nonsense of his humanity. The other is to go in the opposite direction and see him as usurping the divine name, as for instance Stauffer[22] does when he interprets the 'I

[22]*Jesus and His Story*, pp. 142–9.

am' of this Gospel as claiming identification with the 'I am he' (*ani hu*) of Yahweh in the Old Testament. But this I believe to be an equal misreading and can be shown to be such by careful attention to the text.

Of the 'I am' sayings in this gospel, those with a predicate ('I am the bread of life', 'the door', 'the way', 'the good shepherd', etc.) certainly do not imply that the subject is God. As Barrett rightly says, 'ἐγώ εἰμι does not identify Jesus with God, but it does draw attention to him in the strongest possible terms. "I am the one – the one you must look at, and listen to, if you would know God"'.[23] If there is a proto-Gnostic style to this formula (which must remain doubtful, since all the evidence, especially the Mandaean on which Bultmann relied so heavily, is later), it is that of the mystagogue, the initiator into and revealer of the divine secrets, not of God himself.

Of the 'absolute' uses of ἐγώ εἰμι, the majority are simply establishing identification: 'I am he.' This is so of 4.26 (the Messiah you speak of); 6.20 (confirming Jesus' identity on the lake at night, exactly as in Mark 6.50; Matt. 14.27); 9.9 (on the lips not of Jesus but of the blind man); and 18.5–8, the 'I am your man' at the arrest (cf. Acts 10.21), even though it evokes awe (though *not* the reaction to blasphemy) in the arresting party. There is the same usage in the resurrection scene of Luke 24.39, 'It is I myself', where John does *not* have it just where we might expect it, any more than he has an equivalent to the 'I am' of Mark 14.62 at the climax of the Jewish trial. Three other occurrences (8.24, 28; 13.19) are I believe correctly rendered by the NEB 'I am what I am', namely, the truth of what I really am. They do not carry with them the implication that he is Yahweh (indeed in the latter two especially there is *contrast* with the Father who sent him) but, in Johannine terms, 'the Christ, the Son of God'. The sole remaining instance is 8.58, 'Before Abraham was born, I am'. This certainly asserts pre-existence, as in the Baptist's statement of 1.15 and 30, but there, as we saw, the subject is specifically designated 'a man'. That Jesus is arrogating to himself the divine name is nowhere stated or implied in this gospel. Even 'the Jews' do not accuse him of this – only of calling God 'his own Father', and thereby implying equality with god (or as H. Odeberg[24] interprets this from rabbinic parallels, rebellious independence, being 'as good as God') (5.18). What they take to be the blasphemy of making himself 'a god' in 10.33 is again made clear to be a misunderstanding of Jesus calling himself 'God's son' (10.36). It is inconceivable, if Stauffer's interpretation

[23] *The Gospel According to St John*, London and Philadelphia ²1978, p. 342; cf. 98.
[24] *The Fourth Gospel*, p. 203.

were the correct one, either in the evangelist's intention or in the mind of Jesus' opponents, that it should not come out in the charges against him at the trial, where again the worst that can be said about him is that he claimed to be 'God's son' (19.7) again without the article.

If then the 'I' with which Jesus speaks is neither that simply of the individual ego nor of the divine name, what is it? I suggest that it is to be understood as the totality of the self, of which Jung spoke in contrast with the ego. As he saw it,[25] the Christ-figure is an archetypal image of the self, the God-image in us, 'consubstantial' alike with the ground of our being and with our own deepest existence. It is the 'I' of the mystics, who make the most astonishing claims to be one with God, without of course claiming to *be* God, the 'I' of Meister Eckhart and Angelus Silesius, of the Sufis and the Upanishads, where *atman* and *Brahman* are completely 'one', as in John 10.30. Such is Bede Griffiths' interpretation, born of long exposure to this tradition. In his latest book he says of Jesus,

> In the depths of his being, like every human being, he was present to himself, aware of himself, in relation to the eternal ground of his being. In most people this intuitive awareness is inchoate or imperfect, but in the great prophet and mystic, in the seer like Gautama Buddha or the seers of the Upanishads, this intuitive knowledge of the ground of being becomes a pure intuition, a total awareness. Such according to the tradition of St John's Gospel (which in its origin is now considered to be as old as that of the other gospels) was the nature of the knowledge of Jesus. He knew himself in the depth of his spirit as one with the eternal ground of his being.[26]

Westcott indeed believed that the great commentary on St John waited to be written by an Indian – though I doubt if this will happen until Indian theology has risen above its tendency to depreciate the historical or to absorb the 'thou' of personal union to the 'that' of impersonal identity. But it is Buber the Jew – shall we say 'the Israelite without guile' of this gospel? – who perhaps gets nearest to what John is indicating by his ἐγώ εἰμι:

How powerful, even to being overpowering, and how legitimate,

---

[25]As he is always careful to insist, *he* is writing at the level of psychology not theology, but these categories can usefully be employed in a theological context to what is true at the level of πνεῦμα and not simply σάρχ.

[26]*The Marriage of East and West*, London and New York 1982, p. 189.

even to being self-evident, is the saying of *I* by Jesus! For it is the *I* of unconditional relation in which the man calls his *Thou* Father in such a way that he is simply Son, and nothing else but Son. Whenever he says *I* he can only mean the *I* of the holy primary word that has been raised for him into unconditional being.[27]

There is nothing here that is not utterly and 'superly' human, as well as being totally transparent of God. To have seen the one is to have seen the other, without either being dissolved in the other. The 'I' that says 'I and the Father are one' is as unequivocally human as the 'I' that says 'I thirst'. There can be no residue or trace of a christology that says that Jesus said or did some things as God and some things as man. That is wholly alien to the interpretation of John. He did everything as the integral human being who was totally one with his Father and with all other men, so that in him the fullness of deity as well as the fullness of humanity becomes visible. The distinctive thing about that 'I' is not that it was *not* human but that it was *wholly* one with the self-expressive activity of God, and thus *uniquely* human. What he was the Logos was and what the Logos was God was, so that in his 'I' God is speaking and acting. Bultmann in his commentary on John gets it succinctly by making a careful distinction: 'In Jesus' words God speaks the ἐγώ εἰμι. We should, however, reject the view that ἐγώ εἰμι means "I (Jesus) am God".'[28]

Thus I believe that we must insist that the human filial self-awareness of Jesus is the linch-pin of John's christology (what, to return to the jargon of our theological youth, constitutes the *Anknüpfungspunkt*, or point of contact, between God and man), and that here as elsewhere John is but drawing out and making explicit what is central to the entire gospel tradition. To declare it tabu is to risk missing everything and to be thrown back on the false alternative of a 'mere man' christology with no unique divine relationship or one which sees him as a heavenly visitant whose genuine humanity is constantly in question. Both I believe are false not only to John but, more importantly, to Jesus.

[27] *I and Thou*, ET, R. Gregor Smith, Edinburgh 1937, pp. 66f.
[28] *The Gospel of John*, p. 327 n. 5.

12

The Fourth Gospel and the Church's
Doctrine of the Trinity

I am grateful to George Caird for so many things – not least for his three splendidly clear articles in the *Expository Times*[1] on 'The Study of the Gospels' setting out the current state of Source, Form and Redaction Criticism, which I have constantly used as introductory teaching material for students; for they took more seriously than anything else I have read the hypothesis on synoptic relationships which I tentatively put forward in my article on 'The Parable of the Wicked Husbandmen'.[2] Nor can I forget the value for my own *Redating the New Testament* of his entry on 'The Chronology of the New Testament in the Apostolic Age' in *The Interpreter's Dictionary of the Bible*,[3] which was a model of clarity and sound judgment; nor again, among many other articles, for that on 'The Glory of God in the Fourth Gospel: An Exercise in Biblical Semantics',[4] which has been valuable for my forthcoming Bampton Lectures on *The Priority of John*.

But it is from none of these that I should like to start here, but from his lecture to the Modern Churchmen's Conference of 1967 on 'The Development of the Doctrine of Christ in the New Testament'.[5] I read this when it first came out, but its impact only hit me, as I explained in my *Human Face of God*,[6] when I realized that it had said with much greater authority than I could muster in relation to the intertestamental period what I had been arguing for in my chapter on pre-existence. By this I mean that, until about the end of the first century AD, Jewish and Christian language about pre-

---

[1] *ExpT* 87, 1976, pp. 99–104, 137–41, 168–72.
[2] *NTS* 21, 1974–5, pp. 443–61; reprinted as ch. 2 above.
[3] Vol. I, New York 1962, pp. 599–607.
[4] *NTS* 15, 1968–9, pp. 265–77, especially pp. 271–3.
[5] *Christ for Us Today*, ed. N. Pittenger, London 1968, pp. 66–80 (especially 75–80).
[6] Op. cit., pp. 178f.

existence was not referring to separate hypostatic persons, divine or heavenly, but to personifications[7] of what Norman Pittenger has described as 'the self-expressive activity of God'.[8]

What I should like to do here is to venture further into the implications for the doctrine of the Trinity of the insights there disclosed. If I have hitherto sheered off doing this in my writings it is because I have had the gravest uncertainty about many aspects of the traditional *doctrine* (as opposed to the perennial reality it seeks to express) but have not been able to say what I would put in its place. In fact my last serious writing on the doctrine[9] was forty years ago in my Ph.D. thesis,[10] in which I sought, I then believed convincingly, to defend the classical statements of St Thomas Aquinas and Karl Barth (as I still would) against a 'social' model that would postulate 'I-Thou' relations between the Persons as individual centres of consciousness and relationship in the modern sense of the word. But the biblical basis of all this, which did not trouble Aquinas much but should have troubled Barth had he been more of a New Testament exegete, has increasingly disturbed me and been brought to a head as I have wrestled with the great Johannine texts on which so much of it was based.

The justification of my interpretation of John's christology must be allowed to speak for itself in my Bampton lectures. But on any interpretation it is clear that patristic theology of whatever school abused these texts by taking them out of context and giving them a meaning which it is evident that John never intended. Functional language about the Son and the Spirit being sent into the world by the Father was transposed into that of eternal and internal relationships between Persons of the Godhead and words like 'generation' and 'procession' made into technical terms which New Testament usage simply will not substantiate.

Unless, against the textual evidence, we allow in John 1.13 the

[7]*The Human Face of God*, ch. 5; cf. subsequently G. W. H. Lampe, *God as Spirit*, Oxford 1977, London 1983, ch. 2; J. Dunn, *Christology in the Making*, ch. 6, especially pp. 163–76 (Dunn also dates the transition at the end of the first century, but largely because he sets the Gospel of John there, which he regards as an exception to the rest of the New Testament); and J. P. Mackey, *The Christian Experience of God as Trinity*, London and New York 1983, ch. 6.

[8]*The Word Incarnate*, New York and London 1959, p. 187, *et passim*.

[9]I exclude my popular exposition of the *meaning* of the Trinity in *But that I Can't Believe!*, London and New York 1967, p. 86–90.

[10]*Thou who Art: the Notion of Personality and its Relation to Christian Theology, with Particular Reference to (a) Contemporary I-and-Thou Philosophy and (b) the Doctrine of the Trinity and the Person of Christ*, unpublished Ph.D thesis for the University of Cambridge, 1945.

singular 'was born' referring the verse to the Logos and not to believers, the sole use of γεννάω of Jesus in the Fourth Gospel, 'For this was I born; for this I came into the world' (18.37), clearly relates to his physical birth. In I John 5.18 there is the ambiguous text, 'We know that everyone who has been born (γεγεννημένος) of God does not sin, but he who was born (γεννηθείς) of God keeps him.' The latter probably in my judgment does refer to Jesus (though the commentators are divided),[11] but its interpretation turns on that of other language about 'sonship' and being 'born of God' or 'from above' in the Johannine canon. It cannot of itself provide any secure foundation for a unique eternal generation of the Second Person of the Trinity. The situation is further bedevilled by the fact that under the influence of the Arian controversy Jerome translated μονογενής of Jesus (though only of Jesus) as *unigenitus* (John 1.14, 18; 3.16, 18; I John 4.9; Heb. 11.17) (elsewhere in the Vulgate he preserves the *unicus* of the Old Latin [Luke 7.12; 8.42; 9.38], as well as in the texts from the Apocrypha);[12] and this became perpetuated in the AV as 'only begotten'. Yet the word does not derive from γεννᾶν but γένος; it means 'one of its kind.' Edward Schillebeeckx says outright that 'there is no basis in Johannine theology for the later scholastic theology of the procession of the Son from the Father within the Trinity *per modum generationis* (birth)'.[13]

As for the difference between coming forth (ἐξέρχομαι) and proceeding (ἐκπορεύομαι), this represents typical Johannine stylistic variation compounded by subsequent translational inconsistency. Ἐξέρχομαι is John's usual word (of Jesus in relation to the Father (8.42; 13.3; 16.27f., 30; 17.8), though ἔρχομαι and πορεύομαι are used interchangeably of this in 16.28, and generally elsewhere. Ἐκπορεύεται which has traditionally been rendered by 'proceeds', is used of the Spirit in 15.26, though the Vulgate, followed again by the

[11]Cf. the most recent survey in R. E. Brown, *The Epistles of John*, New York 1982, London 1983, pp. 620–2. He himself comes down on balance against this interpretation on the ground that 'if the Johannine writers [*sic*] thought that Jesus had been begotten by God, they would never elsewhere have used that language in the many passages on the subject'. But the improbability in context that the reference is to the Christian or to 'the begetting' (of the Christian by God) seems to me a good deal greater.

[12]The only exception is of Isaac in Heb. 11.17, in line with his rendering of Gen. 22.2, 12, 16. But in these latter cases the LXX has ἀγαπητόν. For the detailed evidence, cf. F. J. A. Hort, *Two Dissertations:* 1 *ΜΟΝΟΓΕΝΗΣ ΘΕΟΣ in Scripture and Tradition*, Cambridge and London 1876, p. 48–53.

[13]*The Christ*, ET London and New York 1980, p. 875 n. 57; cf. D. Moody, 'God's Only Son: The Translation of John 3.16 in the RSV', *JBL* 72, 1953, pp. 213–9; Brown, *The Gospel According to John*, pp. 13f; Mackey, *God as Trinity*, pp. 58f.

AV, also says of Jesus that he 'proceeded forth (*processi*) and came from God' to render ἐζῆλθον in 8.42. It is hard to believe that these distinctions, which in any case have no reference to non-temporal metaphysical realities, are anything but verbal, or to disagree with Geoffrey Lampe that no one has ever been able to define any substantial difference between 'generation' and 'procession'.[14]

Nor, I believe, is there any ground in John for thinking of two, let alone three,[15] Persons in heaven, hypostatically pre-existent before all time, who entered history by assuming or indwelling human nature. This obviously is more debatable and cannot be defended here.[16] (The question has again been distorted by the so-called 'Johannine Comma' in I John 5.7, where the interpolation 'There are three that bear record in heaven, the Father, the Word and the Holy Ghost' (AV) has a history unique even to the eccentricities of textual criticism.)[17] I believe that Caird was entirely correct in saying that 'personification' (i.e. making into a person) rather than 'personalization' (being a person) is the key to the interpretation of the language of word, wisdom, sonship, etc., derived from the Wisdom-tradition of the Old Testament; moreover that Schoonenberg[18] and Lampe[19] were right in judging that the Incarnation means the anhypostatic λόγος becoming hypostatic, as the self-expressive activity of God is focused in the historical Jesus as 'a person' in the full sense.[20] His human personality was then retrojected on to the pre-existent Logos – rather than a pre-existent divine Being taking on an 'impersonal' humanity. And, unlike others, I do not believe that either Paul (as Caird thought) or John (as Dunn supposes)[21] represents an exception to this view.[22]

Since this transposition from the Johannine vocabulary has been the traditional foundation for the doctrine of the Trinity, what is left from the wreckage? And what should we put in its place, first for our

---

[14]*God as Spirit*, p. 224, quoting Ambrose, *De Spir.* 1.11.

[15]On the hypostatization of the Spirit in John, cf. Mackey, op. cit., pp. 82–7.

[16]Cf. my forthcoming *Priority of John*, ch. 8.

[17]Cf. C. H. Dodd, *The Johannine Epistles*, London and New York 1946, pp. 127f.; Brown, *Epistles of John*, Appendix IV, p. 775–87, and the literature there cited.

[18]P. Schoonenberg, *The Christ*, ET New York 1971, London 1972, especially pp. 54–66, 80–91.

[19]*God as Spirit*, ch. 5.

[20]Cf., earlier, Caird in *Christ for Us Today*, p. 80.

[21]*Christology in the Making*, pp. 239–46.

[22]Mackey agrees with me in finding the New Testament writers at one at this point.

understanding of John and then for our own?

In the first place it should be noted that John is as undeviating a witness as any in the New Testament to the fundamental tenet of Judaism, of unitary monotheism (cf. Rom. 3.30; James 2.19). There is the one, true and only God (John 5.44; 17.3): everything else is idols (I John 5.21). In fact nowhere is the Jewishness of John, which has emerged in all recent study, more clear. The only possible exception is in I John 5.20, where οὗτός ἐστιν ὁ ἀληθινὸς Θεός could grammatically relate not to the Father but to the immediately preceding words 'his Son Jesus Christ', though the 'his' in 'his Son' must refer to τῷ ἀληθινῷ, i.e., God the Father, as everywhere else. The ambiguities of phrasing in the Johannine Epistles are notorious, but I find it very difficult to be persuaded by such as Schnackenburg, Bultmann and Brown in their commentaries on the Johannine Epistles (ad loc.) that it is Christ who is being designated 'the true God'. Rather, I am convinced with Westcott, Brooke and Dodd that the remaining Johannine usage (particularly 'This is the true God, this is eternal life' (I John 5.20) and 'This is eternal life: to know thee who alone art truly God' (John 17.3), which I believe the former deliberately echoes) requires the reference to be to the Father. There is also the parallel of II John 7, where 'This is the deceiver and the Antichrist' must refer to the secessionists and not to the immediately preceding words, 'Jesus Christ coming in the flesh'.

Yet, despite the clear evidence of the gospel that Jesus refuses the claim to *be* God (10.33) or in any way to usurp the position of the Father, this is clearly for John not the whole picture. From the opening verse it is made explicit that the Logos, to be identified with this man in 1.14, is θεός (1.1). Moreover, the climax to the main body of the gospel is Thomas' confession of Jesus as 'my Lord and my God' (20.28) – and that despite the fact that Jesus himself has used 'my God' of the Father only a few verses earlier (20.17). Then there is the notorious textual crux of 1.18, whether we read with the majority of the manuscripts ὁ μονογενὴς υἱός or with the best ὁ μονογενὴς θεός. Theologically I agree with Hort[23] that not much is at stake here, since the Logos has already been described as θεός (though not as μονογενὴς θεός. But exegetically there is almost everything to be said in favour of υἱός, which seems to be demanded by the contrast with τοῦ πατρός, as in 1.14; 3.16, 18; and I John 4.9. I shall be arguing in *The Priority of John* that there is every justification for all recent editions of the Greek text preferring θεός as

[23]*Two Dissertations*, pp. 13–16.

the best-attested reading, but that it is not mere perversity that, in face of this, both the RSV and NEB still prefer 'Son' in the text as opposed to the margin. In other words, θεός is what has come down to us from earliest times and may well have stood in the autograph, but υἱός is probably what John meant to write (there is only the difference between ΥC and ΘC) – and that he would have been the first to correct it. There is no reason to expect any extended piece of writing or dictating (and the latter aplies even more to the difference between ἔχωμεν and ἔχομεν in Rom. 5.1, where I think we have a similar situation) to be without slip.

Be that as it may, there is no doubt that for John as for Paul and the other New Testament writers, Jesus, like the Spirit, has the equivalence of God. That is to say, language applied to one can be applied to the others, or can alternate with similar language (Rom. 8.9–11 is the classic example), even though the reference of ὁ θεός to any but the Father is notoriously doubtful. Moreover their experienced effects are virtually indistinguishable. For John this equivalence comes out in the conviction that he who has seen the Father has seen the Son (12.45; 14.9) – despite the fact that it is a fundamental tenet of John as of Judaism that no one has ever seen God (1.18; 6.46; I John 4.12). Similarly, spirit, which God is (4.24), as much as he is λόγος (1.1), has the same functions as do both the Father and the Son. Thus the spirit 'gives life' (6.63; cf. 5.21) and, as in the Old Testament, stands for the divine in contrast with the 'flesh' (6.63). The Spirit, that is, God as spirit, represents, without being identical with, both the Father and the Son, just as Jesus represents, without being identical with, the Father. The one can stand for the other, be the agent of the other, so that there is no distinction in dealing; just as the Son and the Spirit can both function as paraclete (14.16, 26; 15.26; 16.7; I John 2.1). This is why Jesus is prepared to ignore the charge that by calling God his own Father he is claiming equality with God (5.18) and accepts that of being the son of God (10.36), while vigorously denying the blasphemy of being God or his substitute.

In sum, what he was the Logos was, and what the Logos was God was (1.1; the NEB rightly here I believe gets the sense of identity without identification), so that in Jesus' 'I' God is speaking and acting.

But, as I said earlier,[24] Bultmann, I think, gets to the heart of the matter when he makes the careful distinction: 'In Jesus' words God speaks the ἐγώ εἰμί. We should, however, reject the view that ἐγώ

[24]Cf. ch. 11 above, p. 170.

εἰμί means "I (Jesus) am God".'[25] Rather, Jesus perfectly images, expresses, incarnates God, so that what one is the other is. The love (14.23; 15.9f.; 17.23f.), the glory (1.14; 7.18; 8.54; 13.31f.; 14.13; 17.1, 5, 22, 24), the words (3.34; 7.28; 8.28; 12.48–50; 14.10, 24; 17.1, 8, 14; cf. 16.13 of the Spirit), the works (4.34; 5.19, 36; 8.28f.; 10.25, 32, 37f.; 14.10f.; 17.4), the witness (5.31f., 36; 8.14, 18) of the one are those of the other. There is what John Hick has styled ὁμοαγάπη and not simply ὁμοιοαγάπη.[26] This holds because *everything* Jesus has is the Father's and *everything* the Father has is Jesus' (3.35; 13.3; 16.15; 17.2, 7, 10; cf. Matt. 11.27 = Luke 10.22, which shows this is no purely Johannine creation). He can do nothing 'of himself' (5.19, 36; 8.28f.; 12.49). Yet though they are totally one (10.30, 38; 14.10, 20), the Father is greater than he (14.28). Christ is *totus deus*, God through and through, without trace of anything ungodlike, and yet not *totum dei*, the whole of God, so that outside him there is nothing of God.

This equation without identity on the one hand or mere similarity on the other is summed up in the pregnant Johannine καθώς, which is used with theological significance in the gospel twenty-one times, with ὥσπερ twice. The synoptic ὅμοιος or ὁμοιόω, signifying the *likeness* or correlation between the things of man or nature and the things of God, is never employed theologically in the Fourth Gospel. *Just as* the Father is, so for John is the Son, and *vice versa*. But the same also extends to believers (17.11, 21–3). By mutual incorporation and indwelling (6.56; 15.4f.; I John 3.24) they too share the *same* love and unity. The goal is that *all* may be one as *we* are – not the Father on the one side and believers on the other, with the Son serving as intermediary. And this is because there are not two classes of sonship – a unique, metaphysical divine sonship which belongs to Jesus alone and a common human sonship that is ours.[27] It is true that Jesus alone is called 'son' in the Johannine vocabulary, while believers are 'children'. But this is because he alone truly embodies what sonship should be. He is the only perfect representation, reflection or 'glory' of his father,[28] the one complete example of filial love and obedience. He claims to be no more than the son that all men including 'the Jews' (8.47), should be. Notice the absence of the

[25] *The Gospel of John*, p. 327 n. 5.
[26] 'Christology at the Cross Roads' in F. G. Healey (ed.), *Prospect for Theology: Essays in Honour of H. H. Farmer*, London 1966, ch. 6.
[27] Again I must leave this to be argued in detail in *The Priority of John*.
[28] For this interpretation of John 1.14 cf. again my *Human Face of God*, p. 187f.

article in 10.36 on which the argument turns: there is nothing blasphemous about claiming to be what everyone is called to be, son or a son of God. If he is unique, it is because he alone is normal, not because he is metaphysically or physically abnormal – for he is genuinely representative both of God and of man. It is lack of moral correspondence that would really disprove his claim to be the Father's surrogate and discredit his sonship. To use a distinction which John does not develop, but which the New Testament everywhere presupposes as a both-and rather than an either-or, he is μονογενής, the only son of God, and πρωτότοκος, the first-born son of God, which both Adam (Luke 3.38) and Israel were called but failed to be, the eldest among many brothers (Rom. 8.29; cf. Heb. 2.10). This does not mean that, to quote the Athanasian Creed, 'none is afore or after another: none is greater or less than another'. Indeed the Father is clearly greater than Jesus as son (John 14.28). But there is a unity between God and Jesus and between Jesus and men which is the linch-pin of all Johannine theology. Moreover in this, I am convinced, John is a typical representative of the New Testament, not the anomalous exception, with one foot in the world of Greek philosophy and Nicene theology, that he is so often presented. Nor does it mean that John supposes there is no distinction between Jesus and the rest of humanity: he is after all μονογενής, *uniquely* normal. Nor does it imply that John's theology is purely functionalist, with no implications as far as he is concerned for metaphysics. For Jesus is above all the representative of the realm of ἀλήθεια: he is the true, or real, light and all the rest. But the 'really real' is not expressed for him in the later distinction between 'ontological' and (merely) 'moral' categories (such as unity by φύσις, nature, in contrast with συνάφεια, moral affinity). Rather, love and will and fully personal union *are* for him the *ens realissimum*.

Clearly there is much more than Johannine evidence to be taken into account when formulating our own doctrine of the Trinity. But since it is this evidence that has been primarily used, or abused, in the church's construction, where does it leave us today?

As Lampe saw,[29] but, alas, did not have the time to work through as he would have been uniquely qualified to do, with his biblical and patristic learning, feeding a vivid concern for the contemporary formulation of Christian doctrine,[30] it clearly points, if we are to use

---

[29]*God as Spirit*, pp. 224–8; also his sermon, originally preached at my request in the chapel of Trinity College, Cambridge, 'What Future for the Trinity?'; reprinted in his *Explorations in Theology* 8, London 1981, pp. 30–7.

[30]Cf. his introduction to the new edition of the report *Doctrine in the Church of England*, London 1982, pp. ix–lx, especially xlvif.

the traditional language, towards a more monarchian, subordinatio-
nist, unitarian understanding of the Godhead. But all these terms,
like those they opposed, carry overtones and associations which
today are postively misleading, especially when spelt with capital
letters. As he said, 'If we do substitute unitarianism for trinitarianism
it must not be the unitarianism that denies the divinity of Christ' or
'postulates a deistically-conceived God remote from the world'
which effectively rules out the divine indwelling Spirit.[31]

We must start, with him and the entire scriptural and Christian
tradition, with the unconditional being of *God*. This is what John
calls the μόνον ἀληθινόν or ἡ ἀλήθεια, the ultimate reality. How and
in what human categories or analogies this is expressed – be it word
(1.1) or spirit (4.24), light (I John 1.5; cf. John 8.12), life (5.26; cf.
11.25; 14.6) or love (I John 4.8, 16) – is purely secondary. It is all
θεός. What is significant is that he applies this language not only to
what later theology would call 'the fount of deity', the First Person,
but to Christ and the Spirit – yet only to these. While many other
things may be true (ἀληθής, ἀληθινός), that is to say partake of
ultimacy, Christ and the Spirit alone are designated ἡ ἀλήθεια (1.17;
8.32 [cf. 8.36]; 14.6; I John 5.6). They embody and represent
(though they do not exhaust) divine reality in microcosm. To
encounter Christ and the Spirit is to meet God. Thus they are
interchangeable, though not identical, with God. And this, in later
language, is what is meant by their divinity.

This is not to say that Christ *is* God dressed up in human clothes, a
heavenly being who takes on manhood but in origin is not genuinely
totus in nostris; nor that he is a 'divine man', a θεῖος ἄνθρωπος, who
has 'God with him', though he does (3.2; 8.29; 16.32); let alone a
'mere man' (ψιλὸς ἄνθρωπος) who arrogates to himself the divine
name (10.33). He is the humanity of God, the human face of God,
God for us, and can be acknowledged as such without blasphemy
(20.28). And the same applies to the Spirit, who 'stands in' both for
Christ and the Father. We can therefore say '*There* was God, *there* is
God', completely though not exclusively: God *as* son, God *as* spirit.
Or, as Paul puts it, there is here visible and incarnate πᾶν τὸ πλήρωμα,
dwelling σωματικῶς (Col. 2.9; cf. 1.19), both corporeally and
corporately. This, as Augustine saw, is the distinctive thing about
Christianity, whether in comparison with Platonism or with
Judaism, Hinduism, Buddhism or Islam. The doctrine of the Trinity
remains uniquely Christian, whatever *vestigia* or adumbrations are

[31]*Explorations in Theology* 8, p. 36.

gladly to be recognized elsewhere. But it has been far too narrowly, statically, and I believe falsely, formulated if it is to do justice not only to the coming context of 'world theology'[32] but to its own sources and roots. Much honest rethinking will be required. This essay is but a contribution, from one angle, to the debate that lies ahead. Nowhere perhaps is there so much dead wood, to use John's own metaphor (15.1–6), to be pruned away if the fruiting branches are to be made more fruitful still.

[32]Cf. W. Cantwell Smith, *Towards a World Theology*, London and Philadelphia 1981.

INDEX